# Changing Clinical Care

# Changing Clinical Care
## Experiences and lessons of systematisation

Edited by

## ANDREW GRAY

*Academic Services for Public Management*
*Visiting Professorial Fellow, North East Public Health Observatory*


## PIETER DEGELING

*Health Services Consultant*
*Visiting Professor, Health Care Innovation Unit, Southampton University*
*Former Professor of Health Management and Director, Centre for Clinical*
*Management Development, University of Durham*


and


## HAL COLEBATCH

*Professor, Department of Public Policy*
*Robert Gordon University, Aberdeen*

Radcliffe Publishing
Oxford • New York

**Radcliffe Publishing Ltd**
18 Marcham Road
Abingdon
Oxon OX14 1AA
United Kingdom

**www.radcliffe-oxford.com**

Electronic catalogue and worldwide online ordering facility.

British Library Cataloguing in Publication Data

A catalogue record for this book is available from the British Library.

ISBN-13: 978 184619 202 9


Typeset by Pindar New Zealand (Egan Reid), Auckland, New Zealand
Printed and bound by TJI Digital, Padstow, Cornwall, UK

# Contents

# List of contributors

**Dr Graham Archard** is a part-time GP in Christchurch, Dorset and Vice Chairman of the Royal College of General Practitioners. He works closely with the Department of Health and, in particular, the National Institute of Clinical Excellence (NICE) for whom he serves on several committees. He became interested in systematisation following inclusion of his project 'Succeed' in the National Service Framework for heart disease and has lectured widely on the subject both at home and abroad.

**Dame Carol M Black** is at the Centre for Rheumatology, Royal Free & University College Medical School, London, where she maintains a deep interest in both the clinical and research aspects of connective tissue diseases. She is the Government's first National Director for Health and Work, leading the Government's Health Work and Well-Being strategy – a joint initiative across government to improve the health and well-being of working age people. She is also Chairman of the Academy of Medical Royal Colleges, the Nuffield Trust and past president of the Royal College of Physicians of England.

**Mr Nick Carty** is Consultant General Surgeon at Salisbury District Hospital. His special interests are in Surgical Oncology, particularly breast cancer and minimal access surgery – upper gastro-intestinal and hernia. He has been involved with a variety of projects that have attempted to improve the efficiency of surgical processes, first in breast cancer (Salisbury was a Beacon site and through the Cancer Collaborative) and more recently in the Emergency Services Collaborative.

**Dr Helen Close** is Research Associate, Centre for Integrated Health Care, Durham University. She qualified as a nurse in 1993. She has a background in both district nursing and palliative care and holds specialist practitioner and nurse prescribing qualifications. She completed her PhD in 2005 and is currently working on ways of understanding and improving the experiences of people with long-term conditions.

**Janine Cochrane** is a senior manager at the Velindre Cancer Centre, Wales. She was Clinical Care Pathway Coordinator at HealthCare Otago from 1996 to 1998.

**Professor Hal Colebatch** (co-editor) holds a part-time appointment as Professor in the Department of Public Policy at Robert Gordon University, Aberdeen, and visiting appointments in the School of Public Health and Community Medicine and the School of Civil and Environmental Engineering at the University of New South Wales. He is Chair of the International Political Science Association's Research Committee on Public Policy and Administration, and has recently edited two books on the nature of policy work: *The Work of Policy: an International Survey* (Lexington Books: Lanham MD, 2006), and *Beyond the Policy Cycle: Policy Work in Australia* (Allen and Unwin, Sydney, 2006).

**Dr David Colin-Thomé** is National Clinical Director for Primary Care, Department of Health, England; a GP in Castlefields, Runcorn; Honorary Visiting Professor, School of Health, University of Durham; Honorary Visiting Professor, Centre for Public Policy and Management, Manchester University; and Adviser to Manchester University Hospital.

**Barbara Coyle** is Research Associate, North East Public Health Observatory, based at the Wolfson Research Institute at Durham University. Barbara's current work includes statistical analysis of hospital-based activity to support the development of integrated care pathways.

**Allan Cumming** is currently an Associate Director with the National Leadership and Innovation Agency for Healthcare, Wales. He was a Clinical Practice Group Manager at HealthCare Otago from 1996 to 1999.

**Deidre Degeling** was formerly Director of Health Programs, National Heart Foundation (New South Wales Division) and has extensive background and experience in the theory and practice of primary and secondary prevention.

**Professor Pieter Degeling** (co-editor) is now a freelance health services consultant including as Visiting Professor at the Health Care Innovation unit at Southampton University. From 2001 to 2006 he was Professor of Health Management and Director of the Centre for Clinical Management Development, University of Durham. Prior to 2002 he was Professor of Health Management in the School for Health Services Management at the University of New South Wales and was Foundation Director of its Centre for Clinical

Governance Research. He has published extensively on health care reform, clinician management, clinical pathway development and implementation, and clinical governance.

**Dr Kathryn de Luc** completed her PhD in England and now lives in New Zealand.

**Barrie Dowdeswell** is the Executive Director of the European Health Property Network that links governmental departments and academic centres with interests in the capital financing, design and procurement of health care facilities. He was formerly chief executive of the Royal Victoria Infirmary NHS Trust in Newcastle upon Tyne, UK, and has served as advisor to a number of NHS policy boards.

**Linda Dunn** is Specialist Advisor for Advanced Practice/Non Medical Consultant Roles, Workforce Innovation, NHS West Midlands.

**Nigel Edwards** is Director of Policy for the NHS Confederation, the membership organisation that represents over 90% of NHS organisations in the UK. His role is to influence health policy on behalf of members, develop the Confederation's policy positions on areas of key interest to members and to speak on behalf of NHS organisations, particularly in the media. He is a Director of the Confederation's Future Healthcare Network which supports organisations involved in the largest healthcare building programme for one hundred years. Nigel is an Honorary Visiting Professor at the London School of Hygiene and Tropical Medicine.

**Jonathan Erskine** is Research Associate with the Centre for Integrated Health Care Research at the University of Durham, UK, and administrator for the European Health Property Network. He has written on healthcare design and HAI, the future of regional healthcare networks, and innovative capital investment projects across Europe.

**Chris Fokke** is Director of Clinical Practice and the Nursing Professional Advisor at the Royal National Hospital for Rheumatic Diseases NHS Foundation Trust in Bath, a specialist rehabilitation hospital. His role includes supporting clinical teams in care pathway development and implementation, and advising the Board on progress and opportunities associated with care pathways and clinical models. His nursing career has mainly been in Neuro-Science, although his first honours degree was in Community Health Care and he worked for a short while as a district nurse in Oxford. His second degree is an MSc in Information Technology, and he has applied some of the information systems' technology to clinical models, in particular care pathway development.

**Professor Andrew Gray** (co-editor) is Emeritus Professor of Public Management (University of Durham) and now provides freelance academic services for public management as it struggles with the challenge of being 'business-like but not like a business'. His principal assignments are as (1) Visiting Professorial Fellow, North East Public Health Observatory (based in the Wolfson Research Institute at Durham University), (2) Vice Chairman, County Durham Primary Care Trust, where his particular interests are in clinical governance, commissioning and prison health, and (3) Editor of *Public Money and Management*. He is also Chair of the Durham Forum for Health, Board member of the Public Management and Policy Association, and Steering Group member (and founding chair) of Prison and Offender Research in Social Care and Health (North East, Yorkshire and Humber) – known as PORSCH. He was joint editor (with Professor Stephen Harrison) of *Governing Medicine* (Open University Press, 2004).

**Professor Debra Humphris** is Professor of Health Care Development and Director of the Health Care Innovation Unit at the University of Southampton. The role of the Unit is to be a national and international centre for policy and innovation in healthcare workforce and regulation.

**John Kennedy** is Research Fellow, North East Public Health Observatory, based at the Wolfson Research Institute at Durham University. His current work includes statistical analysis of hospital-based activity.

**Professor Alison Kitson** is Executive Director, Nursing, at the Royal College of Nursing where she leads the transformation of professional services for nursing practice, including by introducing a range of innovative processes and services, and represents the profession of nursing at international and national level. She continues to publish and holds honorary professorships at City and Leicester Universities and the University of Ulster, and is a supernumerary Fellow at Green College, University of Oxford. She was awarded a prestigious Florence Nightingale Leadership Award in 2004.

**Paul McDonald** is Senior Lecturer in Psychology and Health Sciences, University of Worcester.

**Sharyn Maxwell** is Research Fellow in the School for Health at the University of Durham. She has a background in economics, community health and healthcare services management. She became interested in the potential for systematised approaches to improve care delivery when working with people with intellectual disabilities and their families. Her interests range across questions of wider system design, the specifics of delivery of care for people with specified conditions and the change requirements associated with these.

**Mr David J O'Regan** is a Consultant Cardiothoracic Surgeon in Leeds. He graduated from Southampton University in 1985, became a fellow of the Royal College of Surgeons of Edinburgh in 1990 and obtained the FRCS C-Th in 1999. He was awarded a Doctor of Medicine Degree by Imperial College in 2000 and a Masters in Business Administration in 2005 by Leeds University.

**Jane Robinson** was formerly the Modernisation Manager supporting the Professional Executive Committee at Hambleton & Richmondshire PCT. Her work continues as part of North Yorkshire and York PCT.

**Dr Eileen Scott** is Post-doctoral Research Fellow, School for Health, University of Durham, and Research Advisor to North Tees & Hartlepool NHS Trust. She qualified as a nurse in 1989 and her clinical speciality has always been anaesthetics and recovery. Her PhD thesis (2000) was concerned with the care of surgical patients with the focus on the perioperative environment. She is particularly interested in clinical risk management and the prevention of post-operative complications.

**Kate Silvester** originally trained and practised as an ophthalmologist but then retrained as a manufacturing systems engineer. After a career in management consultancy, transferring manufacturing principles to service industries such as banking, airlines and healthcare, she rejoined the UK National Health Service and worked on many national programmes to improve the flow of patients through the system, thus improving timeliness, cost and quality of healthcare. Her specific area of expertise is in the design and management of organisational systems to address the variability in demand and capacity. She is now also an Honorary Senior Lecturer at Warwick Medical School and coaches NHS boards and senior clinicians in systems engineering techniques (including Lean) as part of the Osprey programme.

**Roslyn Sorensen** is Senior Lecturer, Faculty of Nursing, Midwifery and Health at UTS (University of Technology Sydney), Australia.

**Mr Richard Steyn** is Consultant Thoracic Surgeon at Heart of England NHS Foundation Trust with specialist clinical interests in oesophageal cancer and cardiothoracic trauma. He is also an active pre-hospital doctor with West Midlands Ambulance Service and Warwickshire Ambulance Service. He has a particular interest in understanding the effects of variation and flow on the management of demand and capacity and the resulting waiting lists. He has developed computer models to facilitate the understanding and teaching of the concepts that must be addressed to allow effective use of healthcare resources. He was appointed National Clinical Lead Demand, Capacity & Patient Flow with the NHS Modernisation Agency in December 2001, and National Clinical Lead Cancer Modernisation in March 2003. He is also now an Honorary Senior Lecturer with the University of Warwick.

**Paul Walley** is Associate Professor of Operations Management at Warwick Business School. His main interest is clinical systems improvement that involves the analysis of procedures in order to improve process design. Applications have included pathology and emergency care. He has also produced a training course for senior people within the healthcare system who are to be used as trainers within their own organisations on the IPH initiative.

**Dr David Walton** is a psychologist who has worked with both the United Nations and European Commission on conflict resolution and public service institution building. Holding visiting fellowships at two UK Universities, he has worked closely with a number of health communities, cancer networks and NHS Trusts on strategic development, organisational change and clinical leadership.

**Claire Whittle** is Integrated Care Pathways Appraisal Tool (ICPAT) Project Leader, and Lecturer in Nursing, University of Birmingham Medical School. She has worked on Integrated Care Pathways with several hospital trusts in the West Midlands Region including with the Pan Birmingham Palliative Care Network. She has visited Melbourne and Sydney to look at the evaluation and validation of care pathways in Australia and is a member of the European Pathways Association that has involved networking with European colleagues to discuss the development and evaluation of ICPs within Europe. Whittle has worked as a National E Care Pathways facilitator for Connecting for Health and as Care Pathways Knowledge Service and Database Coordinator for the National Library for Health.

**Dr Kai Zhang** is Senior Analyst for Patient Safety with the New South Wales Clinical Excellence Commission, Australia.

# Prologue: clinician views

## Systematisation and its place in acute care
### Dame Carol Black
### Past President, Royal College of Physicians of England

As Degeling and Gray point out, systematisation is not a new idea in healthcare delivery, but in the approach explored thoroughly in their book it signifies a fresh and attractive way of tackling many demanding problems that face clinicians and health managers. Such problems call for close joint engagement simply to assure and improve the safety, quality and clinical and cost effectiveness of care. The need grows if we are to meet high public expectations, and respond promptly to the new opportunities that health science brings.

The principles underlying the systematisation of healthcare are simple and obvious; so are the potential benefits. It might be surprising, therefore, that they are not seen in action everywhere within and between the services that people look to for their health and social care.

Systematisation in this context means an orderly but critical approach to care at the level of patient encounters, or rather the series of encounters that comprise clinical events – the pathway of patient care. Typically, it is seen in the integrated care pathways that increasingly are adopted as the models of clinical care for particular conditions – usually the common conditions that make up a large proportion of clinical work. These models are a natural consequence of the systematisation of clinical science itself. The evidence generated by clinical science allows and even enjoins approaches characterised by authoritative guidance and protocol, albeit tempered by the individuality and idiosyncrasies of patients and the judgements of clinicians.

Although we are far from being able to deal with every pathology in this way, or with the complexities of multiple pathologies or vague symptomatologies, systematic integrated pathways have become a familiar pattern over a large part of elective continuing clinical practice.

Systematisation of clinical knowledge and of practice, and wide access to that knowledge, also underlies the development of team working. When systematisation takes hold it reaches beyond the evidence base of therapeutic intervention to take in the processes of care, their design, the quality and safety of care, and the appropriateness, risks and benefits of particular interventions. It is sensitive to the proper use of resources. Its focus becomes one of improvement in each of these areas, necessarily informed by monitoring and reviewing performance by agreed measures undertaken by the clinical team. Such a shift can bring a fuller expression of team working, provided – as Degeling and Gray say – that this is promoted by a 'a conversation', a dialogue that explores ways to promote these changes.

Systematisation in this usage bears further messages – about cultural change in health services. Systematisation as a means of improvement can only be fully realised by engagement jointly of those clinical and managerial staff who are directly involved in the care of patients and in the processes that make up a clinical service. Put another way, the approach recognises and emphasises their essential role in the shaping, provision and improvement of the elements that constitute an integrated care pathway. Moreover, if systematisation is to yield benefit to patients and health services as a whole, it implies collaboration and cooperation between the several components of care pathways.

Last, more pointedly, systematisation allocates responsibility with authority, where it should lie – with teams at the front line of care. As Degeling and Gray remark, it is a plea for establishing a new responsible autonomy with the inherent motivation which that should release. The approach offers a demonstration of 'intelligent accountability' for clinical quality – accountability that is collective and represents the cooperative nature of modern clinical care, and is transparent. It becomes a key expression of proper clinical governance.

So understood, we should expect to find systematisation in each part of any clinical organisation. In a narrowly defined clinical sense, the management of common long term disorders, and of many elective interventions, has become systematic.

Acute illness presents challenges of a new order. There is a huge amount of acute care. In England, over 80 million people each year seek help with an acute or urgent condition. About 14 million are referred or self-refer to acute hospitals, and about 20% require subsequent admission (1–2% requiring intra-hospital transfer to regional services). Medical emergencies account for 80% of medical bed use, and 60% of beds in the surgical specialties.

In acute illness the challenge to a systematised approach is heightened by the complex nature of arrangements for decision making and intervention. These extend sequentially from the community, through primary care (and its discontinuities), ambulance services, acute hospital services and their interdependencies, and the specialised service hierarchy that reaches from acute district hospital to the places of supra-specialised service. Optimal management of common acute presentations calls for prompt, correct, coordinated action. A systematic approach is surely an even greater imperative in these circumstances. Yet, as the chief authors observe, the relatively small number of common disorders that are amenable to integrated care pathway development and implementation do not account for a great part of acute clinical work. Nor is it realistic to systematise all clinical work into pathways.

We also recognise that, although there is evidence that better outcomes are possible for some kinds of acute illness, with some exceptions we know rather little about the real quality of outcome of much care. These exceptions are notable in having been clinician led. They have demonstrated, in ways unmatched by other (command and control) approaches, that truly participatory governance, devolving responsibility to clinicians at the very front line of care, can give good results.

Even where less is known about the outcomes of care, there are recognised standards of practice and provision, breaches and shortcomings in which threaten quality, safety and efficient use of resources. Highest among those standards are competence, identified responsibilities, completeness and accuracy of clinical records, protocols for verifying therapeutic instructions, sound communication, consistency of information given to patients, and so on. Systematic attention to such generic matters, generally recognised as capable of bringing benefit, can also marshal collective involvement in governance at the front line of care, and command clinical engagement.

A systematic approach should pervade all medicine, both elective and acute, and I commend this book to clinicians and managers alike.

# Systematisation of clinical work in general practice

*Dr David Colin-Thomé*
*National Clinical Director for Primary Care,*
*Department of Health, England*

United Kingdom primary care can be defined as a community-based first contact healthcare. Ninety per cent of all NHS contacts are in primary care, the bulk shared between community pharmacy and general practice. In 2002 the Audit Commission published *A Focus on General Practice in England*. It reported:

> General practice is an important service, accounting for eight out of ten patient contacts with the NHS, but only one-fifth of NHS spending (£8.3 billion).

> Most people see the GP [general practitioner] as the first port of call when they are feeling unwell and 99 per cent of the population are registered with a GP, usually close to where they live.

This registration of the patient population is one of the unique features of UK general practice but its potential has been insufficiently exploited. Registration should not be seen as an inalienable right of general practice, but a benefit for patients. It serves as the basis by which a practice values individual and personal care and at the same time takes responsibility for its population's health. Such a population focus will mean a community oriented approach to improving the public's health, of which the proactive searching for patients who have an undiagnosed or under-treated chronic illness and in particular a focus on the increasing number of patients with comorbidity, is a key element.

In this context there are three challenges to general practice. The first is to ensure that the individual clinicians and support staff are competent. This has particular significance for the general practitioner who in the majority of cases has an ownership and clinical leadership responsibility. The second is the need to ensure the whole organisation has systems and processes in place to deliver optimal care for its patients. The Quality and Outcomes Framework of the GP contract offers incentives to improve organisational capacity and capability. In England practices have the further opportunity to be practice-based commissioners; that is, to take on the responsibility of the entire budget for the total care delivered to their patients, much of this delivered by hospitals. Primary care clinicians will continue to be advocates and navigators for their patients but with hugely increased powers to channel more resources into extended primary care provision from outmoded and inefficient hospital-based care. But such total budgetary responsibility also means they are the custodian of the taxpayers' money which provides a third challenge: an increased accountability and a need to work closely across the NHS and local government with the concomitant need to have new systems, processes and relationships. The key relationship is with the host primary care trust.

The systematisation of care provides a process for successfully meeting all these challenges and the care of patients with long-term conditions (chronic disease) an application with potentially huge benefits. The majority of these individuals are leading full and active lives supported by occasional but systematic contact with health professionals but who provide much of their care themselves by adapting their lifestyles. However, up to a quarter of those affected have more severe symptoms and have a higher risk of hospital admission.

Long-term conditions account for eight out of the top 11 causes of hospital admissions. Services are geared primarily to help patients when their condition reaches crisis point but in the past they have often failed to provide the continuing, coordinated support required to prevent such crises from happening in the first place. However, the NHS is now providing the tools for better care and improved quality of life for patients living with long-term conditions. The aim is to prevent unnecessary hospital admissions that result from patients being insufficiently managed, but even more importantly, to prevent the onset of the condition wherever possible and treat patients sooner, nearer to home and earlier in the course of disease.

Effective delivery of such care calls for health education, earlier detection, good control to minimise the effects of the disease and more effective medicines management. Practices also need to have cooperative plans for patient care that involve primary and secondary care, GPs, consultants, social services, nurses and community pharmacists. Case management will need to be embraced and delivered by case managers from a social or health background. In practical terms, such care requires the following.

▶ Integrated personalised care plans on the basis of the needs, preferences and choices of the patient.
▶ General practice teams working through a multidisciplinary approach of proactive care in the community to patients with the highest burdens of disease.
▶ Cross-boundary working in partnerships with secondary care clinicians and social services, stratifying patient populations to identify those at high risk of unplanned admissions to hospital.
▶ Care teams managing the patient journey proactively and seamlessly though all parts of the health and social care system.

The gap between this systematised care model and present practice is challenging: 50% of people with long-term conditions report they have not been told about treatment options, 25% have no care plan, 50% do not have a self-care plan and 50% of medicines are not taken as intended. Systematising clinical work will thus benefit individual patients and the whole population as personal health services have a relatively greater impact on severity (including death) than on incidence. As inequities in severity of health problems (including disability, death, and comorbidity) are even greater than those in the incidence of health problems, appropriate health services have a major role to play in reducing inequities in health.

Thus, the challenge to all primary care professionals is clear. A defined population confers an opportunity to improve the public's health. What better local population to focus on than that registered with general practice and served by a comprehensive budget?

# Systematisation as necessary, but not sufficient, to ensure patient-centred care

*Professor Alison Kitson*
*Royal College of Nursing*

We are both liberated and enslaved by our ability to imagine perfection; whether it is our ultimate image of the perfect car or holiday or our sense of what it would be like to work in an organisation whose systems and processes are so mature and well developed that they would enable us to achieve what we wanted to do. The benefit of the vision is that it spurs us on to try to improve what we do; the disadvantage of course is imperfection; that is, the reality of our everyday working lives that tends to burden us and make us lose faith in being able to transform ourselves, our teams and our organisations.

Systematisation as described in this volume is one approach that attempts both to understand the complexity of delivering patient-centred care within a healthcare system and offer a methodology and a set of approaches that will help people who work in healthcare systems to be more effective. Of course, the central tenet of systematisation is not unfamiliar: it argues (quite rightly) that taking a systematic, measured approach to understanding and analysing work and work flow within an organisation will improve effects, productivity and efficiency.

Systematisation embodies care pathways and similar approaches that look at a process of care for a particular client group, such as people with chronic obstructive airways diseases, and work out the acceptable standard of care for that group. Ideally, such care pathways extend beyond organisational boundaries so that whole teams delivering integrated care can ensure that the patient and their family remain at the centre of the work.

But systematisation calls for additional integration across the whole healthcare system. As well as the journey through the system that the patient will experience personally, the argument is that all those systems and processes that enable the care to be given have also to be methodically and systematically engineered. So the clinical governance, risk management and safety systems need to be calibrated against the care pathways as well as educational, human resource, IT and administration systems.

From a nursing perspective this all makes perfect sense. High quality nursing care is very sensitive to variations or changes in other systems. We only need to consider the impact of cleaning and catering services on nursing quality of care and patient standards to know that multiple interdependencies exist.

This leads me onto my central point around the systematisation agenda and nursing care. I would like the discourse in the future to make explicit the broader nursing care functions that have to be delivered to all patients regardless of the care pathway they find themselves in. So, for example, I would wish to understand how, from a whole organisational perspective, I could guarantee an acceptable level of care for all my patients around such fundamentals as personal hygiene and comfort, privacy, dignity, confidentiality, adequate nutrition and hydration, acceptable noise levels, rest and relaxation and adequate observation of their condition. I find myself wondering how quality and safety standards around such fundamentals of care are measured now. How do we identify risk to patients, regardless of medical need, when the system can be found to be deficient in basic commodities such as affording dignity to patients or keeping wards clean?

How we calibrate these essentials of care against care pathways and in turn look at them through the prism of quality, safety, clinical governance and cost effectiveness is surely an important agenda to embrace. But one word of caution: the illusion in the world of systematisation is to assume that organisations and all those people who work in them and who use them are logical, systematic, rational, sensible, predictable and dependable. Organisational theorists, of course, will tell us the 'machine' metaphor of organisations has been replaced by a view of the organisation as an organisation that grows, develops and has a life cycle of its own. So just as the 'messiness' of nursing practice needs to be taken into consideration in the colder, more calculated rationalisation of a care pathway, so the emotional, intuitive, spontaneous, irrational organisational and personal response needs due consideration.

There is much to be done and a lot of improvements can be made. We should not stop ourselves from continuing to imagine that perfect team or organisation where our systems and processes work brilliantly and we can deliver the best possible care to our patients.

**PART ONE**

# Concepts and contexts

# CHAPTER 1

# Conceptualising and practising the systematisation of care

*Pieter Degeling and Andrew Gray*

This book is about the systematisation of care: who is interested in it, why interest has increased in recent years, the changed structures and practices that are central to it, how some clinicians and managers have experienced these changes and what they and we have learned from them. This conjunction of systematisation and care, however, begs a number of questions. What, for example, do we mean by the systematisation of care? How does 'systematised care' differ from other approaches? Are we suggesting that these other approaches are devoid of systematisation? Have our conceptions of what can and should be systematised changed over time? What has stimulated the changes and what have been their effects?

Systematisation is not a new idea in healthcare delivery. On the contrary it has a long history, notably in medical knowledge and skills as well as the licensing of practitioners. For example, medicine's standing in modern healthcare delivery owes much to the systematisation of bio-medical knowledge that emerged from the Enlightenment's empiricist reappraisal of the body and the self.[1] Medicine's writ, at the levels of both society and the individual, has since been built on its perceived capacity to generate, harness and apply a systematic body of knowledge in making expert clinical judgements and intervening on the bodies of their patients for therapeutic effect. Equally, medicine has long recognised that its writ depends on systematic profession-based structures for specifying by whom and to what ends medical knowledge can be applied. Until recent times its success in this regard was continually reinforced as actors in health policy circles, clinical settings and therapeutic encounters routinely enacted the ensemble of practices, rules, values and meanings that underwrote medicine's institutionalised mandate to define what constitutes disease and illness and to determine what was required for the proper conduct of its work and that of other clinical occupations.

For its part, the development of nursing as a profession has also involved systematisation of its knowledge base and licensing arrangements. More particularly, since Florence Nightingale collected data on hospital mortality rates and devised the Polar Area Diagram to graphically represent her results, nursing's professionalisation has been founded on the practical systematisation of patient care in respect of, for example, the recording of patient signs and symptoms, infection control, the management of pain, rehabilitation and medications and the development and implementation of more holistic models of care that take account of the experience of both patients and care providers.

Broadly, similar concerns inform the papers presented in this book. Our interest in care systematisation is grounded in a recognition that the pan-professional and across-setting interconnectedness of care provision differs between identified patient groups, such as those undergoing a normal birth delivery, a hip replacement, or an acute exacerbation of an underlying chronic condition. Accordingly, the following discussion proceeds from the view that care delivery for each of these patient populations is systematised in so far as:

▶ the interconnected network of tasks that need to be performed (for each case type) has been prospectively designed, planned, sequenced as a consistent and coordinated whole to optimise their instrumentality in achieving specified therapeutic ends, and

▶ the resulting condition-specific care processes are observed, monitored and routinely reviewed and benchmarked by the people who are involved and affected by their performance to the benefit of improved efficiency, effectiveness and quality.

Construed in these terms, care systematisation depends on structures and practices whose operations are grounded in a recognition of the centrality of frontline medical, nursing, allied health and managerial staff in the design, provision and improvement of care processes to nominated patient types with whom they are directly involved. In the longer term, these bottom-up structures provide means for re-establishing responsible autonomy as a guiding principle in healthcare organisation. This will occur, largely, through the collective self-control that clinical teams exercise as they prospectively design care processes for nominated case types and then in transparent ways hold themselves accountable for their performance.

Such collective self-control also underlines the centrality of multidisciplinary conversations between doctors, nurses, allied health professionals and managers to engage routinely and in systematic multidisciplinary conversations about questions such as the following.

▶ Are we doing the right things? That is, in the light of assessed health needs and existing resource constraints, are we delivering value for money and, on a condition by condition basis, appropriate and effective services?

▶ Are we doing things right? That is, are we managing risk, safety, quality and patient evaluations appropriately and, on a condition by condition

basis, are we performing the sequence of tasks whose occurrence or non-occurrence significantly affects quality, outcome and cost?
▶ Do we have the capacity to get better? That is, on a condition by condition basis, what strategies are in place for improving the care process and clinical skills development?

The realisation of the grounded developmental potential of this model of systematisation, however, runs counter to historically embedded factors in most healthcare systems. From its inception in 1948, for example, care provision within the National Health Service (NHS), has represented the day-to-day working out of high level bargains between, on the one hand, the State and the electorate and, on the other, the State and the medical profession. The State's bargain with the electorate is registered in the continuing provision of a National Health Service equally accessible to all, funded from universal taxation, free at the point of use and provided according to clinical need rather than the ability to pay. The bargain with the medical profession is registered in the commitment of the government when establishing the NHS to give the profession 'all the facilities, resources, apparatus and help I can, and then leave you alone, as professional men and women to use your skills and judgement without hindrance'.[2]

The deference to professional autonomy embedded in this commitment has left successive governments with the problem of finding ways and means of reconciling their national accountability for NHS performance with the autonomy of professionals working locally. Put simply, while the national government provides for the total level of publicly funded health expenditure, doctors control local allocation of these resources through their clinical decisions. The fulfilment of the government's obligation to the electorate requires not merely that it provides adequate funding but also that it takes responsibility for establishing organisation and management processes that, notwithstanding the claimed autonomy of medicine, are capable of delivering services as and where they are needed.

Against the backdrop of these cross-cutting tensions, healthcare reforms have through governments of various political hues progressed from a concern about (a) the systematisation of the NHS as an administrative structure, to (b) systematisation of resource management within delivery organisation, and (c) systematisation of the monitoring arrangements for matters nominated as generic to healthcare quality. In the remainder of this chapter we examine these concerns before presenting some thoughts on where ways forward are likely to be found, particularly in respect of the organisation and management of clinical care.

## SYSTEMATISATION OF CARE AS ADMINISTRATIVE STRUCTURE

At the time of its establishment in 1948, the administrative oversight of the NHS was divided between 850 administrative bodies 'each with its own separate tradition and fiercely protective of its autonomy'.[3] Among others were executive councils (responsible for relations with general practitioners, pharmacists and other independent contractors), local government health authorities (whose writ covered local community-based services), 16 regional hospital boards (responsible for hospital-based services), 36 boards of governors of teaching hospitals and 380 hospital management committees comprising a lay administrator, a medical administrator and a finance officer each of equality of status.

Taken as a totality, the arrangements demonstrated the importance of three principles: (a) the accommodation of institutional interests, (b) the emphasis on localism (the authority of locality-based executive councils, regional hospital boards, local authorities and hospital management committees) and (c) the faith placed in profession, in particular medicine. However, as noted by Klein,[4] these principles produced three effects. First, stripped of its rhetoric, the NHS actually comprised a collection of nationalised but locally oriented hospital services that were only loosely linked to publicly funded primary care services run by general practitioners who operated small businesses. Second, there was a wide diversity of orientations and outcomes of service delivery at local levels. Third, service development at local level was shaped largely by the historical inheritance of individual localities.

It was soon apparent, however, that changing social, economic and political circumstances meant that the inherited status quo was unsustainable. Demographic change (ageing) and patient expectations (medical science and technology) were increasing demand for acute services, and the lack of integration between GPs, acute services and social services was producing outcome failures and inequities. On a more optimistic note, moderate economic growth furnished the prospect of replacing or refurbishing the existing hospital building stock in ways that improved the distribution and scope of hospitals to optimise new technology and promote service efficiency and effectiveness.

In 1959 the Ministry of Health established an advisory committee to report on hospital efficiency that anticipated wider changes within government. Following acceptance of the Plowden Report on the Control of Government Expenditure in 1961, the government established the Public Expenditure Survey as an instrument of long-term expenditure planning and control.[5] From this time onwards, governments of both persuasions significantly expanded the accounting, economics and planning capacities of government departments. The prevailing optimism about planning was matched by an enthusiasm for structural reform. In 1974, at the same time as changes to local government, the patchwork of health consultative arrangements, in place since 1948, was replaced by a structure of 15 regional health authorities, 90 area health authorities each linked with its counterpart family practitioner committee and 200 district management teams each flanked by a community health council. Finally, under the Resource Allocation Working Party (RAWP)-based formula introduced in 1976, funding was allocated to regional health authorities on the basis of their population weighted for a number of social, demographic and epidemiological factors.

The new arrangement established clear lines of planning responsibility and accountability between the centre and the periphery and provided delegations under which the periphery could interpret national priorities and norms in terms of local circumstances and needs. Secondly, it heralded a greater emphasis on the proactive management of healthcare provision rather than the reactive administrative accommodation of service transactions. The new managers increasingly found themselves cast as local representatives of central government. They negotiated national priorities with local stakeholders (in particular local medical specialties), established and maintained across-profession-based management teams and orchestrated their local functioning along lines consistent with national priorities and, finally, set in place mechanisms to satisfy the increasing reporting requirements of central government. Regional and area health authorities produced plans that reflected the new Department of Health and Social Security priorities as well as their adaptation to local circumstances.

These plans, however, were based on at least three assumptions: that (a) economic growth would continue at the level enjoyed since the mid 1950s, (b) the Ministry's compact with medicine and the quiescence of other occupation unions would endure, and (c) the bipartisan political consensus would hold. Events, however, dissolved each of these assumptions. The economy failed to sustain its growth, the compact with medicine was shattered as the Labour Government and British Medical Association (BMA) fought over private patients and the terms and conditions of full-time consultant appointments, and the reformed Conservative Party under Margaret Thatcher broke the bipartisan consensus by extolling the corrective virtues of a more market-oriented approach.

## SYSTEMATISATION OF CARE AS LOCALISED RESOURCE MANAGEMENT

In addition to terminating policy players' enchantment with planning, these events provided grounds for replacing the previous culture of diplomatic administration with one of interventionist management. In 1979, the incoming Conservative Government committed itself to reducing public expenditure by cutting back on bureaucracy. Accordingly, in 1982 it abolished area health authorities (that had sat since 1974 between the regions and districts) and reconstituted district health teams as district health authorities (200 in total) with devolved power to plan, develop and manage service provision for their geographic populations of between 150 000 and 500 000. The aim was to place decisions closer to the point of service delivery.

Following acceptance of Sir Roy Griffiths' Report on NHS management,[6] the people charged with making and implementing these decisions was a cadre of newly appointed general managers. In the period that followed service delivery was increasingly subjected to a range of management concepts and technologies drawn largely from the private sector that were aimed at inserting a logic of productivity into the organisation and management of service provision, particularly at hospital level. Broadly cast service goals were supplanted with explicit measurable output targets, hospitals were increasingly subjected to cash limits and cost improvement programmes. And, under the rubric of the Resource Management Initiative, attention was given to harnessing the dramatically expanded data processing capacity of information technology to establish information systems that could map the range of resources used in treating patients and thus inform clinical and resource decisions.[7]

This focus on improving resource utilisation also underpinned efforts to replace traditional profession-based authority and committee structures by clinical directorates under the leadership of part-time medical managers charged with meeting both budget and clinical output targets. This change was justified on the grounds that the consultative and incremental stances of the existing cadre of administrators were inadequate to satisfy the challenges of a declining economy, an ageing population and the growing demand for services. The new regime of hospital management was expected to be more focused, proactive and directive in controlling the hospital's financial performance.

The principle of managerial responsibility for financial viability and production efficiency was reinforced by subsequent policy, including *Working for Patients*[8] and The National Health Service and Community Care Act 1990. The latter's formal recognition of the clinical directorate structures as the preferred model of hospital organisation and management was matched in April 1991 by a notification to hospitals that they would be charged for their capital assets and an invitation to opt out of the control of district health authorities (DHAs) by establishing themselves as independent NHS Hospital Trusts that would compete for service contracts in a new internal market. The aim was to create incentives that would motivate managers of now independent acute trusts to attend more closely to the resource usage implications of existing approaches to service provision within their Trust.

Despite some twists and turns on matters of detail, broadly similar aspirations and orientations have characterised New Labour's approach to resource management reform. Although its initial government policy statement, *The New NHS: modern, dependable* recalled earlier consensual models, subsequent statements such as *The NHS Plan: a plan for investment, a plan for reform* were expressed and sourced in the same public management thinking that had informed its Conservative predecessors.[9] The NHS Plan, for example, has included strategies that are extensions of previous Conservative efforts to insert a logic of productivity into the organisation and management of service provision. Successful trusts, those receiving the maximum three stars for meeting national financial and performance targets, have been further incentivised to apply for the increased financial and operational freedoms of a foundation trust under the oversight of a board of governors elected by the local community and staff. However, the assessment of candidates for the new status is almost entirely in terms of governance and especially financial viability.

Labour has also established systems of provider incentives for resource management at various levels. Under the rubric of payment by results (PBR), it has developed a case-mix hospital payment system based on the resource requirements of different treatment types defined in clinical terms (Health Resource Groups), a payment system for GPs based on the Quality and Outcomes Framework (QOF) and a new contract for hospital consultants. The systematisation of care as resource management is in these respects more fully developed under Labour than at any time in the history of the NHS.

## SYSTEMATISATION OF CARE AS MONITORING QUALITY

The issues here include those that touch on the evidence base of clinical interventions, variability in clinical practice, avoidable risk and the occurrence of adverse events. Prior to the 1980s these issues were seen as lying within the purview of peer-based reviews within medicine and nursing and hence outside the managerial domain. Since then, however, medicine's right to self-define and monitor its work has been challenged increasingly amid doubts about the variability of clinical practice as well as the efficacy of many medical practices. These factors, combined with the growing impost of acute care delivery on an already strained public purse, have steadily strengthened the perception that medicine's capacity to regulate clinical quality falls short of what is required.

In 1989 the Conservative Government's policy document, *Working for Patients*,[10] foreshadowed an erosion of medicine's clinical preserve by making general managers responsible for clinical audit and quality improvement within their delivery organisations. Hospitals were then required to establish clinical audit processes along lines agreed with professional bodies.[11] However, performance on the ground was far short of the 'systematic, critical analysis of the quality of medical care, including the procedures used for diagnosis and treatment, the use of resources, and the resulting outcome and quality of life for the patient' envisaged by policy makers. While in clinical audit, for example, the aim was to establish across-profession reviews of care to identify and remedy deficiencies, most trusts differentiated between nursing audit (introduced in 1990) and clinical audit (delayed until 1993). Medical participation was voluntary and hence the new system depended on the commitment of individuals and the time they were willing to devote to it.

The take up and focus of quality improvement initiatives also varied widely. Projects ranged over utilisation review, profile analysis, the development and implementation of quality and performance indicators, quality circles, total quality management and continuous quality improvement. Again medical involvement was voluntary and most quality improvement came to be seen as something done by nursing.[12] Similar lacklustre outcomes derived from the evidence-based medicine programme, promoted by the Conservative Government to support a more rigorous application of clinical audit and the dissemination of information about 'best science-based' clinical practice.[13]

A variety of factors account for these indifferent outcomes. First, local implementation of initiatives (audit, quality or evidence) was pursued through the development of a series of 'stand alone' units (a clinical audit department, a quality improvement unit) whose staff gathered data on *issues* falling within their unit remit. Combined with the continuing absence of a 'clinical product'-based hospital payment system, a trust's clinical work thus continued to be conceived and spoken about as an undifferentiated aggregate. The resulting failure to disaggregate care into different patient categories meant that efforts to improve quality and effectiveness could only be pursued through managerial reporting structures that gathered data retrospectively on generic issues such as quality, risk, safety and patient satisfaction.

The New Labour Government's remedy was for more systematised integration of the responsibility and accountability of quality and risk (*see* Figure 1.1). It restructured the role and function of the General Medical Council and established professional revalidation. It set up mechanisms for developing clear national standards of service provision (National Institute for Clinical Excellence [NICE] and National Service Frameworks [NSFs]) and monitoring their implementation (the Commission for Health Improvement and its successor the Healthcare Commission). And it promoted clinical improvement

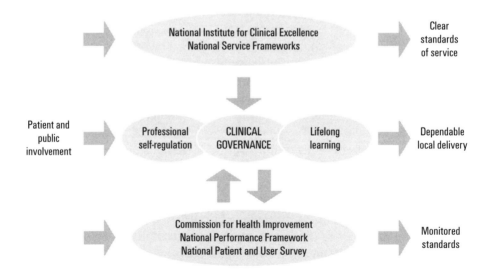

**FIGURE 1.1**  The New Labour modernisation of healthcare[15]

in trusts through clinical governance structures that it claimed would change 'the culture of the organisation in a systematic and demonstrable way, so that quality [of care] is included in all aspects of the organisation's work'.[14] For their part, chief executives of hospitals and other service delivery organisations were made directly accountable for the quality of care provided by their organisation.

Not long after its establishment, the Centre for Health Improvement (CHI) indicated that a trust's efforts in establishing clinical governance would be central to the assessment of its overall performance. It provided advice on the structures through which a trust should focus on risk, clinical audit and effectiveness, and staff development. Unsurprisingly, in following their regulator's advice, trusts developed strikingly similar clinical governance structures that, as illustrated in Figure 1.2, have emphasised the top-down accountability of clinicians and managers for issues identified by the Commission as affecting the overall quality of care. Responsibility for monitoring and addressing these issues has in general been assigned to stand alone committees for clinical governance, risk management, etc., which, in most trusts, are supported by dedicated staff who gather data on the issue falling within their particular committee's remit and ensure that their committee's decisions are implemented within clinical settings. The effect has been, in the jargon of the day, a 'silo' structure of clinical governance.

This top-down, issue-based reporting structure of clinical governance mirrors other aspects of Labour's reforms. Despite its best intentions, it

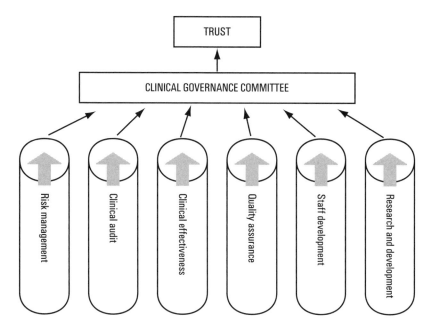

**FIGURE 1.2** Silo structure of clinical governance

maintains the fiction that a trust's clinical work can and should be conceived and spoken of simultaneously as an undifferentiated aggregate (of patients) and as a highly fragmented set of functions based on specific issues such as risk and safety. Because this fiction is far removed from the day-to-day experiences of medical, nursing and allied health staff, it undermines the relevance of clinical governance and leads many of them to regard it as merely adding to paperwork imposed by an increasingly inspectoral and interfering management. Equally, the prevailing model's failure to disaggregate clinical work enables clinician managers to absolve themselves from introducing changes within their units that focus on the particular interconnectedness of what is done by doctors, nurses and allied health staff for the care of identified patient groups that is the condition specific systematisation of care outlined in our opening discussion. In short, the issue-based reports that are produced via the existing model of clinical governance cannot encompass the interconnected network of tasks that are entailed in, for example, treating a patient with a fracture or support-ing a patient in self-managing asthma. Nor do these reports provide means whereby condition specific care processes can be observed and routinely reviewed to improved efficiency, effectiveness and quality.

## TOWARDS AN ALTERNATIVE SYSTEMATISATION

The way forward in the systematisation of care is *not* likely to be found in the abstracted categories that populate the top-down reporting structures that are inflicted on frontline service providers and that more often than not preoccupy local trust management. Rather, the effective and efficient provision of care requires structures and processes that, at the level at which clinical work is performed, facilitate *condition and procedure specific* multidisciplinary con-versations on questions such as the following.

▶ Is our clinical practice for this condition informed by evidence, national guidelines and protocols?
▶ Are we in agreement about the networks of activities and events that are involved in treating patients with this condition and have we documented these activities and events and do we have structures in place to monitor their occurrence or non-occurrence?
▶ Does our clinical practice for this condition incorporate the perspectives of patients, their informal carers and all clinicians?
▶ Have we specified measures for judging quality, safety, effectiveness, appropriateness and economy of the totality of care for this condition and do we know how we are performing on them?
▶ Do we have means for identifying variations from the agreed care for this condition and do we understand how these variations affect service integration, the experience of the patient, quality, safety, risk, clinical effectiveness and technical efficiency?
▶ Do we know what clinical, organisational and behavioural factors have

produced these variations and whether and how we should change them or our approach to them?

Our experience of working with, for example, hospital teams suggests that these conversations are unlikely to occur within clinical units unless there is, first, a clear shift in the *focus* of day-to-day management and in the *methods* by which this shift will be pursued and, second, the provision of *accountability* arrangements whose operations will both *signify* and *authorise* these shifts. On *focus* there is a need to shift explicit attention away from issues management and performance targets (on budgets, activity levels and waiting lists) to systematising the detailed composition of care to nominated high volume patient groups (which will by definition deal with issues and performance). On *methods* there is a need to disaggregate a clinical unit's patient population into high volume case types (for example, in orthopaedics, patients undergoing hip replacements, those undergoing knee replacements, those receiving treatment for fractured neck of femur, etc.). High volume case types then become focal points for developing multidisciplinary integrated care pathways (ICPs) that prospectively:

- describe the composition, timing (and therefore sequencing) and network of activities that are needed to treat the specified condition
- identify the events in this sequence whose occurrence or non-occurrence will significantly affect clinical quality, patient experience and technical efficiency, and
- define the indicators that will be used to assess performance with respect to cost, clinical effectiveness, patient and provider safety, adverse events, patient/carer involvement, satisfaction, complaints and claims.

An accumulating body of evidence points to the way that integrated care pathways (also known as integrated clinical pathways)contribute to improving the evidential basis of clinical practice,[16] as well as contributing directly to improvements in quality[17] and interdisciplinary communication, service integration and learning.[18] ICPs also enable patients and their families to understand and influence what is involved in the full scope of their treatment in ways that benefit both clinical effectiveness and patient satisfaction[19] and reduce inappropriate admissions,[20] resource usage[21] and lengths of stay without a drop in patient satisfaction.[22]

   Yet, a number of ICP issues need to be clarified. First, it is neither realistic nor useful, for example, to systematise as pathways all clinical work: only about half of a hospital's clinical workload is accounted for by the relatively small number of high volume patient types that are amenable to ICP development and implementation. Second, ICPs are not immutable documents setting out inviolable treatment regimens: a pathway does not obviate clinicians' responsibility to make clinical judgements and tailor care according to their assessment of the clinical needs of individual patients. Thus clinical variation remains a 'to be expected' (in the sense of an often required) feature of clinical practice. The matter at issue is what a clinical team can learn from these variations and how they can systematise this learning through, for example, the across-profession conversations described earlier.

Recognition of the importance of condition/treatment specific multidisciplinary conversations along these lines, however, begs questions about who should be authorised and held accountable for generating and orchestrating these conversations and the structural and resource support that these people will require. One approach to addressing these questions is illustrated in Figure 1.3 below.

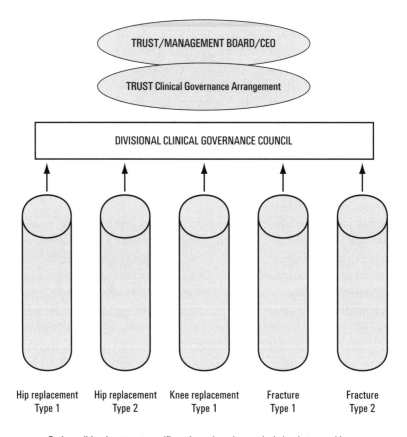

Each condition/treatment-specific pathway-based report includes data on evidence, cost, outcomes, quality, safety, adverse events, variance and complaints/claims

**FIGURE 1.3** Pathway-focused clinical governance in acute settings

The central features of this model are reporting structures and processes for monitoring and reviewing the condition and/or treatment specific clinical production processes of individual clinical units (e.g. of an orthopaedics unit, a paediatric unit or primary care team). Implementation of these accountability arrangements will have a number of effects. It signals the desired shift in managerial attention, first, to a concern for the detailed composition of care for the high volume conditions/procedures that constitute the bulk of each unit's work, and, second, to front line clinician and manger use of ICPs as a means to review and thus improve performance quality, effectiveness and efficiency. Moreover, at the level of a clinical unit (orthopaedics, birthing, renal, etc.) the model embodies a management approach to clinical work that both involves and is orchestrated by the people who do clinical work. As clinicians describe, monitor and review what they do both individually and collectively, control processes come to be centred *not* in a nominated individual (the unit manager as the focal point of knowledge, power and authority) but in a 'distributed system' in which the onus of organising, monitoring and reviewing the systematics of care for high volume case types belongs to the clinicians themselves.

In summary, as medical, nursing and allied health clinicians within a (say, orthopaedic) unit use pathway methodologies to reflect on and develop a shared account of how they can and should carry out hip replacements, they not only will clarify the elements that are critical for the stability, appropriateness and clinical effectiveness of their approach but also will find themselves having to negotiate common understandings about what can and needs to be done to address the resource usage implications of their approach and take ownership of the range of organisational issues (staff skill mix, scheduling, funding and service integration) that will need to be addressed to ensure an ICP's implementation. Finally, in monitoring and reviewing their performance on measures they have specified for an ICP, members of a clinical team not only provide themselves with means for updating and improving an ICP but also enact their acceptance of the need to balance personal professional autonomy with transparent/collective accountability as well as their acceptance of power-sharing implications that are inherent in the multidisciplinary nature of care.

## CONCLUSION

Our account has suggested that over the past half century policy authorities have sought to systematise the NHS as (a) an administrative structure, (b) a process of resource management and (c) a way of monitoring and addressing issues nominated as generic to healthcare delivery. All three have been characterised by tensions between clinical autonomy and the government's electoral accountability for the NHS, by the abstracted 'managerial' categories that they mobilised and the top-down nature of the reporting structures on which they depended, and by the way that clinical work has been conceived and expressed as an undifferentiated aggregate. In combination, these characteristics have reinforced separations between medicine, nursing and allied health and, more broadly, between clinical and managerial domains. Both separations are inimical with care systematisation.

In contrast, as the chapters that follow are designed to show, systematisation embodies a stance on clinical performance improvement that goes beyond the abstracted issues that are the focus of risk managers and quality coordinators. Based in a disaggregated and condition-specific conception of clinical work, it invites the people who perform this work to define, describe, assess and manage what they do as teams. It explicitly recognises clinician centrality to the organisation and its performance and provides clinicians with a medium for integrating the clinical, resource and organisation bases of care. In doing so it provides a way for ensuring that (clinical) management becomes the responsibility of both clinicians and managers. In summary, the systematisation of clinical work that will emerge from developing and implementing ICPs for high volume case types and other expressions of systematisation will enable clinicians to specify the information they require to give substance and form to *responsible autonomy* as the foundational principle of a system of *clinical self-governance*.

The chapters that follow first explicate further the concepts and context of the systematisation of care: they discuss its relation to health policy, to systems ideas, to patient-centred care and nursing, and to data analysis. In Part Two the chapters provide a range of experiences of systematisation in practice, including indifferent branches of surgery and long-term conditions, discuss ways to evaluate pathways, and explore organisational and executive dimensions of effective systematisation. Finally, in Part Three, the implications of systematisation for workforce development and structures of authority are elaborated before we draw general conclusions.

## REFERENCES

1 Porter R. *The Enlightenment.* 2nd ed. Basingstoke: Palgrave; 2001.
2 Webster C. *The National Health Service: a political history.* 2nd ed. Oxford: Oxford University Press; 2002.
3 Ibid.
4 Klein R. *The Politics of the National Health Service.* London: Longman; 1983.
5 Plowden, Lord. *Control of Public Expenditure.* Cm. 1432. London: HMSO; 1960.
6 Griffiths R. *NHS Management Inquiry.* London: Department of Health and Social Security; 1983.
7 Harrison S. *Managing the National Health Service: shifting the frontier.* London: Chapman and Hall; 1988.
8 Department of Health. *Working for Patients.* London: Department of Health; 1989.
9 Department of Health. *The New NHS: modern, dependable.* Cm. 3807. London: Stationery Office; 1997. Department of Health. *The NHS Plan: a plan for investment, a plan for reform.* Cm. 4818-I. London: Stationery Office; 2000.
10 Department of Health, *Working for Patients,* op. cit.
11 National Health Service. *Medical Audit.* London: HMSO; 1989.
12 Carr-Hill R, Dalley G. Assessing the effectiveness of quality assurance. *J Management in Medicine.* 1992; **6**(1): 10–18.

13 Department of Health. *The National Health Service: a service with ambitions.* Cm. 3425. London: Stationery Office; 1996.

14 Ibid., 1999.

15 Department of Health. *A First Class Service: quality in the new NHS.* 1999.

16 Collier P. Do clinical pathways for major vascular surgery improve outcomes and reduce cost? *J Vascular Surgery.* 1997; **26**(2): 179–85. Gottlieb L, Roer D, Jega K, *et al.* Clinical pathway for pneumonia: development, implementation, and initial experience. *Best Practices and Benchmarking in Healthcare.* 1996; **1**(5): 262–5. Turley K, Tyndall M, Woo D, *et al.* Radical outcome method: a new approach to critical pathways in congenital heart disease. *Circulation.* 1995; **92**(9 Suppl. S): 245–9.

17 Borkowski V. Implementation of a managed care model in an acute care setting. *J Healthcare Quality.* 1994; **16**(2): 25–7, 30. Chang P, Wang T, Huang S, *et al.* Improvement of health outcomes after continued implementation of a clinical pathway for radical nephrectomy. *World J Urology.* 2000; **18**(6): 417–21. Kelly R, Wenger A, Horton C, *et al.* The effects of a pediatric unilateral inguinal hernia clinical pathway on quality and cost. *J Pediatric Surgery.* 2000; **35**(7): 1045–8.

18 Flynn A, Kilgallen M. Case management: a multidisciplinary approach to the evaluation of cost and quality standards. *J Nursing Care Quality.* 1993; **8**(1): 58–66. Hart R, Musfeldt C. MD-directed critical pathways: it's time. *Hospitals.* 1992; **66**(23): 56. Ireton Jones C, Orr M, Hennessy K. Clinical pathways in home nutrition support. *J American Dietetic Association.* 1997; **97**(9): 1003–7. Poole J. Care profiles, pathways and protocols. *Physiotherapy.* 1994; **80**: 265–6. Santoso U, Iau P, Lim J, *et al.* The mastectomy clinical pathway: what has it achieved? *Annals Academy Medicine.* 2002; **31**(4): 440–5. Woodyard L, Sheetz J. Critical pathway patient outcomes: the missing standard. *J Nursing Care Quality.* 1993; **8**(1): 51–7. Zander K. Critical pathways. In: Melum M, Sinioris M, editors. *Total Quality Management: The Health Care Pioneers.* Chicago: American Hospital; 1992.

19 Guiliano K, Poirier C. Nursing case management: critical pathways to desirable outcomes. *Nursing Management.* 1991; **22**(3): 52–5. Johnson S. Patient focused care without the upheaval. *Nursing Standard.* 1994; **8**(29): 20–2. Nightingale E, Kristjanson L, Toye C. Evaluating the Navigate Care Model: clinical palliative care pathways based on anticipated care outcomes. *Int J Palliative Nursing.* 2003; **9**(7): 298–307.

20 Becker B, Breiterman-White R, Nylander W, *et al.* Care pathway reduces hospitalizations and cost for hemodialysis vascular access surgery. *Am J Kidney Diseases.* 1997; **30**(4): 525–31. Chin R, Browne G, Lam L, *et al.* Effectiveness of a croup clinical pathway in the management of children with croup presenting to an emergency department. *J Paediatrics and Child Health.* 2002; **38**(4): 382–7. Willis B, Kim L, Anthony T, *et al.* A clinical pathway for inguinal hernia repair reduces hospital admissions. *J Surgical Research.* 2000; **88**(1): 13–7.

21 Board N, Brennan N, Caplan G. Use of pathology services in re-engineered clinical pathways. *J Quality Clinical Practice.* 2000; **20**(1): 24–9. Brandsma C, Calhoun B, Vannatta J. Uncomplicated pregnancy: clinical pathway genesis based on the nursing process. *Military Medicine.* 2000; **165**(11): 839–43. Calland J, Tanaka K, Foley E, *et al.* Outpatient laparoscopic cholecystectomy: patient outcomes after implementation of a clinical pathway. *Annals Surgery.* 2001; **233**(5): 704–15.

Calligaro K, Dougherty M, Raviola C, *et al*. Impact of clinical pathways on hospital costs and early outcome after major vascular surgery. *J Vascular Surgery*. 1995; **22**(6): 649–57. Gallagher C. Applying quality improvement tools to quality planning: pediatric femur fracture clinical path development. *J Healthcare Quality*. 1994; **16**(3): 6–14. Ghosh K, Downs L, Padilla L, *et al*. The implementation of critical pathways in gynecologic oncology in a managed care setting: a cost analysis. *Gynecologic Oncology*. 2001; **83**(2): 378–82.

22 Archer S, Burnett R, Flesch L, *et al*. Implementation of a clinical pathway decreases length of stay and hospital charges for patients undergoing total colectomy and ileal pouch/anal anastomosis. *Surgery*. 1997; **122**(4): 699–703. Grant P, Campbell L, Gautney L. Implementing case management and developing clinical pathways. *J Healthcare Quality*. 1995; **17**(6): 10–6. Worwag E, Chodak G. Overnight hospitalization after radical prostatectomy: the impact of two clinical pathways on patient satisfaction, length of hospitalization, and morbidity. *Anesthesia and Analgesia*. 1998; **87**(1): 62–7.

# CHAPTER 2

# Why systematisation matters for health policy

*Nigel Edwards*

One of the curious aspects of the discussion of healthcare policy is how much of it seems to be about structures, incentives and a range of issues that are some distance from the actual delivery of care. This is even more strange when it is observed that many of the problems and issues that are of concern to the public and policy makers are related to the details of care delivery.

Developing more systematic healthcare delivery is a key part of developing and implementing policy which addresses the real challenges facing health systems, in particular:

- poor service experience and adverse public opinion
- various types of unexplained variations in healthcare utilisation and delivery
- poor quality, safety and productivity
- unresponsive services, and
- clinician engagement, particularly doctors, in improving care delivery and ensuring that objectives and incentives are properly aligned.

Creating more systematic ways of organising healthcare at the clinical front line, within organisations and across local systems, is essential if these challenges are to be met. Without this approach attempts to reform the NHS are likely to fail. This chapter considers each of the challenges detailed above and the contribution that systemisation can make to dealing with them.

## POOR SERVICE EXPERIENCE AND ADVERSE PUBLIC OPINION

Surveys by the Picker Institute indicate some fairly serious shortcomings in the experience of patients. These failings include poor clinical outcomes for key conditions such as stroke, heart disease and cancers, pain control, involvement in care, information about their condition and after care, the way they are spoken to and treated, and availability of convenient appointment times in primary care.[1] Polling by MORI also shows a remarkable correlation between patients' perception of acute trusts and a whole series of indicators of the detail of the encounter between a patient and the system: respect and dignity, cleanliness, pain control, purpose of medication properly explained, organisation of Accident and Emergency, and privacy to discuss treatment.[2] The way that professionals behave, communicate and respond to the patient's needs and how the system backing them up is organised are all crucial elements of how the service will be perceived.

---

**BOX 2.1 Key factors in patient experience[3]**

- Fast access to reliable health advice.
- Effective treatment delivered by trusted professionals.
- Involvement in decisions and respect for preferences.
- Clear, comprehensible information and support for self-care.
- Attention to physical and environmental needs.
- Emotional support, empathy and respect.
- Involvement of, and support for, family and carers.
- Continuity of care and smooth transitions.

---

**BOX 2.2 Key findings from the 2005 primary care patient survey[4]**

**Positive experiences**
- 92% said they were treated with dignity and respect by the doctor.
- 82% said the doctor listened carefully to them.
- 74% said they definitely had enough time with the doctor to discuss their problem.
- 76% said they had complete confidence and trust in their doctor.
- 85% had complete confidence and trust in other primary care staff.

**Negative experiences**
- 41% would have liked more say in decisions about medicines.
- 39% of those prescribed new drugs wanted more information about side effects.
- 70% of patients referred to a specialist were not given copies of referral letters.
- 57% of patients who had phoned the practice had had difficulty contacting the practice.
- 19% of smokers who wanted help to quit smoking had not been offered it.

---

The Picker Institute identifies a similar set of determinants of patient experience that also relate to issues about the detailed operation and design of care. Improvements have been most significant in areas that have been the subject of coordinated action, such as hospital waiting times, cancer care, coronary heart disease and mental health, although there is still room for more improvement, particularly in the care of mental health patients and pain relief. Of the key factors (*see* Box 2.1) the continuity of care and smooth transitions appears to be particularly important in cancer care and the management of chronic conditions. In primary care the areas the public want to see improve are also about the detail of how the systems are organised (*see* Box 2.2).

Many of these issues have a significant impact on how the NHS is perceived by patients and the public. They also have implications for how staff see their jobs. Unsurprisingly, staff who feel that their organisation is focused on the needs of patients appear to be much more positive about the jobs and are more likely to be advocates for their organisation to patients and other members of the public.

More systematic care could eliminate a number of the reasons behind poor staff and patient experience and reduce the anxiety of policy makers that lead them to seek more levers to improve patient experience.

## UNEXPLAINED VARIATION

Unexplained variations are a significant feature of healthcare and a source of frustration to politicians and policy makers who would like to see a more rapid spread of innovation. There are three areas where variation is a particular issue: quality, access and utilisation, and efficiency.

Some unexplained variation in clinical work is unavoidable because of its complexity and the impossibility of controlling all the variables that may produce it. Some variation may be explained by the characteristics of patients or by differences in the capability of clinicians. A significant amount of variation will be legitimate and even desirable; for example, it might be unwise to ask slower surgeons to simply work faster. The term 'unwarranted clinical variation' is a useful way of describing the issue; John Wennberg an expert in this area, defines it as 'care that is not consistent with a patient's preference or related to [their] underlying illness'.[5]

Professor Sir Brian Jarman's research[6] indicates very significant variations in risk-adjusted mortality between providers, as follows.

▶ Crude mortality rates varied from 3.4% to 13.6%.
▶ Age/sex standardised mortality ratios for trusts varied from 53 to 137 (England = 100), i.e. a 260% variation.
▶ Standardising for emergency mix and length of stay reduced the variation to 67–119; deaths outside hospital or the patient characteristics do not explain this 180% variation.

Within individual hospitals there may also be significant variations in outcomes by day of admission (admission at weekends can be more dangerous), time of day (night time operating) or, more anecdotally, time of year (related to SHO change-overs).

Risk adjusted mortality rates for surgery are relatively easy to measure but identifying variations in other outcomes is more difficult, particularly as the NHS does not assess the condition of patients before admission and there is no agreed, universally recognised, measure or measurement methods that are consistent between units. The problem is even more difficult for emergency admissions or for patients with chronic conditions. However, it is likely that the variations in avoidable excess morbidity are at least as great as those for mortality.

In addition to variation in mortality and morbidity it is well known that there are unwarranted variations in the utilisation of healthcare and in the thresholds for treatment by:

▶ area: local clinical preferences, distance and supply being important
▶ social class: the 'inverse care law'
▶ gender: e.g. low rates of heart surgery in women
▶ ethnicity: high rates of admission and compulsion in psychiatry, and
▶ age: as a result of different views about capacity to benefit.

Variations of this type are not unique to the UK. US Medicare per capita spending in 2000 was $10550 per enrollee in Manhattan and $4823 in Portland, Oregon. These differences are due to volume effects rather than illness differences, socioeconomic status or the price of services. Unfortunately, this high utilisation was no guarantee of high quality outcomes. Residents in high spending regions received 60% more care but did not have lower mortality rates, better functional status or higher satisfaction.[7] This obviously represents a significant efficiency loss with potential savings of 30% if high spenders reduced expenditure and provided the safe practices of conservative treatment regions. There is also a very significant equity issue with some areas or groups within the population being seriously undertreated and others, equally worryingly, overtreated.

There are also very significant differences in the productivity of individual, teams and organisations, as the following examples show.

▶ In A&E the ratio of patients per nurse varies from less than 1:1000 to more than 1:2000 and from 1:2500 to 1:6000 for medical staff.
▶ In outpatient clinics the doctors' workload varies five-fold.
▶ Outpatient cancellation rates vary more than twofold.
▶ There are large variations in new to follow up ratios in outpatients.
▶ CT equipment usage varies almost twofold.[8]

The causes of unwarranted variation are themselves varied. They include, first, differences in approach to **preference-sensitive care**; that is, conditions where more than one treatment option exists and where clinicians or particular services tend to favour one over others. Higher levels of bed availability are known to lead to an increase in admissions. For some surgical procedures patient or clinician preference may determine which option is actually selected. Second, many clinical decisions seem to be subtly influenced by the availability of clinicians, an indication of **supply-sensitive care**. In one study, for example, doubling the number of cardiologists seemed to be associated with a halving in the interval between appointments.[9] Third, variations in **the use of effective care** appear due to differences in clinical knowledge, differential rates of diffusion and adoption of innovation and an absence of well designed systems. Fourth, variations may be attributed to **managerial and policy decisions**, including those relating to the allocation of resources, medical and nurse staffing levels, and the availability or otherwise of particular technologies or treatments.

Fifth, **organisational culture**, including team working, internal communication, and attitudes to learning from errors or from elsewhere, may also be important. For example, hospitals with high levels of adverse events appear to have lower death rates. This may indicate, sixth, that **internal systems** are important. Combining Professor Jarman's research with Commission for Health Improvement clinical governance scores suggests that high quality audit,* effective research,* the use of information and education** and training** scores may be associated with lower mortality (*p<0.05 **p<0.1).[10] And, seventh, **timing issues** such as days of the week, weekends, opening hours, GP visit timing, holidays, and medical staff rotation also seem to cause variation. Admission at the weekend, for example, as noted above, is often associated with higher levels of mortality.

Systematic approaches to clinical work help to reduce variation of all types. But they also bring significant challenges in terms of the perceived threat they pose to professional autonomy.

## QUALITY, SAFETY AND EFFICIENCY

Most of the measures required to improve the safety, quality and efficiency of healthcare relate to improvements in the systems supporting provision or the extent to which care is delivered in a systematic way. There is a significant evidence base to support the view that more systematic care produces better outcomes. For example, Medicare mortality is lower among hospitals known for good nursing care, particularly the ability to coordinate across units.[11] In a nine-hospital study of patients with total hip and total knee replacement, relational coordination was significantly associated with less post-operative pain, greater post-operative functioning, and shorter length of stay,[12] and similarly trained primary care physicians practising in different organisational environments provided significantly different quality of care for diabetic patients after adjusting for patient characteristics.[13]

Two other examples are worthy of particular attention. In his Chronic Disease Model (*see* Figure 2.1), Wagner shows that the effective management of chronic conditions requires an approach that brings together a number of components which need to be designed in a systematic way, to use evidence-based care, to engage patients in self-management and to mobilise community resources. All of these depend on the process of care delivery being defined in advance and effectively coordinated.[14]

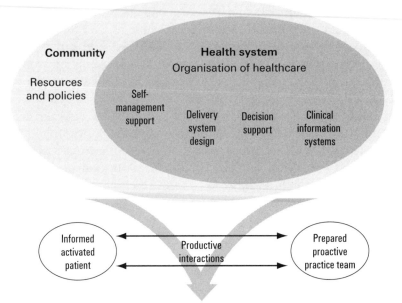

Functional and clinical outcomes

**FIGURE 2.1**  Model for improvement of chronic illness care[15]

A second example is the CMS pay for performance pilots. Early evidence suggests they have produced significant improvements in both efficiency and quality. They require compliance with a range of evidence-based quality indicators shown in Box 2.3. It seems unlikely that compliance with these indicators alone would be sufficient to generate the improvements that have been seen. Discussions with those involved suggest that the focus on a limited range of quality indicators has required hospitals to redesign the entire pathway to make it more systematic as without this it is not possible to create the systems to meet the quality criteria.

## RESPONSIVENESS AND PATIENT INVOLVEMENT

Improved patient choice is a key part of the reform process in England as the choices made by patients lead to change in the flow of funds to providers. The policy on choice is developing from the simple selection of a provider for an episode of care towards models of patient empowerment, shared decision making and greater involvement in choices along the pathway to give patients control over their own care. Systematisation is a key part of an approach to creating greater patient involvement in the way care is designed and delivered as well as meaning that they can take much more responsibility for much more of their own care management. To offer options for care, self-management strategies and a number of other aspects of care required by patients with an increasingly consumerist approach, it will be essential for providers to be able to articulate what the pathway of care looks like and which are the key events where decisions are required.

---

**BOX 2.3  CMS pay for performance quality criteria**

---

**Acute myocardial infarction (AMI)**

- Aspirin at arrival.
- Aspirin prescribed at discharge.
- ACEI for LVSD.
- Smoking cessation advice/counselling.
- Beta blocker at arrival.
- Beta blocker prescribed at discharge.
- Thrombolytic received within 30 minutes of hospital arrival.
- PCI received within 120 minutes of hospital arrival.
- Inpatient mortality rate.
- Coronary artery bypass graft (CABG).
- Aspirin prescribed at discharge.

**CABG internal mammary artery**

- Prophylactic antibiotic received within one hour prior to surgical incision.
- Prophylactic antibiotic selection for surgical patients.
- Prophylactic antibiotics discontinued within 24 hours after surgery end time.
- Inpatient mortality rate.
- Post-operative haemorrhage or haematoma.
- Post-operative physiologic and metabolic derangement.

**Heart failure**

- Left Ventricular Systolic assessment.
- Detailed discharge instructions.
- ACEI or ARB for LVSD.
- Smoking cessation advice/counselling.

**Community-acquired pneumonia**

- Percentage of patients who received an oxygenation assessment within 24 hours prior to or after hospital arrival.
- Initial antibiotic consistent with current recommendations.
- Blood culture collected prior to first antibiotic administration.
- Influenza screening/vaccination.
- Pneumococcal screening/vaccination.
- Antibiotic timing, percentage of pneumonia patients who received first dose of antibiotics within four hours after hospital arrival.
- Smoking cessation advice/counselling.

**Hip and knee replacement**

- Prophylactic antibiotic received within one hour prior to surgical incision.
- Prophylactic antibiotic selection for surgical patients.
- Prophylactic antibiotics discontinued within 24 hours after surgery end time.
- Post-operative haemorrhage or haematoma.
- Post-operative physiologic and metabolic derangement.
- Readmissions 30 days post discharge.

## CLINICIANS LEADING IMPROVEMENT

The need for clinicians to be engaged in the leadership and management of their organisations is clearly very important.[16] Doctors have particularly significant amounts of formal and informal power within the organisation and the ability to make or break attempts to change how it functions. Policy makers in England have become very concerned about the disengagement of clinicians from the reform process. There are many reasons for this but one significant feature is the perceived loss of professional autonomy that is implied by many of the reform proposals. This is a feature of the relationship between the medical profession and organisations, employers and government in many countries.[13] In this respect systematisation may represent a further threat to clinical involvement in reform and improvement if not handled carefully.

In a recent survey for a GP magazine 75% of respondents felt that their professionalism was being undermined and in particular by the way that protocols and guidelines were being implemented.[17] The obstacle that needs to be overcome is the view that the systems of accountability that come with systematisation are not inimical to professionalism and the ability to act autonomously. Pieter Degeling argues compellingly that rather than being opposed to each other the liability to account for decision making is a key safeguard of autonomy. However, much care is based on guidelines a significant number, perhaps a majority, of patients will need to depart from them to some extent. Professional judgement and the autonomy to decide to depart from the pathway are still key skills that cannot be replaced by systems or guidelines. Degeling argues that to protect this key element of professionalism it is important to show why decisions have been taken and to be willing to be held to account for the outcomes.

This view seems entirely consistent with the views of the Royal College of Physicians working party on medical professionalism:

> The practice of medicine is distinguished by the need for judgement in the face of uncertainty. Doctors take responsibility for these judgements and their consequences. A doctor's up-to-date knowledge and skill provide the explicit scientific and often tacit experiential basis for such judgements. But because so much of medicine's unpredictability calls for wisdom as well as technical ability, doctors are vulnerable to the charge that their decisions are neither transparent nor accountable. In an age where deference is dead and league tables are the norm, doctors must be clearer about what they do, and how and why they do it.[18]

Thus, systematisation is a necessary condition for the clinical leadership of improvement and of clinical leadership more generally. Without an agreed and clear statement of the expected process and outcomes of care against which actual delivery can be measured, the provision of any sort of leadership and management will be difficult.

## CONCLUSIONS

There seems to be powerful evidence that a healthcare system that is more systematised, focused on patient outcomes and experience will provide better care. There are a number of obstacles to achieving this that will need to be overcome, including the following.

▶ Increasing the profile and role of clinical leaders.
▶ Designing clinical governance systems that allow discussion of the clinical products of the organisation rather than just elements of organisational processes.
▶ Developing ideas of responsible autonomy supported by accountability systems.
▶ Improving the data to support clinical management and commissioning.
▶ Creating incentive systems to support systematisation.
▶ Developing improvement and process redesign skills among managers and clinicians.

Improved systematisation is a key part of implementing any reforms but too often the content of reform fails to address this directly.

## REFERENCES

1 Coulter A. *Trends in Patients' Experience of the NHS*. Oxford: Picker Institute; 2005.
2 Edwards N. *Lost in Translation: why are patients more satisfied with the NHS than the public?* London: NHS Confederation; 2006.
3 Coulter, op. cit.
4 Coulter A. What do patients and the public want from primary care? *BMJ*. 2005; **331**: 1199–201.
5 Wennberg JE, Barnes BA, Zubkoff M. Professional uncertainty and the problem of supplier-induced demand. *Social Science & Medicine*. 1982; **16**: 811–24.
6 Jarman B, Gault S, Alves B, *et al.* Explaining differences in English hospital death rates using routinely collected data. *BMJ*. 1999; **318**: 1515–20.
7 Ibid. Fisher ES, Wennberg DE, Stukel TA, *et al.* The implications of regional variations in Medicare spending. Part 1: the content, quality, and accessibility of care. *Ann Intern Med.* 2003; **138**: 273–87; Part 2: health outcomes and satisfaction with care. *Ann Intern Med.* 2003; **138**: 288–98.
8 Edwards N, Austin J. *Variation in Healthcare: does it matter and what can be done?* London: NHS Confederation; 2004.
9 Wennberg JE. Unwarranted variations in healthcare delivery: implications for academic medical centres. *BMJ*. 2002; **325**: 961–4.
10 Jarman, *et al.*, op. cit.; Edwards, Austin, op. cit.
11 Aiken L, Sochalski J, Lake E. Studying outcomes of organizational change in health services. *Medical Care*. 1997; **55**: NS6–NS18.
12 Gittell JH, Fairfield KM, Bierbaum B, *et al.* Impact of relational coordination on

quality of care, postoperative pain and functioning, and length of stay: a nine-hospital study of surgical patients. *Medical Care*. 2000; **38**: 807–19.

13 Desai J, O'Connor PJ, Bishop DB. *Variation in Process and Outcomes of Diabetes Care in HMO Owned and Controlled Clinics*. Proceedings CDC Diabetes Trans. Conference; 1997.

14 Wagner EH. Chronic disease management: what will it take to improve care for chronic illness? *Eff Clin Pract*. 1998; **1**: 2–4.

15 Ibid.

16 Edwards N, Kornacki MJ, Silversin J. Unhappy doctors: what are the causes and what can be done? *BMJ*. 2002; **324**: 835–8. Sheaff R, Schofield J, Mannion R, *et al. Organisational Factors and Performance: A Review of the Literature*. National Primary Care Research and Development Centre, Manchester University; 2004.

17 Ford S. GPs fear demise of profession's status. *Doctor*. 24 October 2006.

18 Royal College of Physicians. *Doctors in Society: medical professionalism in a changing world*. London: RCP of England; 2005.

# CHAPTER 3

# Using a systems perspective to improve healthcare processes

*Kate Silvester, Richard Steyn and Paul Walley*

Healthcare professionals have tended not to use commercial management methodologies widely to adapt or improve clinical practices. Yet systems engineers have improved the timeliness, cost, return on net assets and quality of their products and services by understanding and eliminating the pathology of waiting time and quality.[1] Their science can do the same for clinical practice.[2] In particular, the analysis of healthcare situations as a set of processes with system dynamics can make a significant contribution to the reduction of waiting times without compromising quality or patient safety. Recently, large increases in resources have not had the positive impact on quality expected. We suggest that many current problems would have been prevented if the lessons from a process and systems perspective had been more widely accepted.

In the following sections we will demonstrate that the underlying pathology of current waiting time and quality problems are caused by the number of steps in a process, the quality (or errors) at each step in a process, the variation in demand at each step (number × time required), the variation in capacity at each step (skills × hours available), the capacity of the bottleneck step that governs the flow through the entire process and thus the income, and the costs of managing the interactions of the variation within the numerous processes that share resources in any one system.

## PROCESS AND ITS STEPS

A process is a sequence of tasks occurring in series, or in parallel, that transform an object or consumer: metal ore into cars, grass into ice cream, hungry customers into replete ones, and patients into functioning clients and citizens. In industry, the process-based view, which sees every set of operational interactions as a process, is the central perspective of every contemporary, effective management methodology including Lean Thinking, the Theory of Constraints and Business Process Redesign.[3] In contrast most healthcare organisations do not currently have a process-based perspective within their clinical or managerial cultures. Instead, departmental or clinical speciality optimisation is the dominant approach. The patient's journey cuts across a wide variety of departments and specialities, sometimes in several organisations. Consequently, the processes to treat patients are not normally optimally designed to meet the patients' needs.

If we view the patient journey as a process (*see* Figure 3.1), it starts with presentation by the patient and involves taking a history and examination. Following this, there will be events such as making a working diagnosis, giving initial treatment and, for some patients, performing laboratory investigations and imaging the body part concerned. Lastly, there may be more extensive treatment, supporting recovery and reviewing a patient before eventually discharging them. Many with chronic diseases repeat a continuous cycle of investigations and review until death.

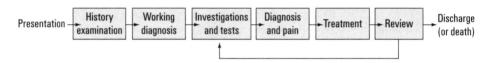

**FIGURE 3.1** A high level view of the clinical process

The issue for healthcare is the variety of patients, their presenting symptoms and treatments required. Some patients require all these steps, some only a few. Others require the application of different skills and technologies to perform these steps and all will require a different time (cycle time) at each step. Hence, healthcare systems are made up of a number of different clinical and supporting processes that share resources but have different processing rates. In order to understand how to manage the interactions within this very complex system, we will begin by understanding the pathology in one process.

When we map the high level process in Figure 3.1 for any one patient undertaking the process from presentation through to discharge, we find hundreds of sequential and parallel tasks. Each task is performed by one person, in one place, at any one time to the patient, their laboratory samples, images and other information. Thus, a patient requiring an X-ray to make the diagnosis may go through the following steps from their general practitioner's (GP) consulting room to the X-ray department:

1 GP fills in X-ray request.
2 GP hands X-ray request to patient.
3 Patient leaves the GP surgery.
4 Patient travels home.
5 Patient phones hospital switchboard.
6 Patient connected to X-ray reception.
7 Patient arranges appointment.

8 Clerk books and confirms appointment.

9 Patient waits for appointment.

10 While the patient is waiting at home, the X-ray receptionist requests the old films from the filing department, porter takes the request to filing department, filing clerk finds old films, clerk puts old films for collection, porter picks up old films and takes them to X-ray department, X-ray clerk puts films in required order for appointment that day.

11 Patient drives to hospital.

12 Patient finds a car parking slot.

13 Patient finds the X-ray department (this may involve several enquiries!).

14 Patient checks in at X-ray reception.

Etc.

Lean Thinking has introduced the notion that steps in a process need to add value for the consumer.[4] Any steps that do not add value can be considered as wasteful and candidates for elimination. In our very simple example, the vast majority of steps add no value at all. Some of these non-value-adding steps are necessary because of the physical locations of the equipment and skills involved (the GP surgery does not have an X-ray machine). Others are there to manage the queues waiting for the resource. Yet, queues (waiting lists) are a symptom of the pathological impact of variation within badly designed processes. On-site analysis can reveal that 80% of existing steps in healthcare processes do not add value.[5]

## VARIATION WITHIN PROCESS

The issue in healthcare, when compared to manufacturing, is the variation in the number and types of patients. However, there are other sources of variation within healthcare. The first is the **inherent or natural variation** of patients and staff. This is the variation in biological make-up and socioeconomic status that impacts the time required by the patient (this affects demand), and level of skill provided by the staff (this affects capacity). This type of variation cannot be eliminated and must be managed.

In contrast, the **iatrogenic variation** is generated by the system itself due to:

▶ staff capacity, i.e. staffing patterns (shifts, holidays, weekends), the availability and quality of staff training, and conditions of employment, etc.

▶ machine and equipment capacity, i.e. processing rates, set ups, maintenance, shutdowns, etc.

▶ information capacity, i.e. the technology involved, processing times, transcribing errors, etc.

▶ clinical processes, i.e. different protocols and pathways

▶ supplies, i.e. different drugs, materials and technologies available.

The vast majority of variation is iatrogenic (i.e. generated by the system), and is thus under the system's control and so it can and should be eliminated.[6]

Both types of variation affect the patient demand (volume × cycle time required at each step) and the resource capacity (i.e. ability of staff to do their job, provide the right capacity to meet the demand at the appropriate quality).

## Defining variation and quality from the consumer's perspective

Most people recognise the patient as both the final end consumer of the health-care process and the object being transformed. With the process view the needs of the consumer are central to the definition of the objectives for the process's outcome and therefore process thinkers would define the patient as the overall *customer* of the process.

Process thinking recognises a very specific and important relationship between the people performing the process – the internal *customers* and suppliers. Each step in the process has a supplier (upstream) and a customer (downstream). The ability of the latter to be able to perform his or her task is dependent on receiving the right information and quality of input from their supplier at the previous step at the right time. Thus it is the internal process customers who define the quality and measure the errors; that is, the mismatches between their requirements to perform their task and what they receive from the previous step.[7] Occasionally, the patient is both an internal supplier (giving a history, personal details, blood sample) and an internal customer (receiving directions, instructions). Just as all other internal customers notice errors and delays in what they have been supplied, so do the patients when they too are the internal customer of a process step.

## The impact of variation on quality

As we illustrated earlier, process analysis often reveals hundreds of sequential and parallel steps in a process, the vast majority of which deliver no value; indeed they delay care, often contributing unacceptable clinical consequences, inadvertently increasing demand, wasting capacity and increasing cost. Moreover, as illustrated in Table 3.1, the number of steps in a process severely impacts the overall quality of the process.

Let us consider the scenario in which a process has only one step (i.e. the whole process is performed by one person, at one place, at one time). If this step is performing at the quality standard used in a clinical trial (i.e. $p = 0.05$ = 0.95 = 5/100 quality errors), then for every 100 patients processed, 5 will experience an error, and 95 will be processed correctly. If, however, the process involves 50 steps (each performed by one person, at one place, at one time) and each step is performing at a quality standard of 95% correct, then overall only 8% of patients will be processed correctly because the impact of variation at every step is cumulative (0.95 to the power of 50). So even if the quality standard at each step is very high, the overall quality of the clinical care and service for any one patient is unpredictable. This is the reported experience for the majority of patients.

**TABLE 3.1** The impact of the number of process steps on quality

| | Probability of performing each step correctly | | | |
|---|---|---|---|---|
| Number of steps in the process | 0.95 | 0.99 | 0.999 | 0.999999 |
| 1 | 95 | 99 | 99.9 | 99.999 |
| 25 | 28 | 78 | 98 | 99.8 |
| 50 | 8 | 61 | 95 | 99.5 |
| 100 | 0.6 | 37 | 90 | 99 |
| | Number/100 patients who are correctly processed | | | |

The majority of patients experience such 'errors' as delays or 'unacceptable service' (e.g. misspelt names and addresses). Most are corrected after costly rework by staff – a constant source of staff frustration and dissatisfaction but accepted as 'the usual way the system works round here'. Other combinations of random errors are more serious and will, by random chance, result in harm and unexpected patient deaths. Yet, the cumulative effect of variation at the hundreds of process steps means that it is impossible to find direct causality (i.e. a direct link) between poor patient outcome or experience and errors at each step. Thus audit is an inappropriate quality strategy. Despite fault-finding, blame and retraining, the process errors continue to occur on an hourly and daily basis on the shop floor. The more serious outcomes lie just waiting to happen again through the mathematical accumulation of random chance (*see* Figure 3.2).

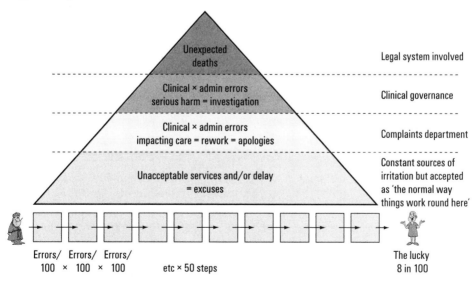

**FIGURE 3.2** The relationship between process flow and quality

Thus, there are only two strategies for improving clinical and service quality: (a) reducing the number of steps in the processes of care, and (b) reducing the number of errors at each step by making each step 'foolproof'.[8] However, many of these process steps have been introduced to manage queues. So, to eliminate these steps, we have to understand the cause of the queues.

## The impact of variation on queues, time and cost

So far, we have discussed how the inherent and iatrogenic causes of variation within the system cause variations in the demand (volume × cycle time required) and capacity at each step in the process. We now consider how variation creates queues and delays in the patient's journey. Just as variation has a cumulative impact on quality, so it affects queues and delays. Unless we do something to reduce the variation, more capacity (i.e. cost) will be required to deal with the queues that are generated.

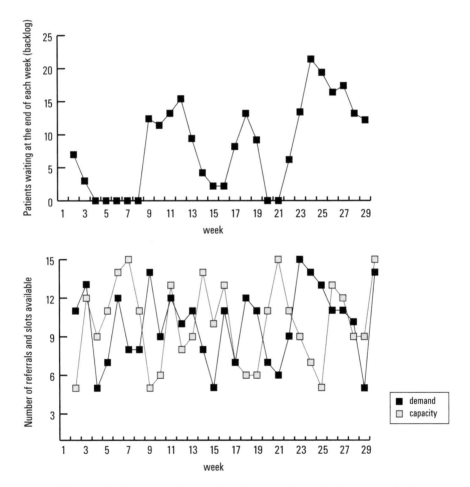

**FIGURE 3.3** Mismatch between demand and capacity variations results in queues (backlog)

The first cause of a queue (i.e. waiting list, inventory, or backlog) is when **average demand is greater than average capacity**. In this case the numbers of patients, paper work or specimens waiting to be processed will increase inexorably over time. This is rare in healthcare since so much of the available capacity is wasted. The second cause is when average demand is equal to average capacity but **there is a mismatch between the variations in demand and capacity**. Even if over time the average demand is equal to average capacity, at any one time there will be variations in both demand and capacity. If at any one time the demand is greater than the capacity, the excess demand is carried forward as a queue or backlog; if the capacity is greater than the demand at any time, capacity cannot be carried forward as it is lost. Over time there is an overall loss of capacity resulting in a queue (as in Figure 3.3). This is the most common cause of queues in healthcare as capacity plans are based on past average activity and fail to take into account the variations in demand or capacity. Therefore the planning process *guarantees* waiting lists and queues.[9]

## MANAGING VARIATION IN DEMAND AND CAPACITY IN COMPLEX SYSTEMS

The demand for healthcare is relatively constant compared to the change in demand for other services and products. However, as we discussed above, there are inherent natural causes of variation in demand for healthcare both in patient volume and case-mix and the latter impacts the cycle time required at each step in the process. Given that the capacity also varies mainly due to the iatrogenic causes in the system but also in a small part due to the natural variation among staff and specialisation of skills, how should we cope with the variable demand and capacity for healthcare?

The default approach to this problem is to group both resources and patients. This is immediately recognisable in industry as a batch production process, where queues are a deliberate tactic to keep an expensive resource utilised. Once there is a queue, then excess capacity can be filled from the queue mitigating, to some extent, the numbers waiting. This gives a false sense of efficiency since the utilisation of the capacity at a single resource is often the organisation's measure of an individual worker's efficiency, rather than the presence of the queue and waiting time which is the patients' measure of efficiency.

In batch production systems, the natural complexity makes the management of the different processes extremely difficult. The journey of one single item or patient is difficult to plan accurately and delays are accepted as inevitable. The system cannot easily be optimised as a single process and so managers tend to optimise the utilisation of capacity at each step in every process.

Although healthcare workers would not necessarily recognise their ubiquitous management style as 'batch thinking', most healthcare workers are all too familiar with the following downsides of batch production.

## The relationship between capacity utilisation and the queue is not linear

In batch production 'utilisation of capacity' (efficiency) is traded for waiting time (the queue). However, Erlang demonstrated that this relationship is not linear, and that once a capacity reaches 85% utilisation, the queue, or number of cancelled patients, grows exponentially (*see* Figure 3.4). This critical point is dependent on the statistical distribution of the variations in demand and capacity and the phase relationship of the mismatch. In very abnormally distributed systems (as is healthcare), the critical point will be far less than 85%.[10]

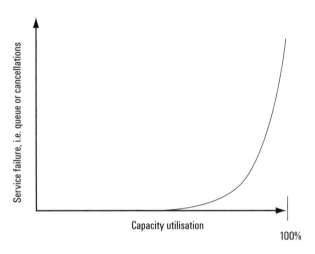

FIGURE 3.4 The non-linear relationship between service failure and capacity utilisation in a system in which demand and capacity vary

The only way to improve the utilisation of any given capacity is to reduce the variation within the process. As the variation falls the amount of capacity required to meet the peaks in demand reduces. Reducing the average demand without changing the variation between the peaks and troughs has no impact on the overall capacity required to ensure a process is capable of meeting the desired waiting time.

## The cost of queues

While optimising the use of capacity at any one step in the process, another downside of a batch production system is that there are queues and these queues incur the following types of cost that are not captured in the activity/cost calculations for any one person, resource, department or organisation within the overall system.

▶ Cost of storing queues including at home, car parks and waiting rooms.
▶ Cost of physical and psychological deterioration in the queue and the cost of rework.
▶ Cost of managing and administering the queue, especially those arising

from a vicious circle in which (a) queues cause delays, (b) more costs are incurred as patients are prioritised, reprioritised and the batch schedule changed at short notice to meet clinical priorities, (c) frustrated consumers request that their supplier's capacity be ring-fenced or carved out to meet the demand for their specific type of patients with yet more capacity wasted as it is not always used, (d) consumers then increase demand by making clinically unnecessary requests and (e) eventually the quality and economies of a batch production system are lost completely.[11]

▶ Cost of downstream capacity as batch production at one step in the process distorts and amplifies the demand on the next step in the process, requiring in turn the next step to be able to ramp up capacity to cope with the batch when it appears; e.g. to respond to a weekly rheumatology clinic's demand for the X-ray of every joint for every patient, the radiology department has either to invest in capacity that stands idle between rheumatology clinics or it stores and compromises other patients (e.g. those from Accident and Emergency) – an effect compounded in batch production systems as variation in demand is amplified as it moves down the batch manufacturing process.[12]

Where the process steps are independent of each other (decoupled) then the queue of patients, paperwork or specimens will be stored at home, in a waiting room or on a shelf while it waits for the next step in the process. In some processes the steps are dependent (coupled). For example, in a surgical inpatient process a patient cannot be moved from theatre to recovery or Intensive Care (ICU) unless there is a bed available. A bed only becomes available if a patient is discharged from a ward. The capacity at each step is predominantly governed by the iatrogenic causes of variation in the system, such as the frequency of doctors' ward rounds. The ability of a patient to move through the coupled process is dependent on capacity being available at exactly the right time at all the subsequent steps. Hence the probability of a patient completing the process is a cumulative function of the availability of capacity at each step.

Thus, in a dependent or coupled process, the queue does not necessarily denote the position of the bottleneck in the overall process. The queue will be in front of the first step in the series of dependent steps. In the emergency process these patients are visible on trolleys in the emergency department, in corridors or 'outliers' on inappropriate wards. In the elective part of the system patients are stored, invisible, at home, until they enter the dependent inpatient part of their process.[13]

Similarly, the wasted capacity is amplified in a dependent system as capacity towards the end of the process can only be used if patients get through all the previous process steps. The temptation is to move this 'wasted' capacity upstream by taking nurses from the wards and putting them in A&E and closing unoccupied nursing home beds. This only reduces the probability of a patient moving through the system and makes the queue at the front of the system even worse.

Thus, failing to recognise the dependent nature of a clinical process can lead to capacity being increased at the wrong point with increased costs and capacity being removed from the wrong point, thereby reducing throughput and income.

## FLOW PRODUCTION

If we can reconfigure our processes to reduce the amount of batching at each step, we eliminate the designed-in waits and delays. Taken to its fullest extent (i.e. a batch of one or single piece flow) we work towards seamless, uniform flow through our processes. The advantages of achieving flow are shorter delays for the patient, fewer non-value-adding costs of managing and storing the queues, improved predictability of time and cost, and greater visibility of the patient's progress through the system.

In Lean processes, the whole focus of the organisation is to deliver precisely when and what the downstream worker (consumer) requires to meet the overall demand. Flow 'thinking' recognises that the flow through the entire process is controlled by the one step with the least capacity – the bottleneck. To optimise the capacity at the bottleneck, a small buffer or queue is deliberately placed upstream of the bottleneck step.[14] Since much of the bottleneck's capacity will be wasted by the iatrogenic causes of variation, these must be worked on until the bottleneck has sufficient effective capacity to meet the rate of demand and the buffer can be removed. Maintaining queues to optimise the use of capacity at any other step is waste since it will have no impact on throughput at the bottleneck or the overall total process and income. In such lean flow production, any type of a queue is a symptom of wasted resource *elsewhere* and thus to be hunted down.

The downside of flow production is that it is often less than robust since resources are carefully balanced across the process with minimal resource buffering. So, if part of a process is unreliable, the whole process might be affected. To ensure that each stage of the flow process is very capable of performing its required tasks without error, considerable effort is devoted to quality assurance when managing flow processes, to minimise the impact of poor quality on output.[15] Similarly, we need to think about the output of the flow process as a whole system, and avoid local optimisation of capacity at single stages, in order to ensure that the movement of items or patients is kept as uniform as possible. From an efficiency perspective, 'flow thinkers' are more concerned with the output from the whole process rather than the capacity utilisation at each step.

## MANAGING CASE-MIX AND CYCLE VARIATION

Although the demand volume for healthcare is extraordinarily predictable in healthcare, case-mix variation unbalances systems due to the variation in cycle time. Furthermore, to deal with the case-mix we have developed specialisation and sub-specialisation that affect the availability of capacity.[16]

In manufacturing, the cycle times at each step in the process are relatively normally and tightly distributed. Any 'abnormal' cycle times are attributable to special causes: events outside the normal statistical performance of the material, operators and their machines.[17] In service industries, however, the cycle times are not normally distributed and are comparatively widely spread. This is because each task along the diagnostic and treatment pathway is subject to the non-normal natural variation of the people being transformed (the consumers) and the staff performing each of the tasks.[18] The 'bulk' of consumers follows a 'normal' distribution for cycle time, but those who require a longer cycle time for any one 'step' (e.g. at a call centre) are not 'unusual' and may be difficult to anticipate. In healthcare the abnormal distribution of cycle times require careful thought and management. Lean Thinking encourages normality in the system, but also depends on regularity in demand.

Involving patients in the design reveals the differences that patients require from the process: skills, technologies and processing time. Patients can be segmented into groups with similar requirements and the system can be divided up into sub-systems or 'value streams' to deliver standardised care for the specific groups. Most patients expect and are reassured that their clinical processes are standardised to some degree. But the standardised care in each value stream can be fine tuned (within the limits of the capacity) to meet every patient's expectations.

If we look at the types of patients by process (i.e. by the skills, technology and cycle time they require), we find that the demand for each process group obeys the Pareto Principle, with 80% of the patients able to follow one standardised process that is capable of coping with a high variation in patient mix. For example, an analysis of accident and emergency demand reveals that the vast majority of patients have a wide range of minor illnesses and injuries, but all of these can be processed very quickly and sequentially by experienced nurses with minimal equipment.[19] In such a system 80% of the demand would provide a steady sequence of work that would only be interrupted by the less common 15% of patients. Only these patients may have to wait until the specialist became available. Once this patient had been dealt with, the specialist would return to the pool to work on the majority of patients. Hence a steady flow would be maintained for 80% of patients with occasional and minimal changes in the rate of throughput.

The last 5% of patients in the Pareto analysis will have a huge range of very rare conditions posing different challenges. These include the staff experience of these rare conditions and thus their capacity to treat them and the impact of these patients, who may have significantly longer cycle times, being introduced into the main flow of patients with the more common conditions. The question then is whether these patients should be dealt with in a separate sub-system.

However, the degree to which the natural variation in patient demand can be limited to a fewer number of value streams or routings is dependent on the skills and capability of the staff involved at each stage in the clinical pathway. The trend of increasing the variation in capacity through specialisation and sub-specialisation with no reference to the demand will produce more 'idle' capacity and expensive waiting for the appropriate patients within the system at any one time.[20] Lean Thinking suggests that patients requiring different skills, technologies and cycle time, and therefore different value streams, should be processed in separate sub-systems or cells. Such an arrangement prevents the chaos of the variation within one process impacting another through a shared resource. Only when the skills, technologies and cycle times are the same should processes be amalgamated.[21]

## CONCLUSION

The existing management approach to healthcare focuses on utilisation of resources at each and every stage in the process. This is a characteristic of batch process thinking. The solution to any of the problems of batch production, as seen in the healthcare system, can be addressed by moving to a process and flow view of the patient's journey. 'Flow thinkers' recognise the cumulative and adverse impact of variation on the timeliness and quality of care, increasing capacity and cost, and reducing throughput and income. To achieve flow in healthcare we have to reduce variation in the system.

In effect this means understanding patient demand by their process characteristics and then standardising each of these separate value-streams. Standardisation improves the quality at each step both in the eyes of the patient being processed and the consumer downstream of each step. Hence capacity losses due to quality errors and reworking are gradually retrieved and the system becomes more tuned to delivering a timely, cost efficient service with a clinical outcome that meets the functional expectations of the patient.

## REFERENCES

1 Swank CK. The Lean Service machine. *Harvard Business Review*. 2003; **8**(10): 123–9.
2 Bowen DE, Youngdahl WE. Lean Service: in defense of a production-line approach. *Int J Service Industry Management*. 1998; **9**(3): 207–25. Levitt T. The industrialisation of service. *Harvard Business Review*. 1976; **54**(5): 75–81. Spear SJ. Fixing health care from the inside, today. *Harvard Business Review*. 2005; **83**(9): 78–91. Weber DO. Toyota-style management drives Virginia Mason. *The Physician Executive*. 2006; **Jan–Feb**: 12–17. Wysocki B. Industrial strength: to fix

health care, hospitals take tips from factory floor; adopting Toyota techniques can cut costs, wait times; ferreting out an infection. *Wall Street Journal*. 2004; 9 April.

3 Womack J, Jones D. *Lean Thinking: banish the waste and create wealth in your organisation*. New York: Simon and Schuster; 1996. Goldratt EY, Cox J. *The Goal*. Croton-on-Hudson: North River Press; 1984.

4 Womack, Jones, op. cit.

5 Radnor Z, Walley P, Stephens A, *et al. Evaluation of the Lean Approach to Business Management and its use in the Public Sector*. Edinburgh: Scottish Executive, Office of Chief Researcher; 2006. For summary see Research Findings No. 20/2006, Edinburgh: Scottish Executive, Office of Chief Researcher.

6 Litvak E, Long MC, Cooper AB, *et al.* Emergency Department diversion: causes and solutions. *Academic Emergency Medicine*. 2001; 8(11): 1108–10. Litvak E, Buerhaus PI, Davidoff F, *et al.* Managing unnecessary variability in patient demand to reduce nursing stress and improve patient safety. *Joint Commission Journal on Quality and Patient Satisfaction*. 2005; 31(6): 330–8. Noon CE, Hankins CT, Cote MJ. Understanding the impact of variation in the delivery of healthcare services. *J Healthcare Management*. 2003; 40(2): 82–98. Wheeler DJ. *Understanding Variation: the key to managing chaos*. 2nd ed. Knoxville: SPC Press; 2000. Deming WE. *Out of the Crisis*. Cambridge: Cambridge University Press; 1986.

7 Bowen, Youngdahl, op. cit. Monden Y. *The Toyota Production System*. Portland: Productivity Press; 1983.

8 Weber, op. cit.

9 Silvester K, Lendon R, Bevan H, *et al.* Reducing waiting times in the NHS: is lack of capacity the problem? *Clinician in Management*. 2004; 12(3): 105–9.

10 Walley P. *Cellular Operation Design in Healthcare*. Warwick: Warwick Business School; 2002.

11 Ibid.

12 Burbidge JL. *The Introduction of Group Technology*. New York: Wiley; 1975.

13 Litvak, Long, Cooper, *et al.*, op. cit. Litvak, Buerhaus, op. cit.

14 Goldratt, op. cit.

15 Spear, op. cit. Weber, op. cit.

16 Silvester, Lendon, Bevan, *et al.*, op. cit.

17 Wheeler, op. cit.

18 Hogg TM. Lean Manufacturing. *Human Systems Management*. 1993; 12(1).

19 Walley, op. cit.

20 Ibid.

21 Hines P, Holweg M, Rich N. Learning to evolve: a review of contemporary Lean Thinking. *Int J Operations and Production Management*. 2004; 24(10): 994–1011.

# CHAPTER 4

# Empowering nursing and patient-centred healthcare through the systematisation of clinical work

*Helen Close and Eileen Scott*

In 2001, Alison Kitson wrote a paper entitled 'Nursing leadership: bringing caring back to the future' setting out her vision for the future of the UK health service in 2012. Her key messages were as follows.

- Improvement of health services is dependent upon the way patient-centred care is understood.
- Traditional healthcare culture and roles need to change if service delivery is to improve.
- Leadership that promotes the values of patient-centred care – respect, dignity, compassion caring – will lead this transformation.
- For nursing, the features that will help this transformation are patient-centred care measures developed as part of performance management and clinical governance, leadership based on personal growth and development principles, and a new clinical career and competency framework for nursing.[1]

The implicit recognition here, that an empowered, autonomous nursing work-force and patient-centred care are inextricably interdependent goals, has been an underpinning feature of attempts to make nursing work explicit, planned and systematic since the days of Florence Nightingale. Along a continuum from 'task' through 'team' to 'named nursing', the work of nursing has been organised to make explicit its *content* while at the same time keep largely hidden the contribution it has made to multidisciplinary quality, continuity, and the coordination of the care *process* experienced by the patient.[2]

Despite attempts to make visible and transparent these aspects via the professionalisation of nursing, its continuing subordination has prevented the realisation of Kitson's vision in several ways. First, clinical decision making and longer term decisions about resources remain covert and implicit and outcomes continue to be largely shaped by the dominant medical perspective.[3] Second, the everyday tension between collective and individual needs is resolved in an ad hoc, covert manner which fails to make explicit the type of 'patient-centred care' that is claimed as an objective. Kitson argues that patient-centred care can only become a reality via a paradigm shift whereby 'caring' is given as great a priority as 'curing' and that 'traditional healthcare culture and roles need to change if service delivery is to improve'.[4]

This chapter explores the role of systematisation, and in particular pathways, in the achievement of this cultural change by allowing nurses to lead the way in articulating the *process* that constitutes the patient journey. Using examples taken from practice, we argue that the need to plan and coordinate collective care and the desire to remain responsive to individual patient needs within the resources available can only be resolved by giving nursing a mechanism, via pathways, with which to renegotiate the power differential between nursing and medicine in such a way that the unique historical contribution of nursing to the systematisation of care delivery is fully recognised.

## A HISTORY OF SYSTEMATISATION AND NURSING

The gendered division of labour, in which nursing was seen as the 'natural' expression of the caring nature of women, has long been attributed to the organisation of clinical work in which nurses were the unseen 'handmaidens' to doctors who 'know best'.[5] Accountability was traditionally structured along hierarchical lines in which Matron or Sister juggled the contrasting requirements of several different consultant physicians or surgeons and had ultimate, but largely invisible, control over the apparently seamless patient journey from admission to discharge.[6] That this control was covert, implicit and devolved the practical work of nursing into a series of simple tasks led to concerns about individualised, patient-centred care, patient advocacy, and the individual autonomy of nurses.[7] The professionalisation of nursing was seen as a way of claiming control over these interrelated issues, and systematisation (i.e. the explicit planning of who will do what, how, where and when) was the mechanism for providing the autonomy and individual accountability on which the definition of nursing as a profession depended.[8]

Significantly, the emergence of the 'nursing process' in the 1980s transformed the articulation of nursing work from a simple task-based focus to a process in which collective decisions were explicitly and overtly informed by the specialist knowledge that was seen as nursing's unique contribution to care. For the first time in the history of nursing, the articulation of this process allowed for evaluation of individual contributions to care, thus allowing nursing to lead the way in a concern for measuring quality of care, as well as becoming increasingly accountable for the delivery and management of care.[9] The resultant professionalisation strategy led to the introduction of 'Project 2000' which, via the development of a specialist body of nursing knowledge, sought to sever the link between nurse education and the handmaiden needs of medicine.[10]

Even long before the introduction of the nursing process, nursing showed an ability to develop ways of providing a systematic approach to the organisation and planning of their work. In various guises and terminology ranging from case management to primary nursing, a commitment to 'systematisation' (i.e. applying a planned, explicit, proactive, coordinated approach to the organisation of nursing work) has been a largely hidden feature of nursing practice since the days of Florence Nightingale. Although these systematic approaches to care went some way to providing visibility about decision making and care delivery, the articulation of that content inherently disregarded the multidisciplinary *process* that characterises the patient journey, both in the community and in a hospital context. This fact has largely conspired to keep the importance of nursing work 'a secret' in regard to the interconnectedness between nursing and medicine.[11] Of particular note here is the implicit, covert historical role of nursing as coordinator of the patient journey and overseer of quality, within a system that privileges medical knowledge over nursing knowledge. In other words, nursing work and nursing decision making (even well planned and systematised decisions) have remained subsidiary to medicine, and the covert, hidden nature of this relationship has thus rendered the totality of the care pathway assumed and, therefore, invisible.

In everyday practice, therefore, two patterns of shared decision making emerge strongly. First, decisions about individual patients are usually made in isolation, with different decisions being made at different stages by different members of the team, with ultimate authority being awarded to the medical members.[12] Importantly, these decisions may be fed back to the patient in a sporadic, retrospective fashion that gives little clue about the illness trajectory that faces them in the future.[13] Secondly, decisions about collective groups of patients (e.g. pathways in hospital, or practice protocols in primary care), are often made by a group of nominated multidisciplinary clinicians working together for a short and finite period of time, with little regard for the totality of care needs as they fluctuate over time.[14] These protocols often form the basis for 'defensive practices' such as overemphasis on record keeping and management of physical risk factors, which seem to result from a climate of litigation risk, rather than a concern for the overall quality of care.[15]

What is at issue here for both clinicians and patients is illustrated in Box 4.1, an anonymised amalgamation of many clinical incidents involving different people at different times.

Three issues emerge as being important here. First, the lack of integration between decisions made by different members of the team at different times is evident in the experiences of Alf and his family for whom decisions about diagnostic referrals, readmission, and discharge from hospital were made in isolation from each other. Second, highly specialised, segmented aspects of care were addressed using current nationally agreed guidelines; for example, Alf was seen by a tissue viability specialist nurse during his hospital stay who instigated a treatment plan based on clinically agreed protocols for the management of pressure ulcers. The fact that each individual member of the team followed agreed best practices made it difficult for Alf's family to complain following Alf's death; each professional group was found to have acted in an accountable, professional manner. Third, the resulting invisibility of the lack of integration, and lack of regard for the patient journey, made an analysis of the overall structural and organisational issues impossible, thus silencing the voices of clinicians who wished to see change. We now turn to these issues.

---

**BOX 4.1  Alf Brown**

**Alf Brown**, a 51-year-old man, who lives with his wife, was diagnosed with COPD two years ago, following a working life in the coalmines. Lately, he suffered with pain, breathlessness, mobility problems, faecal incontinence and pressure ulcers associated with end-stage COPD and was readmitted to Ward 1 for treatment of a chest infection. Once there, he was treated with antibiotics and diuretics but his general condition had deteriorated and he wished to return home to spend his last days with his family. Alf was unknown to the district nursing team until a faxed referral was received from Ward 1, alerting them to Alf's discharge from hospital that same day (a Friday). Equipment and services were unavailable out of hours, and the patient's family tried their best to care for him at home. Sadly, Alf suffered a difficult and complex death at home just days later. The last four days of Alf's life were characterised by breathlessness and panic, difficulty in managing incontinence and exudate from the pressure ulcers, and frightening hallucinations associated with screaming, sweating and difficulty sleeping. Alf's family was very angry with the community staff for allowing him to suffer, and expressed bitterness that they were left to cope in such difficult circumstances.

---

## THE ORGANISATION OF HEALTHCARE AROUND SPECIALIST SKILLS

Historically, Alf's care might have been coordinated by 'Matron' who had a concern not just for the work being done but also its overall quality. Questions about a replacement for the hierarchical, covert coordination role held by matrons have been met with calls for less top-down leadership in which all qualified nurses share individual accountability and autonomy for their practice.[16] At issue here is the emphasis given to evidence-based medicine (EBM) which both privileges medical knowledge over, sometimes, more qualitative experiential knowledge specific to nursing, and also predominantly, and often covertly, shapes decision making as the more powerful discipline.[17] In response to this, *The New NHS: modern, dependable*, urged nurses and other clinicians to work more collaboratively with more flexible approaches to role boundaries while at the same time establishing clear lines of accountability for quality of care.[18]

In its pursuit of a way of articulating the management of the patient journey, and the quality and management of care within that journey, the professional-isation of nursing has been characterised by debates about the need for a specialist body of knowledge that recognises the experiential aspect of care, and a way of articulating that knowledge in a way that was substantively different from medical objectification and dominance over the 'dependent patient'.[19] In other words, nursing as a profession needed to find a new way of exercising its new-found specialist body of knowledge that did not involve 'telling people what to do', but that simultaneously challenged the gendered subordination of a predominantly female workforce. This is a difficult task since nursing traditionally 'fills in the gaps' left in what Williams and Sibbald call 'ambiguous spaces' between the prevailing configuration of services attached to medicine.[20] Attempts to formalise this role have led to considerable pressure to undertake work formerly carried out by medical staff. While this represents a great opportunity for nursing, it has also resulted in uncertainty about role demarcation, autonomy and legal responsibility. Responses to this have emerged in the development of specialist roles, largely formulated around disease specific, medical specialties and focused on technical, diagnostic and pharmacological-based treatment skills.[21]

Two dangers emerge here as the nurse develops an increasing array of technical and specialist skills. First, the focus on individual performance does not equate with influence over wider issues; in fact, there may be a 'distinct lack of empowerment for effective managerial decision making and nursing control'.[22] Concerns over individual, specialist skills do little to challenge the organisational and structural limitations that are placed on patient care, as evidenced in Alf's vignette. Here, events were associated with a failure to refer Alf to a community team much sooner in his care trajectory, poorly coordinated weekend discharge from hospital, unsystematic processes of care which struggled to adapt to the patient's unusual physiology (particularly allergies to standard treatments), lack of integration, lack of information, lack of emergency equipment, as well as perceived lack of support from a line manager whose own clinical background was not in community nursing. Most of these factors seem to be organisational, structural and process oriented: areas that traditionally lie outside of nursing's sphere of influence.

The team members, who suffered anxiety and stress as a result of this incident, were advised by their manager to undertake clinical supervision. This helped them to internalise and take responsibility for 'their shortcomings' in not providing this patient with a 'good death'. This reinforcement of the *individual* burden of responsibility led to depression and clinical stress in some members of the team, which in turn led to high sickness levels, high staff turnover, increased clinical errors and an overall deterioration in staff morale. Although 'reflection-in-action' is seen as being a central tool in the professional armoury of nursing,[23] that reflection can be limited to questions about 'what *I* could have done differently', reinforced by the drive towards individual accountability in nursing, and contributing to the lack of empowerment felt by nurses. This often leads to the covert power games that constrain reflection-in-action, and relegates it to 'reflection-in-your-own time'. This then underlines the personal responsibility of nurses in the face of structural and organisation constraints to the delivery of good quality care where a more appropriate question might be: 'What could *we* have done differently?'[24]

Second, the focus on specialist skills failed to take into account the patient journey and the ways in which essential care needs (more of which later) fluctuated over time. The fact that all this occurred against a backdrop of the professionalisation of nursing, a proliferation of specialist nursing roles (in the form of, for example, tissue viability nurse specialist, respiratory specialist nurse, palliative care specialist), and a claimed erosion of the subordination of nurses within medicine, gives little comfort to Alf and his family who were failed at every stage of the patient journey. For example, Alf's pressure ulcers (which caused so much pain and distress) were managed using a specialist, rather than a systems approach. It is generally accepted that nurses are responsible for pressure ulcers; this collective responsibility was first documented by Florence Nightingale who argued that it was the fault of the nurses if they developed.[25] Certainly, some pressure ulcers arise from a failure to perform what are seen as basic nursing duties.[26]

These omissions can lead to individual nurses being held to account in official complaints, in litigation and to being charged with contravening the profession's Code of Conduct.[27] While there is no doubt that using nurses as scapegoats is too simplistic an approach,[28] the nursing profession's Code of Conduct stresses each individual nurse's accountability for not just an *action* but also an *omission*. We are not arguing for the abolition of specialist skills here; merely that in themselves they are not sufficient to achieve the vision for patient-centred care outlined earlier. Each specialisation will no doubt have its own protocols and plans demonstrating a degree of systematisation, but systematisation within a discipline or a specialism serves little purpose for the streamlining of care as a whole. The unarguable fact that decisions are a function of power differentials between nursing and medicine and that these differentials are acted out covertly, renders 'clear lines of responsibility and accountability in the overall quality of clinical care'[29] an impossible objective. What is required is a collective, whole systems approach to care in which specialist skills and outcomes are an integral part of a patient journey. But this is no easy task without a mechanism for discussing what underpins those roles and responsibilities in relation to beliefs and understandings about healthcare.

## THE MEANINGS ASCRIBED TO HEALTHCARE

Increasingly, clinicians will express their understanding of 'healthcare' in relation to their specialist skills and contributions. The obsession with specialisation can be located in a profession that sees the attributes of the medical profession (that is largely curative focused) as being desirable. But for Alf and his family, 'healthcare' constituted a journey which began on his admission to hospital and ended in his difficult death with 'no one professional who understands or is accountable for the process of care the patient experiences, or indeed the outcome of that process'.[30] But nurses already know there is more to patient-centred care than episodic specialities. One of the commonly identified reasons for the move away from purely task-based styles of organisation referred to earlier was the accusation that the individual needs of patients are largely ignored, a criticism articulated by those concerned with the delivery of 'patient-centred care' that is responsive to individual, changing needs.[31]

For this reason, Kitson outlines a vision which identifies an appreciation of patient-centred care as being the major driver for sustained change in the health service in which *care* is given equal status to *cure*.[32] The development and deployment of specialist knowledge and professional skills about *collective* care is sometimes argued to be at odds with the unique contribution of nursing to be entirely responsive to the *individual* needs of patients as they fluctuate over time. But what increasingly emerge as important are skills in coordinating and integrating the deployment of specialist skills in ways that empower the patient and take into account the patient journey in its entirety as well as the quality of its essential elements. For example, 'Essence of Care', a Department of Health funded benchmarking exercise that arose from a concern to 'get the basics right', focuses on improving the experience of patients via developments in 10 areas including communication, pressure ulcers, privacy and self-care.[33] The challenge for nursing is to find ways of managing both collective and individual needs in a way that manages the contextual and structural elements of care delivery and planning.

## IMPLICATIONS FOR CLINICAL WORK

One of the questions associated with specialisation and role blurring is concerned with shared accountability. Accountability is at the heart of a drive towards clinical governance in the UK. Nurses, like any members of a profession, have always been accountable to their own professional regulating body, but there is an increasing need for a new, collective responsibility and accountability.

The literature addresses both 'downward' accountability (to the local community or to individual patients), and 'upward' accountability (to the NHS hierarchy). However, neither of these is possible without first putting in place mechanisms for establishing and maintaining horizontal accountability across multiprofessional teams, wards and general practices.[34] Scott asserts that this requires a 'cultural shift on the part of practising clinicians towards more open and impartial evaluation of clinical care and its outcome'.[35]

Of course, the cultural climate and the beliefs and values we hold about our work are directly related to the subsequent organisation of that work. So, the way in which relationships with medicine are constructed will influence a nurse's ability to act as an advocate for Alf. These relationships have been the subject of interest for some time; what is missing is a mechanism for enacting the cultural shift so that it becomes both a process and an outcome. This calls for nurses and nursing to 'place caring at the centre of all we plan and do in the National Health Service'[36] and ultimately to reconstruct our ideas about what it means to be a member of a profession. It requires a shift from 'telling' towards a shared 'listening' in which the needs and priorities of the individual is paramount, and leadership is a concern shared by all nurses.

In such a change nurses are given the tools to take responsibility for planned changes in their practices in a way that gives them ownership, a sense of agency, and pride in their work. And these tools include well designed integrated care pathways which are based on best evidence and reflect professional consensus. The authority of integrated care pathways takes over from the authority of Sister but in a way that makes explicit the beliefs and values that we are talking about. Pathways give us the mechanism by which to negotiate the type of involvement, ownership, control and authority that is inherent in Kitson's vision.

Accountability for improvements in patient-centred care as an end in itself focus on the standardisation of practice via guidelines such as those provided in National Service Frameworks.[37] However, Kitson's argument highlights the need to focus on the *means* to that end, such as improved leadership, ownership and control. At heart here is the way in which a 'profession' is construed. Much of the literature cites the tension between the negative attributes of profession (e.g. self-interest and competition) and the more altruistic elements of patient-centred care (e.g. compassion and continuity).[38] Rather than force ourselves into a construction of profession that is inconsistent with our commitment to patient-centred care, we need a reconceptualisation of the nature of profession in which care is organised around competencies, the patient journey and essences of care. Care organised in this way would be based on explicit negotiation of aims, roles and responsibilities, which define us as contributors to a team, rather than as solo players with specialist concerns. The core values of patient-centred care would be defined and redefined within this forum based on shared evaluation, including the perspective of the patient and their family, so that recognition could be given that Alf and his family had a much bigger role to play, much earlier on in his care trajectory.

## IMPLICATIONS FOR ALF, HIS FAMILY AND HIS CLINICIANS

Is this all unattainable dreaming? In Alf's care, the local palliative care team was awarded some funds to invest in the introduction of the Liverpool Care Pathway for the Dying.[39] Some of the community and respiratory specialist nurses volunteered to act as champions for a pathway development because they recognised the chance to understand and deal with some difficult issues. There was some resistance to the pathway among medical staff (and some community nurses), but overall its introduction allowed the team to manage difficult and complex cases so that good deaths became the norm, not the exception. Patient and family satisfaction rose, multidisciplinary working relationships improved, communication and coordination improved, and staff turnover and sickness rates reduced.

For the nurses, pathways added another layer onto essence of care statements about actions and quality by placing a sense of order and rhythm onto the tasks. For example, instead of being told 'Improve the maintenance of dignity for patients' (as in essence of care benchmarking), pathways outline the sequence of events, by whom, in what order, to what level of quality, cost, and outcome, so that dignity can be maintained within a supportive context. This is important; without clear, definable shared goals and objectives, it is very difficult for nurses today to know when they have 'done a good job'. The nurses involved in the vignette reported that using the pathway helped them to plan their own goals (instead of remaining passive and invisible) and demonstrate when and how well they had achieved them.

Of course, the flip side to this is that non-achievement of the activities in the pathway can be used as a performance management tool in a punitive way. However, even this was welcomed by the nurses who felt that a clear, transparent measure of performance helped to remove the fear of an imminent, invisible and indefinable Sword of Damocles.[40] Allaying the concerns of the GPs about 'trusting' the community nurses to follow the guidelines for drug administration in the home took major time and effort. But its net effect was much greater than implementation of the pathway itself; once nurses had proved they could work within the pathway and could do so in a safe and timely manner, they began to be involved in decision making about other matters and were given a greater stake in the running of the organisation.

In a wider sense, pathways that are fundamentally based on patient-centred care and the patient journey have the capability of giving nursing the structure needed to develop visibility and transparency about what we do (i.e. the unique nature of nursing and essences of care), and how well we do it (concerns about quality). The processes involved in constructing and implementing a pathway inherently side-step the hidden decision making and ambiguities that make up so much of nursing work. By being involved in the meetings and decision making that are necessary to action a pathway, nurses can show the sort of ownership, authority and leadership that Kitson and others call for. The defining nature of a profession, using this model, is the ability to construct a collaboratively agreed pathway and to act on it in an individualised way that takes into account the patient's need for privacy, dignity and the essences of care identified earlier. Thus, patient-centred care and systematisation are seen as mutually dependent world views, rather than mutually antagonistic.

## THE FUTURE FOR NURSING AND SYSTEMATISATION

In the debate over professional autonomy and control, it has been argued that the medical profession has resisted systematisation because it fears that the explicit setting out of its work makes it possible 'for forces outside the profession to codify and regulate the labour process'.[41] This debate often focuses on the need to deliver 'individualised' care that is in every case unique and therefore incapable of being described and planned before it happens. This fear has, arguably, led to the maintenance of mystique around everyday professional practice, the monopolisation of indeterminate elements of practice and the delegation of routine elements to nurses. These routine elements, however, lend themselves to systematisation (such as assessment tools, the nursing process, primary nursing) which perhaps has been unwittingly used as a further method to maintain the subordination of nursing.

Yet, all nurses know that even these 'routine elements' require skill and individual judgement about the essences of care such as privacy and dignity that cannot be easily systematised. So the dilemma facing nursing is that its commitment to making visible what it does, and to what level of quality, potentially shifts control to external *elements*, thus making nursing more, not less, vulnerable to encroachments of management (including financial) control, and to the power differentials between medicine and nursing. However, as Alf's care demonstrates, it is not the *elements* of care that define nurses as professionals but the ability and competency to put those collective elements together into a *process* that is individual patient-centred care. Beil-Hildebrand argues that medical clinicians resist systematisation in order to maintain their professional privilege, status and power.[42] **Collective** systematisation, via the use of integrated care pathways, provides a middle ground in which to articulate, and negotiate, individual contributions in a way that breaks down barriers of professional self-interest. It is only then that we can truly develop and deliver the essences of patient-centred care in a way that is visible, valued and respected.

The professionalisation of nursing, with its unique knowledge base, its commitment to quality assurance, to the transparent organisation and planning of care, places nursing at the forefront of the clinical governance agenda. While the literature on clinical governance and accountability is heavily critical of the lack of specificity and the lack of guidance on the blurring of role boundaries, this represents a golden opportunity for nursing to lead the way to achieve collegiate, patient-centred, quality-assured care that allows for true systematisation of the patient journey. However, despite nursing's clear allegiance with systematisation in its various guises, historical gendered divisions of labour and decision making patterns continue to muddy the waters in clinical practice. Despite legal and professional calls for accountability, nurses all too often find themselves in positions as covert, hidden custodians of individual patient-centred care with very little input into more collective strategic decision making. Pathways have the potential to allow for open discussion and negotiation that allow for patient-centred care to be placed at the heart of systematisation, which then becomes a mechanism, rather than a barrier, to achieving Kitson's vision. We began this chapter with the recognition that an empowered, autonomous nursing workforce and patient-centred care are inextricably linked – integrated pathways give us the tools to achieve both in an open, explicit manner.

## ACKNOWLEDGEMENT

We wish to thank Linda Newton (Palliative Care Specialist Nurse) for her comments on an earlier draft.

## REFERENCES

1 Kitson A. Nursing leadership: bringing caring back to the future. *Quality in Health Care.* 2001; **10**: 79–84.
2 Wolf ZR. *Nurses' Work, the Sacred and the Profane.* Philadephia: University of Pennsylvania Press; 1988. Wicks D. *Nurses and Doctors at Work: rethinking professional boundaries.* Buckingham: Open University Press; 1998. Savage J, Moore L. *Interpreting Accountability: an ethnographic study of practice nurses, accountability and multidisciplinary team decision-making in the context of clinical governance.* Research report, London: Royal College of Nursing; 2004.
3 Reed J, Watson D. The impact of the medical model on nursing practice and assessment. *Int J Nursing Studies.* 1994; **31**(1): 57–66.
4 Kitson, op. cit.
5 Wicks, op. cit. Porter S. *Nursing's Relationship with Medicine.* Aldershot: Avebury Publishing; 1995.
6 Wolf, op. cit. Wicks, op. cit.
7 Department of Health. *A Strategy for Nursing: a report from the Steering Committee.* London: Department of Health Nursing Division; 1989. Ersser S, Tutton E. Primary nursing: a second look. In: Ersser S, Tutton E, eds. *Primary Nursing in Perspective.* 2nd ed. Oxford: Scutari Press; 1991. pp. 3–30. Rafferty D. Team and primary nursing. *Senior Nurse.* 1992; **12**(1): 31–4.
8 Arnold D. Nursing and power-use of the so-called poststructuralism theory for the analysis of the power-relationships in the 'female' nursing professional. *Pflege.* 1996; **9**(1): 72–9. Savage, Moore, op. cit.
9 Savage, Moore, op. cit.
10 Wicks, op. cit.
11 Ibid.
12 Savage, Moore, op.cit.
13 Close H, Procter S. Coping strategies used by hospitalised stroke patients: implications for continuity and management of care. *J Advanced Nursing.* 1999; **29**(1): 138–44. Close H. Roles and responsibilities in understanding, accepting and adapting to an uncertain chronic illness trajectory. Unpublished PhD Thesis, Northumbria University; 2005.

14 Dowswell T, Wilkin D, Banks-Smith J. Nurses and English primary care groups: their experiences and perceived influence on policy development. *J Advanced Nursing*. 2002; **37**(1): 35–42.

15 Wiener C, Kayser-Jones J. Defensive work in nursing homes: accountability gone amok. *Social Science and Medicine*. 1989; **28**(1): 37–44. Annandale E. Working on the front-line: risk culture and nursing in the new NHS. *Sociological Review*. 1996; **94**(3): 416–51.

16 Kitson, op. cit.

17 Savage, Moore, op. cit.

18 Department of Health. *The New NHS: modern, dependable*. London: HMSO; 1997.

19 Beil-Hildebrand M. Theorising culture and culture in context: institutional excellence and control. *Nursing Inquiry*. 2002; **9**(4): 257–74.

20 Williams A, Sibbald B. Changing roles and identities in primary health care: exploring a culture of uncertainty. *J Advanced Nursing*. 1999; **29**(3): 737–45.

21 Beil-Hildebrand, op. cit.

22 Lewis M. Flogging the dead horse: the myth of nursing empowerment? *J Nursing Management*. 2000; **8**: 209–13 (quotation from p. 212).

23 Schon DA. *The Reflective Practitioner*. London: Jossey Bass: 1991.

24 Mantzoukas S, Jasper MA. Reflective practice and daily ward reality: a covert power game. *J Clinical Nursing*. 2004; **13**: 925–33.

25 Nightingale F. *Notes on Nursing: what it is and what it is not*. London: Duckworth & Co.; 1970.

26 Moore D. The buck stops with you. *Nursing Times*. 1987; **83**(39): 54–6.

27 Department of Health. Abstract from the Select Committee Report in relation to the Health Service Ombudsman Report for 1994–95. *J Tissue Viability*. 1996; **6**(3). Bhomick BK. Management of pressure sores – who's responsible? *Geriatric Medicine*. 1992; **16**: 19. Dimond B. Pressure sores: a case to answer. *Brit J Nursing*. 1994; **3**(14): 721–7. Taylor JS. Malpractice implications of pressure ulcers. *Advances in Wound Care*. 1994; **7**(5): 43–8.

28 Anthony D. The treatment of decubitus ulcers: a century of misinformation in the textbooks. *J Advanced Nursing*. 1996; **24**: 309–16.

29 National Health Service Executive. *Clinical Governance: quality in the new NHS*. London: HMSO; 1999.

30 Scott I. Clinical governance: an opportunity for nurses to influence the future of healthcare development. *NT Research*. 1999; **4**(3): 170–6 (quotation from p. 171).

31 Pembrey S. The development of nursing practice: a new contribution. *Senior Nurse*. 1989; **9**(8): 3–8.

32 Kitson, op. cit.

33 National Health Service Clinical Support Governance Team. Essence of Care Programme, 2006. http://www.cgsupport.nhs.uk/Programmes/Essence_of_Care_Programme/default.asp (accessed 3 October 2006).

34 Allen P. Accountability for clinical governance: developing collective responsibility for quality in primary care. *BMJ*. 2000; **321**: 608–11.

35 Scott I. Time for a collective approach from medical specialists to clinical governance (editorial). *Int Med J*. 2003; **32**: 499–501 (quotation from p. 499).

36 Kitson, op. cit.

37 Burnhope C, Edmonstone J. 'Feel the fear and do it anyway': the hard business of developing shared governance. *J Nursing Management*. 2003; **11**: 147–57.

38 Beil-Hildebrand, op. cit.

39 Marie Curie. Liverpool Care Pathway for the dying patient (LCP). http://www.lcp-mariecurie.org.uk (accessed 5 January 2005).

40 Annandale, op. cit.

41 Beil-Hildebrand, op. cit.

42 Ibid.

# CHAPTER 5

# Using data to inform systematised approaches to care delivery

*Barbara Coyle, John Kennedy, Sharyn Maxwell and Pieter Degeling*

For more than 10 years policy authorities within the NHS have, and to a large degree still are, focused on the need to balance quality of care with resource efficiency. Over time, the pursuit of these aims has led to a growing awareness of a need to pursue *systemic* productivity and efficiency (DH). Systems are complex entities which, by virtue of the interrelatedness of their components and nonlinearity of cause and effect within them, can be difficult to analyse and understand. However, the growing sophistication in computer programming and wider prevalence of national and local databanks means the NHS now has the means to begin addressing healthcare issues from a systemic perspective.

This chapter reviews the contribution to systemic understanding of NHS healthcare provision, and its improvement within both strategic and clinical contexts, that is available through analysis of Hospital Episode Statistics (HES). HES data contains information on all NHS inpatient admissions within England. As this dataset is of value to both clinical practitioners and healthcare managers, an understanding of the construction of the dataset, the various classification systems for clinical work incorporated within it, and how these can be used to meet managers' and clinicians' specific needs is provided as the chapter unfolds.

## DATA: WHAT WE HAVE AND WHAT WE NEED

What do we mean by data and why do we gather it? When we seek to represent transactions we call the representations data; when we seek to order these data to inform choice we call them information. In our individual lives the gatherer and the user are usually the same person; data collection and use are entwined. This is rarely so within organisations. Thus there are questions about who collects data and who uses them for which purpose, who bears the cost of collection and transformation, and who gets the benefit. People who do not use the data they collect themselves often see the costs of collection as an imposition. For example, project teams charged with making decisions about a new service or treatment may demand more data, while those such as clinicians who then 'populate' the datasets complain that too much of their time is committed to producing the data for others. It is therefore important that users of data are aware of what data are available to them as well as understanding the strengths and limitations of those data and how they can be best used to inform decisions.

## What data do we have?

A great deal of healthcare data is already collected, collated and stored by and can be benchmarked across organisations. What is recorded is likely to be a 'data point,' a patient admitted, a condition diagnosed, a prescription dispensed, etc. However, the resulting datasets are complex.

The main unit of recording within the HES data is the finished consultant episode (a period of admitted patient care under a consultant or allied healthcare professional within an NHS Trust). This is not always the same as a single stay (spell) in hospital because a patient may be transferred from one consultant to another during their stay. In these cases, there will be two or more episode records for the spell of treatment. Trusts are required to code diagnoses according to the International Classification of Diseases, 10th Revision (ICD-10), which is a comprehensive classification of causes of morbidity and mortality published by the World Health Organization, and surgical procedures (operations) according to the Office of Population, Censuses and Surveys: Classification of Surgical Operations and Procedures, 4th Revision (OPCS-4). ICD-10 categories are organised into chapters of related conditions. Each disease that is of public health importance or that occurs frequently has its own category; otherwise categories are assigned to groups of separate but related conditions.

More recently, clinical activity in the UK has been classified into Health Resource Groups (HRGs), essentially as a resource management tool for the NHS. There are 610 HRGs (seven of which describe cases where an HRG cannot be assigned for various reasons, such as incorrect age or primary diagnosis) which are constructed using a standard computer algorithm or 'grouper' that assigns episodes of care involving different treatments (surgical procedures) to groups that are clinically similar and involve roughly the same demands on the hospital in terms of 'resource usage'. The OPCS-4 procedure codes and ICD-10 diagnostic codes that describe each episode of care are used to assign an HRG code to an episode and also to a spell.[1]

Although the HRG system was not designed primarily as the basis for a prospective organisation of clinical work at an operational level, it is a means for retrospectively understanding the throughput of hospitals. Moreover, under Payment by Results (PbR)[2] secondary care is funded on the basis of volumes of completed work at set prices within HRGs. Hospitals' long-term viability therefore depends on them finding a means to ensure that the total cost of discharged patients is at or below the HRG tariff received for the care delivery. This suggests a means must be found to use the HRG system also to manage clinical work and its associated resource costs.

There are thus two different datasets for recording cases, one built on clinical symptoms and one on patterns of treatment and their resource implications. The first is likely to appeal more to clinicians, the second more to managers, but both are relevant, and the task is to mobilise data in ways that can inform both organisational strategy and clinical decision making.

## What is the quality of the data that we have?

Errors in data collection, recording and analysis are the reason most often cited by clinicians and managers for being wary of hospital activity data. Obviously, information depends on what and how well data have been recorded. Under PbR coding errors can lead to a loss of revenue for providers, which can be particularly significant if they are as high as some of those trusts in Figure 5.1 which have more than 5% of activity incorrectly coded. There are many sources of coding error, such as incomplete recording at the point of service, software problems, errors in data entry and invalid primary diagnoses being used, often reflecting poor coding skill.

Figure 5.1 highlights the variable performance in coding between trusts prior to the wider introduction of case-mix-based funding. The variation suggests that good coding performance is attainable and that concentrating some effort on a more systematised approach to recording of information would mean fewer errors and (for trusts) better cash flow. Trusts located at the

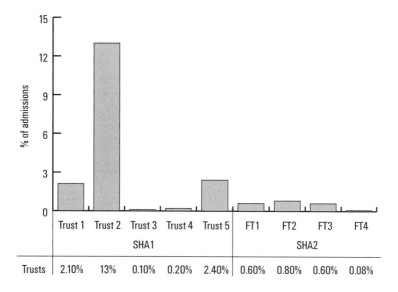

FIGURE 5.1  Percentage of admissions unassigned a valid HRG code, English Acute Trusts, 2004–05

lower end of the graph are mostly foundation trusts (FTs). As FTs have been engaged with PbR for a longer period, their superior coding performance may be an indication that PbR has a positive impact on coding performance.

A recent report by the Audit Commission has identified the need for a centrally coordinated external clinical coding audit programme to ensure that data quality is reliably high.[3] The Commission found evidence of hospital trusts actively working to optimise their coding to maximise income within existing coding rules; hence it is essential that commissioners have the tools and skill base to locally monitor the activity and services for which they are being charged.

## USING DATA TO SUPPORT SYSTEMATISATION IN A STRATEGIC CONTEXT

Within a strategic context, systematised approaches to care delivery involve healthcare organisations asking: 'Are we doing the right things? Are we delivering the most safe, high quality and efficient care that we can?' A great deal of existing data can be used to inform strategic decisions on what and where within a given geographical region services could and should be delivered to ensure productivity, efficiency and quality, and, at another level, to inform individual acute care trusts about what clinical work is worth systematising within the organisation. Analysis of activity may also inform strategic health authorities (SHAs) and primary and secondary care trusts where problems may exist in the standards of care. These may be indicated by significantly high and low volumes of activity, differences in the rates of admission and readmission, or referral patterns from particular GP practices and localities. Thus the data indicate where in the healthcare system important activity management concerns originate and which concerns may benefit from systematisation.

### High volume conditions

The feasibility of systematised approaches to clinical work depends on frequency. Disaggregating hospital activity by clinical condition highlights those high volume conditions which, with the exception of highly technology intensive work, constitute the bulk of the workload and cost. For high volume conditions, there is likely to be some de facto systematisation, insofar as the various members of the team have their standard working practices. These practices need to be made explicit and clearly related to one another according to best practice. Best practice can also be furthered by adopting techniques that routinely review care delivery with a view to reducing clinical practice variation within resource constraints and improving quality of care. ICPs are one way to do this; however, not all clinical conditions are worth such investment of effort. Hence an analysis of an organisation's high-volume activity provides a useful guide for discussions about which conditions should be the focus of efforts to improve clinical management.

Characteristically, for most providers the bulk of emergency, maternity and birth admissions, elective admissions and day cases are contained within a relatively few HRGs. In summary the evidence suggests that, on average, for an English acute trust:

- 40 HRGs (of 603 valid HRGs) account for 46% of all emergency admissions and these HRGs account for 42% of all emergency-generated bed days for a healthcare provider
- 20 of these top 40 emergency HRGs reference long-term conditions with high rates of multiple admissions
- 40 HRGs account for 60% of all elective inpatient admissions and these HRGs account for 40% of all elective inpatient generated bed days
- 40 HRGs account for 84% of elective day cases; and
- 10 HRGs account for 98% of maternity and birth admissions and 97% of maternity and birth bed days.

Further investigation has found that there is a consistency in the HRGs that make up these high-volume conditions across acute trusts.[4] Hence one importance of this dataset for an SHA or commissioner may lie in ensuring consistent quality for high-volume conditions across trusts, via benchmarking of care activity, quality and cost within its geographical area.

## Low volume conditions

The same data used in a different way can be used to demonstrate the conditions that are low volume within a hospital trust or health economy and which raise different questions for strategic management. As demonstrated in Figure 5.2, an examination of activity data from a number of trusts from one SHA indicates that these trusts are doing at least half the possible 603 valid

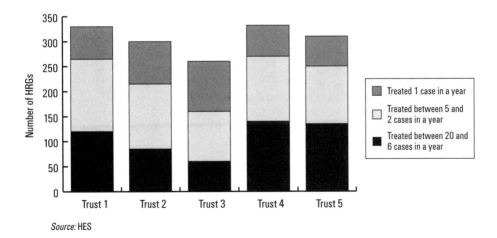

Source: HES

**FIGURE 5.2** Low-volume elective inpatient admissions by hospital trusts from one SHA (2004–05)

HRGs as low-volume case types (defined here as fewer than 20 cases a year). At times the volume is extremely low: in Trust 3, for example, there was only one elective admission in a year for 102 separate HRGs. If some of these HRGs are likely to be specific instances of more general and higher volume procedures and thus not necessarily instances of unrelated low-volume activity, others will be.

Why are low-volume case types significant? When providers treat patients with specific conditions at low volumes, they may lack the specialist skills that these conditions require. This possibility raises questions about the quality and cost of such care: for example, does a lower admission or treatment rate imply a loss of medical skills and expertise in treating these conditions and, if so, does this mean that complications increase, convalescent rates slow, lengths of stay go up and financial costs increase? SHA, hospital trusts and PCTs can get some answers to these questions from available data on length of stay.

Under the PbR financial system, tariffs are calculated on the basis of 'trimmed' data; that is, spells are excluded if the length of stay is in excess of the 'trimpoint' for that condition. Trusts will be reimbursed for most HRGs at a price calculated using trimmed data. An examination of such data enables a commissioner to examine which conditions are giving rise to treatment

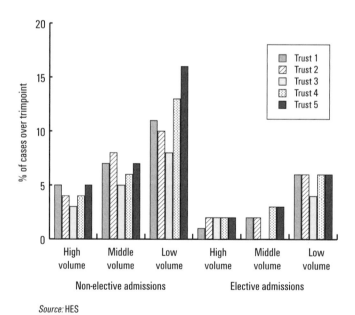

Source: HES

Low volume case types: HRGs with more than one but fewer than 20 admissions within one year.
High volume case types: HRGs with the top 40 highest frequency of admissions.
Middle volume case types: all other HRGs.

**FIGURE 5.3** Percentage of cases above trimpoint by admission type and by volume category for trusts from one SHA (2004–05, using 2003–04 trimpoint)

in excess of the systematised norms of the PbR system. The extent of the differences in the incidence of exceptional cases within and between trusts and how this may be being affected by the volume of cases in each HRG can be mapped by measuring the percentage of trimmed cases by admission type and volume category.

Using data from a number of trusts from one SHA, Figure 5.3 demonstrates that in 2004–05 these trusts displayed very similar patterns in the percentage of cases that were above the trimpoint for each HRG. The more important finding is that, for both emergency and elective admissions, the percentage of cases above the trimpoint increases as the volume of activity decreases. In other words, HRGs with fewer than 20 cases a year were associated with a marked increase in length of stay above the national average. This suggests that patients with these conditions are not always treated efficiently. The impact of this inefficiency must, a priori, be borne by the patient: disruption, pain, inconvenience and loss of work days. At a minimum there is an additional financial cost for the PCT in terms of excess bed days tariff. Further, increasingly greater financial costs may result if the longer than expected lengths of stay are occasioned by poorer quality outcomes necessitating increased treatment needs and/or generating complaints and even litigation.

Although it would be difficult to role-delineate emergency care, this is not the case for elective care. By definition, elective inpatient admissions could be provided in the hospital that is regarded as the most appropriate. This would be likely to improve the effectiveness of clinical practice and to reduce the length of stay and the cost of treatment. These data suggest that an appropriate strategy to increase efficiency (and, we surmise, quality) would be to concentrate low volume elective cases in particular hospitals, where they would become medium to high volume cases. Through this role delineation within a health economy or SHA region, staff could then develop and/or maintain a level of expertise in treating these conditions to the benefit of both the patients and the health service.

We recognise that relocating some conditions and/or services between hospitals (with its potential to either limit choice or herald a future hospital closure) is currently a very contentious issue in the UK and needs careful consultation and management with the communities affected. However, we suggest that some of the 'heat' may be taken out of role delineation discussions if the stakeholders were to receive reliable data about the size of the problem in terms of patients affected, costs and quality.

## Shifts between acute and primary care

It is a broad policy objective that healthcare should be provided as close to the user as possible, and that acute care should be used only when primary care is unsuitable. Admission data show, however, that people are frequently admitted to hospital for conditions that could be more appropriately and economically dealt with in primary care. Patients routinely admitted to acute care with the same condition may thus be an indication of inadequate facilities in primary care with the result that the acute facility becomes the provider of first resort.

As demonstrated in Figure 5.4, the percentage of emergency admissions that are attributable to subsequent admissions within one year range from a high of 40% to a low of 5%. Most secondary care trusts have more than 25% of their total emergency activity generated by multiple admissions. This variation in multiple admission rates has very significant resource implications for both the acute provider and the NHS as a whole, as treating people in acute care when primary care would have been more appropriate puts an additional and unnecessary strain on (costly) acute facilities.

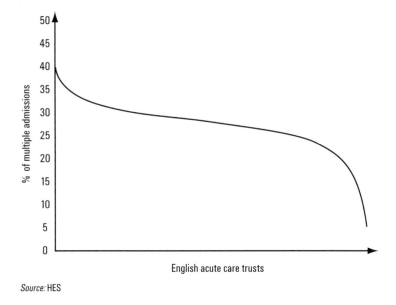

*Source:* HES

**FIGURE 5.4** Percentage of emergency admissions attributable to multiple admission by English acute care trusts (within one-year period, 2004–05)

Hospital inpatient data further show that this tendency for multiple admissions is not evenly distributed, and that some GP practices, for instance, have higher rates than others. Figure 5.5 shows the potential reduction in admissions to hospital by GP practices from several sample PCTs. The data was derived by calculating the difference in admissions in the event that the rate of multiple admissions could be reduced to a rate that is expected if all admissions were independent from one another (derived from a Poisson distribution – *see* appendix to this chapter).

Figure 5.5 illustrates that for this sample of GP practices, the associated PCTs could aim to achieve an average reduction of between 20% and 45% of emergency admissions. For commissioners in a PbR environment, reducing admissions is equivalent to reducing payment and hence those figures reflect

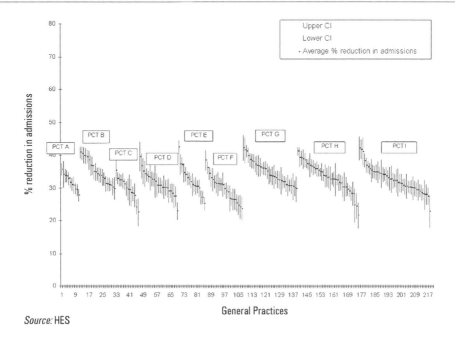

Source: HES

**FIGURE 5.5** Average potential reduction in admissions per GP practice from one SHA (2004–05) (GP practices are clustered according to their associated PCT)

the potential reinvestment opportunities for PCTs. As noted previously, 20 of the top 40 emergency HRGs reference long-term conditions with high rates of multiple admissions and it is these that would be the best starting place attempting to reduce multiple admissions to hospital.

In essence the data suggest that systematisation should focus not simply on how to improve hospital efficiency but also on how the demand for acute services might be better managed. These findings also support the argument for the development and implementation of a systematised approach for orchestrating, funding, supporting and monitoring service provision to patients with long-term conditions, such as the Year of Care model described in Chapter 9.

## USING DATA TO SUPPORT SYSTEMATISATION IN A CLINICAL CONTEXT: DESIGNING INTEGRATED CARE PATHWAYS

We turn now to a review of how HES data can be relevant to a clinical team in its day-to-day practice. The successful construction and implementation of individual care pathways requires frontline clinical staff to identify the degree of patient and clinical complexity appropriate for each specific pathway. HES data can be used as a means for informing these decisions but first clinical staff must resolve issues surrounding the appropriate classification system of clinical work, in particular whether pathways should be constructed around HRGs or ICD-10 codes or combinations of these.

## What data should inform pathway design?

HRGs are resource-based constructs; they comprise different clinical conditions that use similar amounts of clinical financial resource. The same clinical condition can be split between two HRGs if there are several comorbidities or complications which increase the average amount of resources required; hence one HRG will include those patients without comorbidities or complications, another will include patients with them.

Each HRG consists of spells that have various ICD-10 codes as the primary diagnoses. In practice, the HRG and ICD-10 classifications overlap to a large degree; thus somewhat similar depictions of activity can result from either classification. However, for a small percentage of patients, the choice of one classification system over the other can have important clinical and organisational ramifications.

**TABLE 5.1** Breakdown of HRG by primary diagnosis: emergency admissions for HRG D40 (COPD or bronchitis without complications) 1999–00 to 2004–05

| ICD-10 code | Description | Number of admissions | Admissions % within HRG | Average length of stay (days) |
|---|---|---|---|---|
| J441 | Chronic obstructive pulmonary disease (COPD) with acute exacerbation, unspecified | 1087 | 69.4% | 8.9 |
| J449 | COPD unspecified | 226 | 14.4% | 9.4 |
| J440 | COPD with acute lower respiratory infection | 201 | 12.9% | 9.4 |
| J439 | Emphysema, unspecified | 23 | 1.5% | 7.7 |
| J209 | Acute bronchitis, unspecified | 12 | 0.8% | 4.3 |
| J40X | Bronchitis, not specified as acute or chronic | 6 | 0.4% | 5.2 |
| J041 | Acute tracheitis | 2 | 0.1% | 2.0 |
| J219 | Acute bronchiolitis, unspecified | 2 | 0.1% | 13.0 |
| J42X | Unspecified chronic bronchitis | 2 | 0.1% | 7.0 |
| J208 | Acute bronchitis due to other specified organisms | 1 | 0.1% | 1.0 |
| J210 | Acute bronchiolitis due to respiratory syncytial virus | 1 | 0.1% | 0 |
| J438 | Other emphysema | 1 | 0.1% | 1.0 |
| J448 | Other specified COPD | 1 | 0.1% | 11.0 |
| Total | | 1565 | 100% | |

We can illustrate some of the issues here using chronic obstructive pulmonary disease (COPD). In the ICD-10 classification system, COPD codes fall within the respiratory chapter, *J44: Other Chronic obstructive pulmonary disease*, and is mainly classified into three primary codes, J441, J449 and J440. Under the HRG system, COPD is classified according to two HRGs, *D40 COPD or Bronchitis Without Co-morbidities and Complications* and *D39 COPD or Bronchitis with Co-morbidities and Complications*. There is also a third HRG which *may* include COPD: HRG D99 references complex elderly cases with a primary diagnosis concerning the respiratory system.

Table 5.1 shows that, over a five year period for one sample trust, the three main COPD ICD-10 codes accounted for 96.7% of admissions within the HRG D40. The remaining 3.3% of COPD admissions, relating to people with COPD and other respiratory conditions, formed a long 'tail' of ICD-10 codes, all respiratory diseases, some of which are, to a non-clinician, apparently little different from conditions classified as other ICD-10 respiratory codes. The same was true for admissions recorded under HRG D39 (not depicted); these patients had longer average lengths of stay, reflecting the presence of comorbidities and/or complications.

A primary diagnosis code of J44, however, is not confined to HRG D39 or HRG D40. Table 5.2 shows that this code was also assigned to 12 other HRGs although, with the exception of D99 Complex Elderly with a Respiratory System Primary Diagnosis, only in small numbers. Patients with COPD falling into these alternative HRG codes may have been under investigation or having treatment for some other condition simultaneously with their COPD. Alternatively, the HRG may reference a procedure that takes precedence over the primary diagnosis, as is the case with H88 (an emergency due to a fractured neck of femur).

The close clinical similarities between the various manifestations of COPD and the prevalence of patients with an unspecified acute exacerbation suggests that only one pathway would be required to manage patients with COPD. From the data above, this pathway should be structured around ICD-10 code J44 *and* its care components and sequences should be such that the average cost of treatment per patient is equal to, or lower than, the price received by the trust for treating such patients (i.e. the HRG payment). However, in the light of the potential additional complexity in care for those patients classified as either complex elderly patients or requiring additional procedure (indicated by various applicable ICD-10 codes), some patients may be best cared for under another pathway for a higher priority condition or should not be managed according to a pathways-based approach at all.

Hence the depth of clinical detail that ICD-10 codes provide can assist clinicians to make a prospective decision about which management approach is most appropriate for which patients. The validity of these decisions can be checked in a number of ways including the routine analysis of pathways variance, a review of case records for patients treated in a more traditional approach and an analysis of average (realised) costs per pathway.

**TABLE 5.2** Primary diagnosis of J44: other chronic obstructive pulmonary disease by HRG (1999–00 to 2003–04)

| HRG | HRG label | Number of admissions | Admission % within ICD-10 | Average length of stay (days) |
|---|---|---|---|---|
| D40 | Chronic obstructive pulmonary disease or bronchitis without complications | 1516 | 65.71 | 9.03 |
| D39 | Chronic obstructive pulmonary disease or bronchitis with complications | 415 | 17.99 | 13.01 |
| D99 | Complex elderly with a respiratory system primary diagnosis | 356 | 15.43 | 17.69 |
| L20 | Bladder minor endoscopic procedure with complications | 7 | 0.30 | 26.14 |
| C59 | Exteriorisation of trachea | 4 | 0.17 | 19.00 |
| B13 | Phakoemulsification cataract extraction and insertion of lens | 1 | 0.04 | 8.00 |
| C22 | Intermediate nose procedures | 1 | 0.04 | 19.00 |
| D03 | Major thoracic procedures | 1 | 0.04 | 45.00 |
| D07 | Fibre-optic bronchoscopy | 1 | 0.04 | 0.00 |
| E38 | Electrophysiological and other percutaneous cardiac procedures >18 | 1 | 0.04 | 24.00 |
| H16 | Soft tissue or other bone procedures – Category 1 >69 or with complications | 1 | 0.04 | 101.00 |
| H88 | Other neck of femur fracture with complications | 1 | 0.04 | 65.00 |
| L05 | Kidney intermediate endoscopic procedure >69 or with complications | 1 | 0.04 | 14.00 |
| P04 | Lower respiratory tract disorders without acute bronchiolitis | 1 | 0.04 | 1.00 |
| Total | | 2307 | 100 | |

## The significance of comorbidities and complications

The relevance and importance of complications and comorbidities in pathway design can be further examined by considering the numbers and types of secondary diagnosis. Table 5.3 shows the frequency of secondary diagnoses for ICD-10 primary diagnosis J44 COPD (1999/00 to 2003/04). The table shows that 36% of patients with COPD had no secondary diagnoses, 30% had one secondary diagnosis, 19% had two, and so on. There were no instances in which a person with COPD had seven or more secondary diagnoses. As might have been expected, the average length of stay (ALOS) of these patients increased as their degree of clinical complexity increased.

**TABLE 5.3** Frequency of secondary diagnoses for primary diagnosis J44 COPD (1999–00 to 2003–04)

| No. of secondary diagnoses | 0 | 1 | 2 | 3 | 4 | 5 | 6 | 7+ |
|---|---|---|---|---|---|---|---|---|
| Frequency | 577 | 491 | 308 | 154 | 57 | 23 | 8 | 0 |
| Percentage | 35.66 | 30.35 | 19.04 | 9.52 | 3.52 | 1.42 | 0.49 | 0 |
| Average length of stay | 8.40 | 9.80 | 12.46 | 14.86 | 16.11 | 12.43 | 20.38 | 0 |
| Mean age | 70.5 | 73.7 | 75.0 | 74.8 | 77.3 | 73.2 | 77.1 | 0 |

Further exploration of the secondary diagnoses would indicate which other conditions or comorbidities afflicted this population of people. Clinical judgement then provides an assessment regarding which of these secondary diagnoses have relatively little impact on the treatment and care of patients with COPD. Patients with this category of comorbidities conditions can be included in the primary pathway. Similarly, clinical judgement is required about which of these secondary diagnoses has sufficiently significant effect upon patient treatment and care to preclude patients with these conditions from being included on a clinical pathway, or whether the clinical effect of any secondary diagnosis is indeterminate. The efficacy of such initial decisions can again be assessed via future HES data analysis in combination with data on pathway variance.

## Other data points of relevance for pathway development

One final issue that may be relevant to the inclusion or exclusion of specific patients within a clinical pathway approach to care management is the mode of admission. For example, COPD patients are generally admitted as emergencies. Given the very small volume of patients with COPD admitted as elective cases, it would appear that elective patients could also be included in a COPD pathway; the efficacy of this decision could again be tested once the pathway was implemented.

## CONCLUSIONS

The above discussion has demonstrated how data can be used to inform systematisation at various levels of healthcare provision. HES data can be used to identify the clinical conditions that, via systematised approaches to care delivery and management (such as ICPs) and associated routine and reiterative improvements in productivity, efficiency and quality in acute care, should provide significant gains to both individual healthcare providers and the wider health economy. Analysis of HES data also make explicit certain contradictions that may occur within a health economy when planning systematised approaches to care delivery. For example, under case-mix-based funding systems such as PbR, if PCTs implemented interventions that reduced the multiple admissions of their patients and hence generated real savings, trusts providing acute care would lose income faster than they can (initially at least) cut costs.

Questions remain about information that would be useful to have, but on which we have no data. Most national healthcare-related data is based on aggregation of incidents over the whole population of patients treated: it is not organised around the experience of any individual patient. In such aggregations there is little scope for the voice of the patient to be heard: patients may express their views of their treatment, and doctors and nurses may listen, but none of this is systematically collected as data. Systematised approaches to care delivery such as integrated care pathways can deliver the functionality required to include various 'voices' in collections of data. This includes the patients' and carers' perspectives of care in addition to that of the multidisciplinary professional team. This information, when used in conjunction with variance analysis, provides a rounded and holistic method for planning and monitoring patient care at a patient level.

Understanding and improving complex systems such as healthcare will always require more than simply interrogating data. However, the use of robust data adds an important dimension to debates about how the provision of healthcare can be improved. The examples of real data in this chapter have demonstrated how SHAs, trusts, managers and clinicians can use information to help guide the implementation of systematisation of healthcare at various levels of organisation and provision to the benefit of multiple and ongoing patient and policy concerns.

## NOTE

All data represented in the figures and tables were generated from hospital episode statistics by the Centre for Clinical Management Development, Durham University. Please contact authors for further details.

## APPENDIX

The Poisson distribution is derived from the assumption that the risk of having multiple admissions is constant and independent for all admissions; that is, the risk of every patient being admitted once, twice, three, four, etc. times for a specific condition does not change over the time period, regardless of the number of previous admissions. The discrepancy between the Poisson distribution and the actual distribution can therefore be used to assess the risks of patients with a specific condition being admitted within a given time period. These risks can, by simple calculations, be 'converted' to represent admissions that could be saved if the patients' multiple admission pattern reflected that of a Poisson distribution.

# REFERENCES

1 The Information Centre. http://www.ic.nhs.uk.casemix
2 Department of Health. *Reforming NHS Financial Flows: introducing payment by results*. London: Department of Health; 2002.
3 Audit Commission. *Payment by Results Assurance Framework: pilot results and recommendations*. London: Audit Commission; 2006 http://www.audit-commission.gov.uk/pbr/assuranceframework.asp
4 Maxwell S, Degeling P, Kennedy J, *et al. Improving Clinical Management: the role of ICP-based clinical management systems*. Centre for Clinical Management Development, Durham University; 2005.

**PART TWO**

# Experiences

# CHAPTER 6

# Searching for systematisation, and its impact

*Sharyn Maxwell, Pieter Degeling, Roslyn Sorensen, Kai Zhang and Barbara Coyle*

Calls to 'work smarter, not harder' via the application of systems thinking to healthcare and clinical work are now cliché, at least within the English NHS. The rationale is increasingly accepted by healthcare professionals of all persuasions, even if healthcare cultures are frequently, and for good reasons, oriented in other directions. A troubling reality for reformers is that despite the provision of incentives and extra funding for systematising work practices, the practices and processes on the ground in hospitals seem to remain unchanged; the rhetoric, however much accepted, is very distant from the reality. Without underestimating the implementation problems of new ideas, power relations within organisations, or resistance to the realignments of power and authority that may be generated by new ways of doing, the problem is often more fundamental.

For many healthcare professionals, both managers and clinicians, seeing, thinking and doing in a new way is not easy. This is not a problem specific to healthcare; it is the case in many endeavours and knowledge fields. How does one imagine what currently is not? How can one think like an Inuit if one is an Australian or like a ballet dancer if one is an engineer? It is similar to the problem of inventions; once an invention is known, used and has become the norm, it is impossible to imagine how one could not have seen and known it previously and yet, before that time, few could have imagined it so. Older readers will probably recognise this truism with such things as the development of antibiotics and the digitalisation of information. In the field of education, the transforming power of a new concept that opens up new and previously inaccessible views, thereby fundamentally altering how one thinks and acts, is called a 'transforming portal' of knowledge or a 'threshold concept'.[1] For many in the health field, systematisation is such a threshold concept.

Grasping a threshold concept often involves struggle, wrestling with seemingly counterintuitive ideas and the sense of displacement and disorientation that comes with being in a foreign or alien place with only a phrase book guide to the language. In such a situation often the best way to understand and to learn is to plunge in, play, explore and experience. In an academic context, case studies and examples are often particularly helpful. This chapter is an overview of how we, as researchers, attempted to grasp what systematisation looked like in the real world in hospitals and, from that, enhance our understanding (and that of others) of what might help and hinder the application of systemisation in particular hospital settings.

## LOOKING FOR SYSTEMATISATION

In order to look for something, you need to have an idea of *what* it is you are looking for, what you are *not* looking for, and *where* and *how* you should look.

### What?

From a literature review[2] we defined systematisation in healthcare concep-tually as any and all techniques and processes that routinely and prospectively structure, underpin and monitor the evidence basis of care, reduce unexplained and/or unjustified provider-sourced variation, enable resource savings without adverse clinical impact, and improve the conduct and outcomes of clinical processes as well as other desirable objectives. This was helpful in that it gave both an idea of what it entailed and what its outcomes should be, but it is a very broad definition. Furthermore, the number of techniques and methods that can be considered forms of systematisation in healthcare is numerous and steadily increasing. They include integrated care pathways, pharmaceutical protocols, clinical guidelines, classifications of disease (such as ICD-10) and, in the UK, National Service Frameworks that specify national standards for high-volume patient conditions. We therefore decided on a ground-up approach that looked across a number of common hospital procedures, for evidence of systematisation according to both its projected processes and outcomes, and to determine the extent to which this may lead to one ideal type of systematisation, namely integrated care pathways.

### Where?

We chose 12 clinical settings in seven publicly funded hospitals in New South Wales, Australia in 1999–2000. We also selected three common surgical procedures for study, chosen for their high volume of cases and relative clinical homogeneity of patients across settings. In the results section that follows, Settings 1–4 were settings performing appendicectomy, Settings 5–8 transurethral resections of the prostate, and Settings 9–12 elective Caesarean sections. The 12 settings were located in seven different hospitals.

## How?

Initially, we randomly selected a minimum of 40 criteria-appropriate patients from each setting. However, due to difficulties in obtaining records in some settings, we subsequently increased this to 50. The relevant time frame for selection was two medical staff rotations in each setting. We used a mixture of qualitative and quantitative techniques: observation studies, organisational documentation reviews, medical record reviews (483), a stratified survey and interview of up to 30 staff (plus their managers) identified from the medical records (283), patient surveys (257), and cost analysis in four blind studies.

The four studies were:

1 *Structures and processes of care*
   a  An assessment of the completeness of relevant care documentation.
   b  An assessment of structures and practices relating to the continuity of care.
   c  Observations of relevant clinical meetings.
   d  An assessment of the means to monitor and report process and outcomes.
   e  A staff survey, with supplementary interviews, about the management orientation of their hospital, their perceptions about how care was organised, and factors that may impinge upon the organisation of care and working relationships.

2 *Cost of care*
   a  Hospital estimates of the costs of eight care components: ward, procedure, clinical, pharmacy, imaging, pathology, emergency department and allied health costs.
   b  Comparative average total costs of each procedure as reported by the 1998/99 New South Wales Diagnostic Resource Group. These were obtained from the New South Wales Department of Health.

3 *Composition of care*
The following data were obtained from a review of the patients' medical records which sought to identify the resources used in each patient's care and, from this, variations in the resources used both within and across setting:
   a  Types and volumes of drugs and tests.
   b  Duration of particular stages of care (e.g. time in theatre, time in recovery and waiting time).
   c  Pre-admission and discharge procedures.

4 *Quality of care*
   a  The quality of care processes recorded within the medical record was reviewed in two ways by two independent reviewers to assess the quality of documentation and coding and apply the methodology and criteria of the Quality in Australian Health Care Study.[3]

b The patient assessment of quality of care was a Likert scale patient questionnaire with additional open-ended questions; it sought data on patients' perceptions of the quality of care they experienced, the coordination of care between treating staff and the resulting changes in their health.

c The outcomes of care were assessed via data gathered from both the medical record and the patient survey; although we tried to obtain procedure specific outcome measures we had to rely on high level outcomes such as unexpected returns to theatre, infections and readmissions.

Within each study we scored each setting's performance on the relevant criteria according to either the presence or absence of relevant items or the degree of consistency across patients for that category of care, as appropriate. In the *structure and processes* study, a setting scored 1 or 0 (for presence or absence) of, among others, prospective specification of the various components of care and their sequencing, specification of a standard cost, collection of variance data, and presence of supportive managerial structures and procedures, such as clinician 'owned' databases and regular review meetings.

We were not able to use the cost data derived from hospital sources as they were too variable (more on this later in the chapter). However, we were able to use the average total cost for the setting according to the official data. We ranked each setting according to its percentage variation above or below the official average total cost.

The analysis of consistency for each component of care within each patient record and across settings was scored –1, 0 or 1 after the application of non-parametric statistical tests. A score of +1 on drugs usage indicated that this unit was relatively consistent in the type, number of administrations or dosage rates (as applicable) of pharmaceuticals. A score of –1 indicated that this unit was relatively inconsistent in the application a particular care component. A score of zero indicated that statistically this unit was neither consistent nor inconsistent compared to other settings. The quality studies were scored similarly.

The criteria items in each study were categorised and each setting's item scores within each category was summed. The individual settings' scores for a particular category were then rated relative to each other's according to five bands (labelled –2 to +2). This was to avoid overly weighting any one item within a category. The category ratings were then summed to give a sub-study rating for each setting. The various sub-study ratings for the composition and quality of care were then also summed and adjusted to prevent the absolute scores for any one category skewing the overall results.

Because we believe that to be successful, significant new ways of working require support across all relevant levels of organisation, we measured propensity towards systematisation as the combined score of managerial orientations within each setting and its wider organisation, the presence of stable work organisation (defined as consistency in patients' location within wards and consistency in treating staff across patients), and consistency in treating staff's orientations towards the management of clinical work. This last measurement was calculated in such a way as to account for profession-based difference and in effect was a measure of occupational integration in staff's views of how work should be structured in that setting. We then compared the composition of care and quality scores for each setting against its propensity to systematise score and against its relative deviation from the state-wide average cost. We used the qualitative data to add depth and insight to these quantitative results.

## WHAT WE FOUND

### Propensity to systematise

Our first key finding was that there was little evidence in any setting of a propensity towards systematisation in the way we had defined it. Across most clinical settings and all the wider hospital organisations within which the settings were located, there was little evidence of senior or unit management support for structures and processes that focused attention directly upon the management of clinical work as a production process. For instance, we found little evidence in any of the sites that:

- the timing and sequencing of key tasks to be performed by all relevant disciplines had been agreed
- occupational responsibility for potentially contentious aspects of care (such as 'ownership' of intravenous lines and discharge criteria) had been clarified
- the organisation had invested in IT support for systematised care processes (as an example, only one setting had a database capable of providing procedure-specific clinical data and this was a nursing initiative), or
- routine collection of data to perform variance analysis of process performance or outcomes was either collected or analysed.

Rather, management orientations were overwhelmingly focused on managing and on reporting items of key budgetary significance such as costs and activity levels; there was very little reporting of quality information. The limited quality information that was available was at a highly abstracted level such as hospital-wide infection rates and unplanned readmissions to theatre.

Further, despite widespread organisational restructuring into clinical directorates and supposedly devolved clinical and resource decision making there was little, if any, common focus between management and medicine. Management remained broadly focused on administrative tasks and resource issues associated with the overall patient load while clinicians remained narrowly focused on individual patients' clinical needs. In the absence of a clinical champion, divisional medical directors demonstrated only token interest in, and limited capacity for, systematically organising, appraising and, in that sense, managing clinical work. In some settings, particularly Caesarean section, nursing professionals had made attempts to introduce an integrated approach to care provision but in most cases had met with resistance and/or disinterest from other professionals, particularly doctors. Hence in all settings occupational integration on a number of care dimensions about how clinical work should be managed, including acceptable forms of communication, was generally weak, though some settings were better on this than others.

Compounding this were bed management policies that focused on ensuring maximum throughput in all the study hospitals. This meant that patients undergoing the same procedure in a relatively short time span were frequently dispersed over multiple wards. A consequence of such wide dispersion of patients across wards was large numbers of medical and nursing staff caring for relatively small patient numbers. For example, in Setting 4, 314 nurses and 111 doctors treated the 49 patients in the sample. Patients undergoing Caesarean section were the least dispersed across wards and consequently there was greater consistency in the treating staff for these patients. However, even in the setting with greatest staffing stability, only 10% (13 nurses, eight doctors and two allied health professionals) of the 233 treating staff saw more than 10 patients from the sample.

Thus the setting scores for systematisation were low compared to the potential score. The settings that showed a stronger propensity to systematisation scored better as a result of relatively small initiatives such as the nursing database for condition specific data, the presence of a clinical champion for product-focused management, and an ability by specialists and/or nurses to ensure 'protected beds'.

## Cost of care

As noted earlier, the component cost data provided by the study hospitals were widely inconsistent across settings, though it was evident that ward, procedure and clinical costs constituted the bulk of the cost per patient and/or procedure. We asked each hospital for a description of how they allocated costs. Some were able to give us this immediately, some struggled to provide a clear explanation and one never provided it. From the information we did receive it was apparent most hospitals used activity-based costing procedures, although it appeared that one had used a cost driver approach. One attempted to cost each patient 'from the ground up'; others costed only on average. Even when hospitals used the same approach, they made different assumptions, and hence differing internal applications, of that costing method. Given the diversity and incompleteness of the data provided, we decided to disregard this data source. Although this experience raised some doubts for us about the reliability of the official cost data, given the Department of Health's assurance that the state-wide data was sound, we turned to the New South Wales Diagnostic Resource Group average cost data.

These data showed that the *hospital* was a more important factor in controlling costs than the setting or the procedure. (Two of the seven study hospitals accounted for half of the study settings.) Five of the hospitals displayed a reasonably stringent financial stance with average costs for the study procedures at or below the average. Two of the hospitals displayed a less stringent stance being significantly above the average for these procedures.

## Consistency in the composition of care

Figure 6.1 shows that most settings were at or below average cost and that, within these, most had lower rates of variability in the composition of their care. Despite the cost and reduced variability in the composition of care arguments made in favour of systematisation, most of these settings scored poorly on their propensity to systematise as we defined it. This meant that these hospitals' managers had found means, other than systematisation via clinical integration and wider organisational support for condition-based clinical management, to produce the reduced cost and variability results.

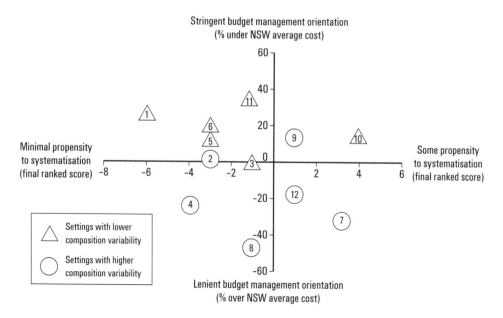

FIGURE 6.1 Consistency in the composition of care, by setting

It did not mean, however, that there was no use of other means for systematising care. Several hospitals used pharmaceutical protocols promoting generic pharmaceuticals as the 'first' (almost only) option for medication, with strict limits on the dosages administered. Protocols for diagnostic tests were also evident. Yet other cost control means were not associated with systematised care. These included discharging all patients after a given length of stay regardless of how many days post surgery that may have been and, in one hospital, a 'cost education' programme. This programme entailed ensuring that ward and theatre store rooms' shelves were not only labelled with the product stored on it but the price of that item. The items concerned ranged through individual band-aids (sticky plasters) to cotton bandages to prosthetics to self-administered analgesic pumps.

The impact of this education programme in changing both cost awareness and traditional professional behaviour was illustrated during an interview between a researcher and a nurse manager. The interview was interrupted for a few minutes while the nurse manager informed a doctor that the diagnostic test he had just ordered cost $150, and questioned whether a test costing slightly over $10 would do just as well. The doctor agreed and quickly rewrote his referral for the relevant patient. Noticing the surprise on the researcher's face, the nurse manager commented that this was by far the most effective way they had found to save money, as without it staff had no idea of what they were spending and so had no way of taking cost into account. Further, the equanimity within the nurse-doctor interaction suggested that the cost education programme had also engendered a (perhaps small) change in traditional medical-nursing power relations.

## Quality

Cost and variability reductions are not the only, or perhaps most significant, care outcomes pursued by proponents of systematisation. For clinicians and patients quality of process and outcome is much more important. Figure 6.2 shows each setting's score for quality juxtaposed against its propensity for systematisation and its deviation from state-wide average cost.

These quality assessment results were constructed from the process (as recorded in the medical record), outcomes and patient experience facets of quality. Statistically speaking, we found no significant difference in outcomes across any of the settings, despite differences in the degree of systematisation. We did, however, find differences in the remaining two measures. On the assumption that only settings that scored positively on both the medical record review and the patient assessment could, with any confidence, be regarded as offering quality care, we characterised Settings 7, 9 and 10 as having good quality, Settings 2, 3, 4, 5, 6, 8, 11 and 12 as having variable quality, and Setting 1 as having poor quality (negative scores for both). In other words, settings that displayed consistently good quality were those where management demonstrated some (even if small) propensity to support clinical staff of all professions in deciding among themselves how they best wanted to treat patients. The setting with the least propensity for this, despite performing well in terms of reduced variability in care and financial efficiency, performed worst in terms of quality.

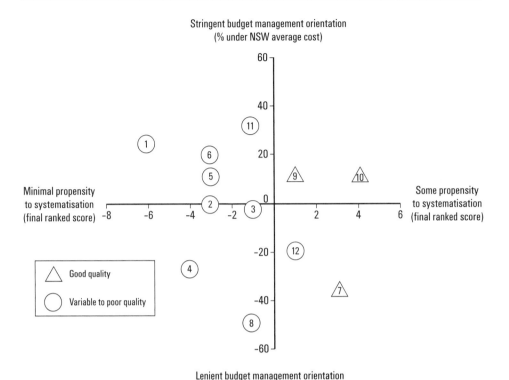

**FIGURE 6.2** Quality of care, by settings

Hence we realised that neither financial efficiency nor reduced variability of care is necessarily an indicator of either quality care or of systematisation along product lines. Further, cost control via cash flow *without* clinical integration and a degree of clinical/management cohesion about how clinical work will be measured, monitored and managed appears to be self-defeating in terms of the production of good quality care. We suspect that in the long run it may be self-defeating in terms of overall cost control as well. As the highest cost in the care of relatively well patients is usually the bed day cost, failure to work with clinical and other staff to eliminate unnecessary 'waits' and/or steps in the care process is also a failure to address one of most expensive and heavily used resources in hospitals.

## DISCUSSION

Integrated care pathways are one way to resolve both this immediate problem and the need for cohesion and agreement between treating professions and management. Yet none of the settings in this study used ICPs; at best they had nursing care plans that integrated allied healthcare. Interviews with staff suggested that this lack was not simply the result of an unwillingness of managers to support clinicians in designing better systems for organising and managing clinical work. As mentioned previously, none of the hospitals had ensured that restructuring into clinical directorate structures had achieved the desired integration between clinical and resource decision making. Managers in clinical directorates remained focused on the administrative tasks and resource issues associated with the overall patient load while clinicians remained narrowly focused on individual patients' clinical needs. This was compounded firstly by the pressure upon management to ensure the financial and activity targets set by the Department of Health (and to keep their hospitals' names out of the papers) and secondly by a poor definition and understanding of the role of clinical managers by both management and clinicians. This poor definition was exacerbated and perpetuated by a lack of work management skills among clinical managers and an inadequate recognition of, and time allocation for, the duties currently performed by clinical managers and those they could potentially perform in a new 'regime'. This is a lamentable lack, as the results showed that even a relatively small propensity to manage clinical work along a product line basis (e.g. management about 'how we do "Caesars" here') had an effect on quality as measured by process and patient experience criteria.

We undertook this study in order to gain a better picture of what systematisation in hospitals might look like and what might help or hinder its progress. Despite some tantalising indications of what might be possible and a better understanding of what needs to change in order for hospitals to reap fully the claimed benefits of systematisation, we failed to find a shining exemplar. Fundamentally, both managers and clinicians in this study suffered from the same impediment as others elsewhere – they found it difficult to envisage a new way of managing the objectives of hospitals by devolving and sharing responsibility on a product line basis. They did use several types of systematisation but primarily to manage cash flow, not to improve the management of clinical work. In terms of our introduction, they hadn't yet gained that threshold knowledge that could/would transform how they thought and worked.

## REFERENCES

1 Meyer J, Land R. *Threshold Concepts and Troublesome Knowledge: linkages to ways of thinking and practising within the disciplines.* Universities of Edinburgh, Coventry and Durham; 2003.
2 Bergman DA. Evidence-based guidelines and critical pathways for quality improvement. *Pediatrics.* 1999; **103**: 225–32. Borokowski V. Implementation of a managed care model in an acute care setting. *J Healthcare Quality.* 1994; **16**(2): 25–7, 30. Citrome L. Practice protocols, parameters, pathways, and guidelines: a review. *Administration & Policy in Mental Health.* 1998; **25**(3): 257–69. Feder G, Eccles M, Grol R, *et al.* Clinical guidelines: using clinical guidelines. *BMJ.* 1999; **318**(7185): 728–30. Leatherman S, Berwick D, Iles D, *et al.* The business case for quality: case studies and an analysis. *Health Affairs.* 2003; **22**(2): 17–30. Mulhall A,

Alexander C, Le May A. Prescriptive care? Guidelines and protocols. *Nursing Standard*. 1997; **11**(18): 43–6. Timmermans S, Berg M. *The Gold Standard: the challenge of evidence-based medicine and standardization in health care.* Philadelphia: Temple University Press; 2001. Wilson B, Rogowski D, Popplewell R. Integrated service pathways (ISPs): a best practice model. *Australian Health Review*. 2003; **26**(1). Woolf SH. The need for perspective in evidence-based medicine. *BMJ*. 1999; **2358**(65): 22–9. Woolf SH, Grol R, Hutchinson A, *et al.* Clinical guidelines: potential benefits, limitations, and harms of clinical guidelines. *BMJ*. 1999; **318**(7182): 527–30.

3 Wilson RM, Runciman WB, Gibberd RW, *et al.* The Quality in Australian Health Care Study. *Med J Australia*. 1995; **163**(9): 458–71.

# CHAPTER 7

# Pathways in general surgery

*Nick Carty*

Surgery is an ideal field for the application of care pathways. There is typically a single evaluation and diagnostic episode followed by a defined treatment. Where follow-up is required, this usually has a predictable schedule. In contrast, many other medical specialities are concerned with the treatment of diseases, which, by their nature, are less easily defined.

This chapter describes how surgical processes have been improved in Salisbury, England, using pathways in three areas of care: (1) symptomatic breast disease, (2) high-volume general surgical conditions and (3) emergency general surgical admissions. A pathway for breast cancer was first developed in Salisbury in 1997. This resulted in Salisbury being one of the first waves of eight national cancer beacon sites and in the unit receiving the Department of Health award for improving the lives of patents with cancer in 2001. Salisbury was in the phase 1 of the National Cancer Collaborative and the author was a National Clinical lead for breast cancer in phase 2. The author was also responsible for one of the Action-on General Surgery projects conducted with the Modernisation Agency from 2003 to 2005 that led to marked changes in practice in the management of routine and emergency general surgery in Salisbury. Each of these pathway experiences will be described separately before common principles are identified.

## BREAST SURGERY

### Referral

When a general practitioner is faced with a patient who presents with a breast symptom, the doctor must initially decide if the patient requires assessment in secondary care and if so, with what degree of urgency. The referral has traditionally been accomplished by the generation of a free-form letter often aided by referral guidelines that have been issued by secondary care. This is a satisfactory method of communication, but has several disadvantages. For primary care the generation of a letter is time-consuming. The specialist has to read through the letter and, using the contained information, assess urgency. This assessment can be accurate, but to be successful involves high level medical input.[1] Finally, the letter is passed to the administrative staff to make an appointment.

A simpler system can be devised using a simple tick box referral, listing clinical criteria reflecting urgent versus non-urgent features. A member of the administrative staff can assign the appointment; a tick against any symptom suggestive of a serious condition, such as a discrete breast lump, equates to an urgent appointment, while other patients are seen routinely. This system saves time for both the primary and secondary teams, but it has the disadvantage of generating a large number of urgent referrals in order to minimise the number of patients with serious pathologies who are given a non-urgent appointment.

**TABLE 7.1**  Simplified version of the referral template to the breast clinic

| Symptoms and signs | Yes score |
| --- | --- |
| Discrete lump | 5 |
| Asymmetrical nodularity | 3 |
| Definite signs of malignancy (ulceration, skin or distortion) | 10 |
| Past history of breast cancer plus new symptom or sign | 10 |
| Age over 40 | 5 |
| Suspected breast abscess | 10 |
| Severe mastalgia | 1 |
| Persistent unilateral mastalgia in a post-menopausal woman | 1 |
| Nipple discharge – if age over 50 or blood-stained or single duct | 1 |
| Nipple retraction, distortion, or eczema | 1 |
| Family history of breast cancer | 2 |
| **Total score** |  |

It is possible to develop a scoring system to significantly refine selection. This system can be adapted to local circumstances and to changes in central guidance. It can also be easily applied to a variety of other conditions; a similar referral has been devised for patients with bowel symptoms. Table 7.1 shows a simplified version of our current referral template. Patients with a total score of 10 or more receive an urgent clinic appointment. An interesting corollary of a scoring system of this type is that it can convey nuances of information that may not have been known to the individual filling in the form. For example, it may not have been appreciated that a discrete lump in a women over the age of 40 is, in the current guidance, a justification for an urgent referral.[2] Reference to Table 7.1 shows that this patient would be allocated a score of 10. In other words, the referral template contains embedded referral guidance, an important consideration within a busy GP surgery, which may use a variety of providers. There is also the further implication that it may well have been possible for the referral template to have been filled in with similar accuracy by an untrained individual or, indeed, the patient.

Table 7.2 shows the distribution of patients assessed in clinic according to the referral template used, referral priority and final diagnosis. The scoring system reduces the number of patients who are given an urgent appointment compared to a tick box, while maintaining an acceptable sensitivity in the selection of patients whose final diagnosis is cancer.

**TABLE 7.2** Comparison of a simple tick box with the scoring referral template

| Referral priority | | Final diagnosis – number of patients | |
|---|---|---|---|
| | | Malignant | Benign |
| Simple tick box n=633 | Urgent n=438 (69%) | 40 | 398 |
| | Soon n=188 (31%) | 3 | 192 |
| Scoring referral template n=496 | Score>=10 n=194 (39%) | 28 | 166 |
| | Score<10 n=302 (61%) | 5 | 297 |

## Clinic assessment

An important aspiration of the hospital clinical assessment is that it should involve the minimum number of trips to hospital and ideally be one-stop. This has several advantages for the patient and the service. Most importantly, the patient is able to know the diagnosis as soon as possible. Obviously, this is of comfort to those with benign problems, but also allows more serious conditions to be dealt with rapidly. There is a reduction in outpatient clinic workload as the number of repeat clinic visits purely for diagnosis is minimised. Finally, it is not necessary to communicate with the patient or the GP repeatedly to update them with the results of outstanding investigations and to make further treatment plans. This gives savings in administrative time and improves efficiency, thereby reducing the scope for errors.

A one-stop service requires careful organisation. It is necessary to match investigative capacity with the demand. In practice in the breast clinic this means that there needs to be the correct number of imaging appointments available at the time of the clinic and also support from pathology to report cytology specimens. Capacity for supply of time consuming investigations, such as mammography, can be increased without extending the clinic, by prearranging some of these tests in the hour or so before the clinic on the basis of the referral information. Similar protocols can be devised for use in other specialist clinics.

## Admission

Prior to admission it is of great value to have a pre-operative assessment. It is unlikely that patients with malignancy will have their operation cancelled on medical grounds, in contrast to a patient being treated electively for a non-malignant condition (see below). There may, however, be some medical problems that can be optimised or at least highlighted to the anaesthetist. The main role therefore of pre-operative assessment in this group of patients is the provision of information, counselling and emotional support.

Given their level of experience and training, junior doctors are not generally well suited to perform these roles. Breast care nurses, in conjunction with trained assessment nurses, are better equipped to perform the pre-operative assessment. The breast care nurse provides psychological and specialist inputs, while the assessment nurses check fitness for anaesthesia and complete the nursing process. This avoids any duplication of information gathering on the day of admission. The junior doctors are excluded from the service part of this process, but attend a limited number of pre-operative assessment clinics to fulfil their educational need. This is an important consideration in the era of the European work time directive and modernisation of the medical career.

In a carefully planned pre-operative assessment, a major aim should be to start preparation for discharge. For example, although it has long been known that it is safe for patients to be discharged on the day following surgery with a wound drain *in situ*,[3] when we presented this option to patients around the time of operation the uptake was poor. However, we have found that if patients and their partners are shown how the drain works prior to admission they are much more likely to accept early discharge. Currently, all patients, except those with social issues, are admitted the day of surgery and 90% are discharged within 24 hours of operation. There has been no increase in wound morbidity since the introduction of this approach and, especially with concerns over MRSA, patients have accepted early discharge very well.

A plan for the whole of the above patient journey is made as soon as the diagnosis has been made. A typical pattern of care is illustrated below; since the pathway is very predictable, all the key dates can be arranged between the patient and the coordinator on day two.

Day 1     The diagnosis is made, counselling with surgeon and breast care nurse takes place.

Day 2     Unit coordinator faxes GP letter to their surgery and telephones the patient to confirm admission arrangements.

Day 8     The pre-operative assessment clinic at which (1) the patient is issued with detailed information in the form of a breast cancer diary that includes general information, confirms the date and ward of admission, and details of the first post-operative clinic appointment, and (2) the specialist nurse begins the process of gaining consent.

Day 10    Admission and operation.

Day 11    Patient is seen by breast care nurse and discharged home.

Day 17    Multidisciplinary meeting (MDM) at which the team discusses the results of the operation and a provisional treatment plan is formulated.

Day 18   First post-operative visit during which (1) the wound drain is removed and pathology results are discussed with the patient and entered in the patient diary and (2) appointments are given for further therapy as decided at the MDM.

## Continuing care

The patient-held diary contains a full follow-up schedule, so that the patient can participate in the treatment plan. Follow-up is delivered in a flexible fashion to suit the patient and based on three service models. The majority of patients follow the first model; they are seen regularly by one of the breast care nurses in a clinic running parallel with that of the consultant. The nurses provide a level of continuity throughout the patient's treatment that cannot be given by junior medical staff. They are also able to allow more time for the patient and thus provide better psychological support as well as safe and effective follow-up.[4]

Second, some patients elect for early discharge from active follow-up to a system of rapid return to the clinic in the event of symptoms, supported by a fixed plan of regular screening with mammograms. This strategy is rational since the majority of recurrences are detected by the patient themselves or on mammography. However, it may not give optimal psychological support and may give false reassurance with loss of confidence in our unit in the minority of patients who develop a late recurrence.

Third, a limited number of patients decide to undertake follow-up under the direction of their GP with the hospital available as necessary. This has the advantage of convenience and continuity, but the quality of follow-up may be less good. To ensure a high standard, each GP involved needs some additional training. It may be more sensible to make a much smaller group of specialist nurses competent.

Each of these models has the advantage of freeing up senior medical time. This allows the consultant to concentrate attention on more complex problems and to undertake training of junior staff. Many of these considerations can be extended more generally and similar patterns of follow-up devised for other common conditions.

## GENERAL SURGICAL CONDITIONS

Now we consider the treatment of patients referred with two high volume, low complexity elective surgical conditions: groin hernia and gallstone disease. The underlying aims of the pathway development were to streamline the patient journey by reducing the number of visits to the hospital while improving patient information and the quality of consent.

## Referral and assessment of condition

The pattern developed in the breast clinic referral has been adapted to apply to the GP referral document for these general surgical conditions. Free-text letters are inefficient and fail to consistently give the required information. The referral template was therefore redesigned to a tick box pattern to allow the clinic to specify the information needed and to simplify its extraction. The information sought was that required to determine the need for an operation and, if so, whether this was likely to be as an inpatient or day case. The former depends on the severity of symptoms and how typical they are for the condition. For example, a patient with pain in the groin that was severe, made worse by exertion and associated with a lump, would usually be offered a hernia repair. Past medical conditions, current general medical problems and social factors can help guide the type of admission. While prior knowledge of this information is not essential, it does allow better planning of the clinic, especially if it is linked to a pre-operative assessment clinic.

Specialist nurses have been trained to assess the symptoms of these groups of patients. The training consisted of theoretical knowledge teaching and practical experience in the consultant clinic. In the learning phase the accuracy of trainee assessment was tested by a blinded comparison of their treatment recommendations with that of the consultant. There was excellent agreement in the need for operation (concordance of 90%). Interestingly the nurses were more likely to recommend day case operation, having had previous experience of assessment in that department. The encouragement of day surgery activity has positive implications for the efficiency of a surgical unit.

Following nurse evaluation, the patient is discussed with the consultant who then briefly reviews the patient to confirm the clinical findings. A treatment plan is then finalised. The duration of consultant input to each patient has been reduced from a mean of 15 minutes to five minutes by the introduction of the nurse assessor role. Patient satisfaction with the combined nurse and consultant assessment is equivalent to that of the consultant alone.

A validated health questionnaire (SF-36) has been used to measure the health benefit of patients having hernia repair. At three months, patients had improved physical functioning score but, importantly, 30% had an increase in bodily pain. Further analysis revealed that this group was made up largely of patients who had operations for an initially minimally symptomatic hernia. Chronic groin pain has recently been found to be a significant problem after hernia surgery.[5] This finding has led us to defer operation for this group of patients. They are now given an information leaflet to explain this strategy, symptoms to look out for and the mechanism for early hospital review if these develop. A conservative policy for the initial management of minimally symptomatic hernias has recently been reported; it has been found to be safe and effective.[6]

Once a decision has been made to proceed with surgery, the nurse issues the patient with an in-depth information leaflet, which is explained fully to them. This leaflet has been produced with the aid of patient focus groups that gave feedback on its breadth and readability. The nurse then checks that the patient remains content with the proposed treatment plan. The patient has the opportunity to see the consultant again at this point if necessary. The information leaflet is linked to a consent form, which summarises the recognised benefits and risks of the operation. The nurse can sign off the first part of this consent form, confirming that the risks have been explained to the patient. The consent form is finally signed by the patient and surgeon on the day of operation. Consent has become a smooth process, rather than a single episode. This has the benefit of providing a well-informed consent and from a risk management viewpoint the disclosure and discussion of risk is full and standardised. Moreover, these improvements have been accompanied by reduced medical input. A knowledge questionnaire has been used to assess the level of understanding of patients after assessment: the mean knowledge scores improved from 45% for those attending a standard clinic with a haphazard system of information delivery to 80% for those attending the new style clinic.

## Pre-operative assessment

After clinic assessment the patient is issued with a pre-operative assessment (POA) booklet and directed to the central pre-operative assessment clinic. The front cover of the booklet is an admission card that replaces the loose operation request forms previously used. This booklet follows the patient journey through assessment, the day of admission, pre-theatre checks and the recovery room. The booklet has allowed standardisation of documentation in our trust. Additional separate pathway documents can be used for specialist patient groups covering only those aspects of care additional to standard; for example, for patients with breast cancer, colorectal cancer and vascular disease.

The pre-operative assessment takes place in a central unit staffed by specially trained nurses. They are supported on one session per week by a consultant anaesthetist, who can be asked to review any more complex clinical problems and also gives educational input both to the nurses and to the junior doctors. As with the pre-operative assessment of patients for breast surgery, junior doctors have been removed from the service aspect of assessment, but have enhanced educational opportunities; they can find out what factors make a patient fit for anaesthetic from the perspective of an anaesthetist. Important considerations for an anaesthetist include crowns on teeth, mouth opening and assessment of the airway, factors not traditionally well assessed by junior surgical staff.

Patients benefit from being given a consistent assessment and information package, allowing them to anticipate more accurately the course of their admission. Pre-operative assessment identifies and allows the correction of any medical problem to minimise the risk of the intervention and reduces the rate of medical cancellations. A further benefit is that the rate of same day admissions for surgery can be increased for a wide range of complexity of operation. In our trust this has been further facilitated by a surgical admission lounge (SAL) into which surgical patients are admitted on the morning of their operation. This unit, separate from the surgical wards, eliminates the problem of patients competing for beds first thing in the morning while the ward nurses are busy trying to organise the discharge of current inpatients. Surgeons and anaesthetists can easily find and assess patients on the theatre list, and the nurses on the unit have as their only responsibility preparation of patients for theatre. Early patient feedback indicated that when all patients were admitted at 7.30 a.m., those later in the list had to wait excessively long on the SAL before surgery. Admission times are now staggered according to the times patients can conveniently arrive on the unit and the order of the operating list adjusted accordingly. The desired increase in the rate of admission on the day of surgery has been confirmed. Now about 80% of patients are admitted on the day of surgery, which amounts to a mean of 50 patients a week. The change in practice has been most noticeable in plastic surgery; 70% of patients had been admitted the day before surgery, now 70% come in on the day of operation.

In general surgery we have tended to make the POA at the time of the initial clinic visit, often some months before the operation. A check shortly before operation can be by telephone or by asking the patient to return a form supplied at the POA, confirming their intention to proceed with operation and highlighting any changes in health status. In other specialities, for example orthopaedics, it has proved more sensible for POA to be booked shortly before operation to allow checking, for example, of MRSA status. It is also possible to be flexible in the relative roles of generic POA nurses, who mainly check fitness for operation and specialist nurses, whose primary role is disease counselling, in the POA process.

The overall patient satisfaction with the hernia and gall-bladder pathway is now very high. A survey of our patients using the national survey gave results above the 95% centile of all NHS trusts.

## EMERGENCY ADMISSIONS

The usual model for the management of emergency general surgical patients is that referrals are accepted from the GP by the house surgeon. Their initial evaluation is then undertaken in the emergency department by the house staff. Patient flow can be erratic for a variety of reasons. These transient and inexperienced staff are not necessarily well aware of the scope of patients that fall within general surgery, they may have a poor understanding of their role within the hospital, for example with bed bureaus, the wards, theatres and investigative services, and they have other calls on their time. Usually, patients are admitted via the busy emergency department and then moved on to a variety of surgical wards, making it difficult to keep track of their clinical progress and the results of their investigation. The experience for both the patient and staff can be stressful and a happy conclusion is not guaranteed.

We have sought to improve on this model by appointing and training a surgical nurse navigator and by developing a small surgical admissions unit.

## Surgical nurse navigator

Surgical nurse navigators act as a point of continuity in the care of emergency surgical admissions. They are members of the surgical nursing staff who, subject to a competitive interview, are seconded to this role, initially for a one year period. The time limit is to encourage innovation and allow the development of the surgical unit staff as a whole. Their input in the patient journey starts when they take the GP call, using departmental guidelines to decide if the admission is appropriate for our speciality. Their good communication with the ward, the surgical teams and bed bureau helps the nurses to manage patient flows. Their discretion also helps the process: they may find it possible, for example, to delay a less acute problem, such as an abscess, to allow patients already on the unit to complete their initial assessment and be moved onward. They have access to consultant clinic timetables and are able to arrange urgent clinic appointments for some patients who would otherwise be sent in as emergencies.

If on admission the patient is assessed as being seriously unwell, senior advice is rapidly sought. In other circumstances the nurse navigator prints and starts to fill in an emergency pathway document for each new admission, formulates a provisional diagnosis (on the basis of an assessment tool), attaches the appropriate treatment algorithm and institutes appropriate investigations and therapies. Finally a member of the medical staff is contacted.

Once a treatment plan has fully matured the navigator continues to assist the patient through his or her journey; for example, by arranging transfer to the ward, facilitating discharge or booking an operation with theatre.

The presence of a member of staff dedicated to the management of emergencies has allowed us to develop some new disease specific pathways. After initial assessment, patients with an uncomplicated abscess are considered for admission delayed to the following day. Previously, due to their low priority in theatre, a patient with an abscess would commonly be in hospital for two nights. A 'planned emergency admission' allows them to be put first on the emergency list and the majority of these patients now go home following day case treatment.

Patients with suspected biliary pathology are fast-tracked for rapid investigation and treatment. The navigator arranges an early ultra-sound to confirm the diagnosis. We have negotiated that a vascular assessment radiographer does a flexible number of scans from the surgical admissions unit at the start and end of each working day, rather than need to rely on the busy general X-ray department. Patients with compatible clinical features and a positive scan are then placed by the nurse navigator on a common list for urgent cholecystectomy to be performed by one of the specialist upper gastro-intestinal surgeons. A successful early operation reduces the risk of emergency readmission for the same problem, avoids a second planned readmission for elective cholecystectomy and thus reduces the overall patient stay and risk. During the last year the author has performed 67 consecutive urgent laparoscopic cholecystectomies. There have been no conversions to open and only one significant complication and that related to the umbilical port rather than to the gall-bladder surgery *per se*. These early data compare very favourably with those in the literature.[7]

## Surgical admissions unit (SAU)

Following successful pilot studies, the SAU is now a four-bedded annex situated within the surgical ward. This location allows direct input from the team of surgical nurses and is more convenient for the junior medical staff. Another benefit is that, with care, it is possible to use the area in a multi-functional fashion. The area can, for example, be used for minor procedures such as change of urinary catheter and superficial abscess drainage.

Having this cohort of patients with acute surgical problems in one area facilitates their management. It is easier to maintain a high ratio of nurses to these patients who require regular reassessment and whose condition is subject to rapid change. Finally it is easier to keep track of the result of their investigations and so rapidly reach a definitive diagnosis.

## DISCUSSION: OVERARCHING PRINCIPLES

Some aspects of these and other pathways are of particular importance and have similar solutions. Particularly notable are the use of communication, information and patient involvement.

## Communication

Many of the developments described above and their improvements to clinical outcomes and patient experiences can be attributed to the management of three important domains of communication. The first is that between primary and secondary care. The use of simple referral templates, which contain embedded guidelines, reduces the work for GPs and improves the quality of information transmitted. Secondary care must similarly communicate rapidly to their colleagues in primary care. The GPs of patients diagnosed with breast cancer are telephoned within 12 hours and receive a faxed clinic letter within 24 hours. We produce newsletters to GPs, hold GP training events and visit their surgeries to give them further information when requested.

The second domain is that between members of the multidisciplinary team in secondary care. The care pathway document has been designed to be filled in by all members of the team and all members of the team are encouraged to contribute to discussions on patient management. Regular multidisciplinary team meetings, planning sessions and away days are of value for individual patient management, to monitor performance of the pathway and to continue to identify ways of improving care. Nurses and surgeons attend the weekly general surgical morbidity and mortality meeting to discuss any complications among surgical patients. Monthly, one of these sessions is allocated to the control of nurses and other, non-medical staff.

The third domain is that between members of the multidisciplinary team and the patient. It is essential to have a full and open communication with the patient. It is useful to encourage patients to take up the offer of a copy of the letter to their GP. This is particularly valuable for new patients. The letter confirms the treatment and follow-up plan, and can highlight any areas of concern, such as the risks of the proposed intervention. Moreover, after a clinic survey indicated that 80% of patients had Internet access and would use it to gain information and give feedback to us, we have developed breast and general surgical websites.

## Information

All phases of the patient journey should be supported by information. The interval from referral to the clinic visit can provoke unnecessary anxiety if one does not know what to expect. Our patients are sent information leaflets (now also available via the web) to show them how to get to our department, to inform them of the type of procedures and processes that they will go through in clinic, and advise them of the likely outcomes of their visit. Patients attending the breast clinic are told that it is one-stop, and advised that they may be reassured and discharged, admitted for diagnostic operation, or for a minority, told that they have cancer. They are therefore prepared to spend some time in clinic and to bring their partner or a close a friend with them.

From the time of definitive diagnosis a different type of information is required. Diagnosis specific information will help a patient with a hernia to make considered treatment choices and facilitate informed consent. Having a detailed and individualised diary will help a patient with cancer understand their condition and be a full member of the team treating their disease.

Information should be provided on what to expect after operation. This should be given well in advance; for example, information for patients who will be discharged with a drain in place is of little value when given peri-operatively. Information is helpful for a patient to plan recovery. How long will it be before they can return to normal activities? How do they care for their wound? What post-operative problems should they look out for and what should they do if they suspect complications? How will their pain be controlled? There are reasonably predictable answers that can be given to each of these questions for any particular patient group.

## Patient involvement

Patients should be involved throughout the development and monitoring of a pathway. There is a variety of tools that allow the team to see the process from a patient perspective and plan the journey accordingly. Patient shadowing is a useful early strategy. It helps to identify bottlenecks, areas of duplication, wasted effort and sources of irritation. Focus groups can be of value to identify what users really want from the service we provide. The answers can be unexpected. Common complaints relate to toilet facilities, confidentiality, privacy and dignity. For example, patients find standard back fastening theatre gowns quite understandably embarrassing, particularly now that we encourage patients to walk to theatre. Regular satisfaction surveys involving both the patients and the staff are useful to monitor that we continue to maintain and improve upon the service.

Based on these principles one can construct a patient-centred pathway that will make the patient journey less stressful, more comfortable and more productive and lead to more reproducibly successful outcomes. Staff within a good pathway should each have to perform less frantically, working within but extending their skills and thus have enhanced job satisfaction. It is generally possible for these benefits to be achieved at worst in a cost-neutral fashion, but usually with substantial savings.

## ACKNOWLEDGEMENTS

Mrs Debbie Postlethwaite has been involved from the outset in the development of the breast and 'action-on' surgical pathways. Miss Vanessa Rogers read through the draft chapter and made constructive suggestions.

## REFERENCES

1 Marsh SK, Archer TJ. Accuracy of general practitioner referrals to a breast clinic. *Ann R Coll Surg Engl.* 1996; **78**: 203–5.

2 Anstoker J, Mansel RE. *Guidelines for Referral of Patients with Breast Problems.* 2nd ed. London: NHSBSP Publication; 1999.

3 Bonnema J, van Wersch AMEA, van Geel AN, *et al.* Medical and psychological effects of early discharge after surgery for breast cancer: randomised trial. *BMJ.* 1998; **316**: 1267–70.

4 Earnshaw JJ, Stephenson Y. First two years of a follow-up breast clinic led by a nurse practitioner. *J Roy Soc Med.* 1997; **90**: 258–9.

5 Courtney CA, Duffy K, Serpell MG, *et al.* Outcome of patients with severe chronic pain following repair of groin hernia. *Br J Surg.* 2002; **89**: 1310–14.

6 Fitzgibbons RJ, Giobbie-Hurder A, Gibbs JO, *et al.* Watchful waiting vs. repair of inguinal hernia in minimally symptomatic men. *JAMA.* 2006; **295**: 285–92.

7 Mercer SJ, Knight JS, Toh SKC, Walter AM, Sadek SA, Somers SS. Implementation of a specialist-led service for the management of acute gallstone disease. *Br J Surg.* 2004; **91**: 504–8.

# CHAPTER 8

# A multidisciplinary process approach to cardiac surgical services

*David J O'Regan*

With the advent of low cost airlines, most people have negotiated and managed the complex decisions and interactions of travel from home to the destination and return. The hospital, in restoring health, should also be aiming to achieve the same sense of expectation of well-being and satisfaction. This principle is not easy to apply in healthcare partly because responsibility for 'the self' is projected onto and reinforced by a third party, the clinicians. However, the principle is reinforced by a resource-based view of hospitalisation: a patient's entry to and discharge from the healthcare process should be a 'value creating transformational process' where the outcomes are audited and the output has direct feedback on input into the process (*see* Figure 8.1).

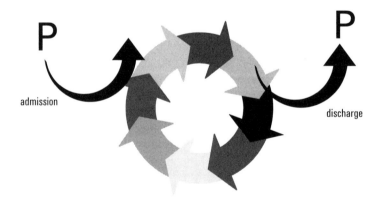

a value creating transformational process

**FIGURE 8.1** Patient in and patient out: a value creating process

This chapter will illustrate how patient care pathways give the patient the opportunity to choose and plan the 'journey' if we can change patient attitudes by presenting the situation, process and function of the hospital and educate healthcare professionals in the value of the process. The study describes four years of clinical cardiac practice before, during and after the introduction of a patient care pathway in January 2003 and analyses its impact on the working practices, clinical and operational performance of a single surgeon and associated nursing and managerial staff.

## THE NEW CLINIC

Before January 2003 patients referred for cardiac surgery were processed in a traditional manner: they were seen and assessed in an outpatient clinic on a time-scale governed by the degree of urgency and placed on a waiting list. One week prior to admission to hospital, the patient attended a nurse-led Preadmission Clinic, the main function of which was to perform all of the investigations such as blood tests, chest radiographs and electrocardiograms in preparation for the forthcoming operation. Admission to hospital occurred on the day before surgery and it was only at this stage that each patient underwent a full history and examination and gave consent for the surgery, the onus of which was borne by the most junior member of the medical team. The whole process was then ratified by the consultant at the end of a busy clinical day with the result that not infrequently abnormalities in the process became apparent at a very late stage leading to cancellation of the surgery. The discharge date and arrangements for patients that underwent surgery were determined by medical staff usually on the evening ward round on the day beforehand. This not only delayed the patient's discharge but also meant that the nursing staff spent not an inconsiderable amount of time at the last minute trying to find solutions to the patient's social and domestic problems.

This process is represented in Figure 8.2. The shaded areas show the actors involved (vertical axis) in the variety of clinical areas (horizontal axis). The majority of the input is provided at the end of the pathway and the decision to proceed (taken by the surgeon and demarcated by the dotted vertical line) was not taken until the patient was occupying a bed the night before the scheduled surgery.

On 29 January 2003, the author changed his clinical practice by introducing the POP-in clinic. The aim of the clinic was to bring together in one place and at the same time all of the staff involved in the patient care pathway with a view to coordinating the patient's admission to, and discharge from, hospital prior to his or her actual admission. The rationale was that such a set-up would improve the efficiency of the surgeon's practice, identify and resolve prior to admission (i.e. before occupying a bed) any clinical, social or domestic problems affecting the procedure and discharge, and provide patients without any problems with a clear idea of their admission and anticipated discharge dates before they left the clinic.

The new pathway is represented in Figure 8.3. Again, the shaded areas show the actors involved (vertical axis) in the variety of clinical areas (horizontal

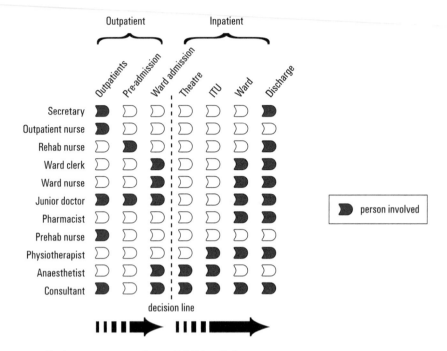

**FIGURE 8.2** Patient process prior to POP-in clinic

axis). In this pathway the majority of the input is at the beginning of the pathway (i.e. prior to admission), and the decision to proceed (dotted vertical line) is taken before the patient occupies a bed.

Currently, a new-patient clinic alternates with a combined 'POP-in' clinic and follow-up patient clinic on a fortnightly basis. Routinely, 10 patients are assessed in the new clinic and each is given a 30-minute appointment. Between eight and 10 patients are prepared for surgery in every POP-in clinic along with 10 or so follow-up patients. Patients, therefore, get seen for the first time following their referral in the new-patient clinic and are then invited to attend the POP-in clinic within two weeks of their admission. The new-patient clinic also focuses on the needs of patients accepted for surgery by offering risk management and secondary prevention advice.

On the day of the POP-in clinic, patients attend the hospital mid-morning and undergo all of the required pre-operative investigations, the results of which are available later on the same day. They are then seen by the rehabilitation team that explains in detail the various stages of the patient journey. Lunch and refreshments are provided before commencement of the clinic proper in the afternoon. The junior doctor, under consultant supervision, checks the patient. The pharmacist checks the prescribed drug chart that will accompany the patient throughout the hospital stay. Finally, once the preparatory work has been completed the patient meets with the consultant. It is at this time, with all

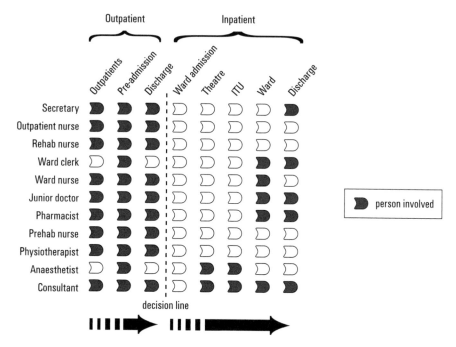

**FIGURE 8.3** Patient pathway after POP-in clinic

of the information readily available, that the consultant discusses the operation with its attendant risks and benefits prior to obtaining consent from the patient. Family members are encouraged to attend this part of the process.

## IMPACT OF THE CHANGE

The method for identifying the impact of the change is set out in the Appendix to this chapter. Table 8.1 summarises the impact of the introduction of the POP-in clinic. The total number of cases processed pre- and post-introduction of the POP-in clinic was 424 and 379 patients respectively. The number of cases classed as urgent, emergency or salvage increased from 70/424 (17%) to 109/379 (28.8%) (P<0.05 chi-square test). The total number of deaths in each period was 6 (1.4%) and 10 (2.6%) respectively. Elective surgery accounted for 338/424 (80%) and 260/379 (68.6%) of the workload in respect of time periods. The majority of the work involved surgical revascularisation (CABG). During both periods some patients were treated at other centres as part of the NHS waiting list initiative. These cases were 'cherry picked' on clinical factors other than Euroscore and although clinical outcomes and process improvement has been demonstrated in all elective CABG patients as a result of the introduction of the clinic, only those patients operated on at the Leeds General Infirmary are represented.

The total number of patients is 247/424 (58%) pre-POP group and 173/379 (45.6%) in the post-POP group. The age and sex distribution of the patients presenting for surgery in the respective periods was the same. However, the total number of patients with the Euroscore greater than 5 increased from 13/247 (5.3%) to 20/173 (11.6%) in the post-POP period. This difference is statistically significant applying a chi-square test to the absolute numbers but is not borne out in multiple regression analysis. Overall, however, the unit has experienced an increased complexity in the nature of cases presenting for cardiac surgery.

TABLE 8.1 Summarised effect of the introduction of the POP-in clinic

| | Pre-POP | | Post-POP | | |
| --- | --- | --- | --- | --- | --- |
| | No. | % | No. | % | Significance |
| Total number of cases | 424 | | 379 | | |
| Deaths | 6 | 1.4 | 10 | 2.6 | |
| Emergency surgery | 70 | 17 | 109 | 28.8 | P<0.05 |
| Elective surgery | 338 | 80 | 260 | 68.6 | |
| CABG | 307 | 72 | 214 | 56.5 | |
| CABG + Valve | 7 | 1.7 | 20 | 5.3 | |
| CABG +Valve +other | 1 | 0.2 | 0 | 0.0 | |
| CABG + Other | 0 | 0 | 1 | 0.3 | |
| Valve only | 23 | 5.4 | 23 | 6.1 | |
| Other | 0 | 0 | 2 | 0.5 | |
| | | | | | |
| **CABG at Leeds General Infirmary only** | 247 | 58 | 173 | 45.6 | |
| Male | 203 | 82 | 136 | 78.6 | Ns |
| Female | 44 | 18 | 37 | 21.4 | Ns |
| Age >70 | 57 | 23 | 35 | 20.2 | Ns |
| Euroscore >5 | 13 | 5.3 | 20 | 11.6 | P<0.05 |
| Discharge Day 4 | 6 | 2.4 | 12 | 6.9 | P<0.05 |
| Post-op <7 days | 168 | 68 | 121 | 69.9 | P<0.05* |
| Post-op >7days | 79 | 32 | 52 | 30.1 | Ns |
| Post-op clinical incidents | 109 | 44 | 60 | 34.7 | P<0.05** |
| Medical not fit/cancelled | 14 | 5.7 | 3 | 1.7 | P<0.05*** |

* Multiple regression analysis confirms that this difference is due only to the introduction of the clinic.

** Binary logistic regression analysis confirms this difference is due only to the introduction of the clinic.

*** Chi-square test.

The post-operative length of stay has reduced. Figure 8.4 represents the pre- and post-operative stay of elective cardiac bypass graft patients attending the Leeds General Infirmary. Multiple regression analysis confirms this shift is due to the introduction of the clinic alone (P=0.015). The pre-POP and post-POP curves intersect at day 7 and thus for analysis the post-operative length of stay was divided into two periods, the number of people discharged before day 7 and the number of people discharged after day 7. The higher number of patients that are now discharged either day 4 or day 5 is statistically significant. Average length of hospital stay after the introduction of consultant led pre-op assessment clinics was significantly shorter in patients who stayed in for less than seven days after their operation (6.3 days before and 6.1 days after the introduction of the POP-in clinic; p-value=0.002; ANOVA; figure 18). Statistical analysis showed that the introduction of the POP-in clinic was the only significant factor related to reduction in hospital stay (p-value=0.015). None of the other factors (age, gender, Euroscore, post-operative clinical incidences) were found to have a positive correlation to the length of hospital stay in this group of patients (p-value>0.05).

There was, however, a significant difference in the average length of hospital stay after the introduction of consultant led pre-op assessment clinics in those patients who stayed in hospital for more than seven days after their operation from 10 to 13 days (p-value=0.002; ANOVA; figure 19). None of the described factors was found to be related to the above rise in hospital stay (p-value>0.05).

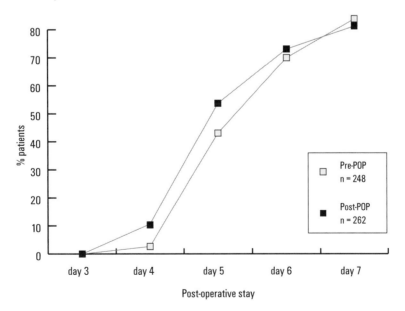

FIGURE 8.4 Change in post-operative length of stay

Runs analysis of the clinical incidents for the pre-POP and post-POP periods demonstrates a fall in the median number of post-operative clinical incidents from 50% to 33%. Statistical analysis showed a significant reduction in the incidence of post-operative clinical incidences in elective CABG patients from 42% to 32%. Binary logistic regression revealed that the only factor which significantly correlated with this reduction was the introduction of the POP-in clinic (p-value 0.01). There was no significant correlation between this reduction and other studied factors (age, gender, Euroscore; p-value>0.05). There was no change in the incidence of post-valvular surgery clinical incidences after the introduction of the POP-in clinic (p-value>0.5).

Further analysis revealed a significant fall in the incidents of arrhythmias, in particular atrial fibrillation. This may be related to the fact the drug chart is written in the clinic and prophylactic beta-blockers are recommenced early. There is a similarly significant fall in pulmonary complications, in particular respiratory tract infections.

The number of elective coronary artery bypass graft patients that were cancelled during the respective time periods fell from 14/247 (5.7%) to 3/173 (1.7%) (P<0.05, chi-square test). This improvement of productivity is also reflected in the waiting times for surgery for these respective time periods. Figure 8.5 also shows that waiting list spikes have levelled off in the post-POP period, a feature absent in the data relating to another consultant who was appointed at the same time.

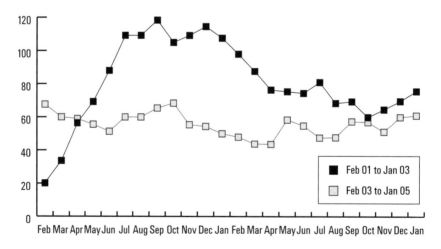

**FIGURE 8.5** Waiting list times

## The patient

The patient has a better understanding of the process and leaves the clinic with a 'script' outlining his or her prospective journey. In contrast to previous practice, the clinic also provides an opportunity for the patient to reflect on the operation and to solicit information first hand from patients (identified by a smiling badge) who are concurrently attending the follow-up clinic. Two patients felt able to question the need for surgery; a detailed history confirmed that they were asymptomatic and did not fulfil the indications for potentially risky surgery. Prior to instituting the POP-in process, they would have been hospitalised the night before surgery, half dressed and bed bound as an anaesthetist and surgeon obtained consent. The timing and the situation could not be more terrifying as the process drove them inexorably to surgery. Thus the stress of admission is obviated.

Patients feel far more reassured about the process and consequently are more likely to tolerate any operational difficulties that may delay their admission. This satisfaction is reflected in the positive responses to a questionnaire that was designed on a Likert scale (1 = strongly agree to 5 = strongly disagree). Table 8.2 presents the responses of 52 male and 13 female patients between the aged of 46 and 80. Sixty-eight per cent of patients brought a relative with them to the clinic; in 60% of cases this was their spouse who also found the clinic useful. Fourteen of the 65 also proffered free comments: they found the clinic very helpful; informative and helpful courteous staff allayed their fears.

**TABLE 8.2** Patient satisfaction survey

| Question | Average rating | Responses Total = 65 |
|---|---|---|
| **Notification** | | |
| The letter about the clinic arrived in time. | 1.27 | 64 |
| The instructions in the letter were clear. | 1.25 | 62 |
| **Time of clinic** | | |
| The time of the clinic was convenient. | 1.39 | 62 |
| I was seen promptly when I arrived. | 1.53 | 62 |
| When I arrived I was told what would happen in the clinic. | 1.7 | 64 |
| I felt that I wasted a lot of time during the day. | 3.76 | 49 |
| **Information** | | |
| I was encouraged to ask any questions that I wanted to. | 1.46 | 59 |
| I understood the information that I was given. | 1.59 | 63 |
| I think that I was given too much information. | 3.69 | 58 |
| My family would have liked more information. | 3.58 | 52 |
| Did anything happen during your stay in hospital that we had not told you about or prepared you for? | 98.31% said NO | 58 |
| **Satisfaction** | | |
| Looking back, now that my operation is over, I think the clinic helped to prepare me for going into hospital. | 1.41 | 59 |

## Cancellations

The number of patients deemed at the last minute 'medically not fit' for surgery has fallen from 14 to three. All of the latter were due to the patient failing to declare a change in symptoms. In total, there were 32 clinical incidences where the admission was manipulated to optimise pre-operative preparation. These improvements saved more than £260 000 of opportunity costs measured in terms of NHS tariffs.

## Training

The introduction of the clinic has had a positive impact on training of junior doctors as the consultant supervises the evaluation of the patient in the clinic. The senior house officer and the registrar also regularly see new patients and are observed taking histories and examining patients. Clinical acumen and judgement, based on evidence, is readily assessed by joint consultation.

## Integrated notes

The POP-in clinical record summarises medical, pharmaceutical, nursing, social and anaesthetic requirements on a single A4 page that follows the patient. This is a first in terms of proper integrated notes for the unit. Drug charts written in clinic now follow the patient. Previously, the patient had charts written in each clinical area and could accumulate up to five different charts on their journey. The pharmacist confirms accuracy and checks compliance. Transcription and prescription errors are removed.

## STAFF ENGAGEMENT

The POP-in clinic has had a positive impact on all the staff. Many have reported a greater degree of job satisfaction from their involvement in the planning of the patient journey. This has contributed of a healthier working environment where every member of the staff feels valued as a member of a multidisciplinary team. A new culture is evolving and staff have spontaneously taken to wearing unique identifying badges (a smiley face set within a heart).

An analysis of the testimonies of staff (summarised in Figure 8.6) shows the attributes that are valued in the new process and specifically how team members have realised their own professional needs and enhanced their sense of worth. One sister in Outpatients commented:

> At first . . . we all thought that [the change] would involve more work, would be confusing and time consuming and we had reservations about how helpful the patients would find the new regime. On the whole, our worries were allayed on the first day. The patients turned up on time, blood tests, ECGs and X-rays were performed and results obtained ready for their consultation. The patients attending the POP-in clinic seemed to enjoy talking to patients who were attending clinic following their surgery and there was quite a

noticeable 'buzz' in the air that was not there in other surgical clinics. The Health Care Assistant in charge of the clinic really enjoyed herself. This clinic gave her added responsibility and much of the success of it was down to her coordinating the clinic and working closely with the secretary. Patients attending post-operatively seemed pleased to see them both and lots of them mentioned that they wanted to have their 'Smiley Face' badge . . . This was a change that had been made at no extra expense to the organisation. It had introduced 'added value' to the service. Feedback from the wards was positive and certainly saved nurses' and doctors' time. A patient satisfaction questionnaire gave us positive feedback from the patients, which was also reassuring . . . After more that 30 years of nursing, it is good to still be challenged in my work and to be working in an innovative way. You can teach an old dog new tricks!

Similarly, a secretary reported:

I really enjoy my involvement in the POP-in clinic and feel very proud of the way the clinic runs. I feel part of a team, especially as I was involved in the initial meetings to set up the clinic. It has been a learning experience, working closely with clinic staff, ward nurses and liaison nurses, who I might not otherwise have worked with. There is a real team spirit which helps the clinic run smoothly, when there is somebody missing from the team other staff fill in, therefore making the process run efficiently. We have been able to adapt the clinic to fit around the consultant's other commitments . . . The POP-in clinic has made the admission lists more adaptable. I feel the worst part of my job as a secretary is when I have to cancel patients for one reason or another. The POP-in clinic has made this a lot easier. Patients are more relaxed about the change, they have seen the consultant and ward staff and are reassured . . . I also have the opportunity to meet some of the patients in the clinic – this is nice as I can put names to faces of the patients I have built up a rapport with over the telephone, and this makes my job more interesting!

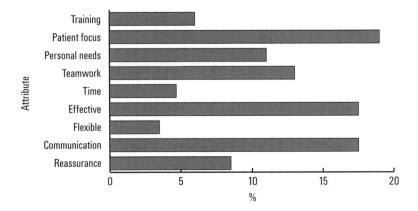

**FIGURE 8.6** Summary of the POP-in clinic attributes used in staff testimonies

## DISCUSSION

The introduction of process thinking into clinical environments has yielded significant improvements in both the clinical process and the operational management of the patient. These centres also noted a fall in intensive care stay, an increase in the number of patients extubated six hours following operation and an improvement in drug compliance.[1]

Despite the increasingly complex nature of the cases, the number of elective coronary artery bypass grafting surgery patients that are going through the POP-in process without incident has improved. This may in part be explained by the increasing experience of the author and the team but is more likely due to fact that the team is 'tightly coupled' and focused on performance.[2]

Patients can now be discharged home on day 4 and 5, a result of the 'virtual admission' through the POP-in process. A total hospital stay of five days increased from 3.4% of admissions pre-POP to 6.7% post-POP (P<0.05, chi-square test), a result of some patients being admitted on the day of surgery (previously not possible) and others being discharged on the evening of the fourth post-operative day. Although the numbers are still small, it highlights the value of educating staff and patients and providing a clear and transparent formal protocol.

There were further gains. The total number of operations that were cancelled for medical reasons was significantly reduced and the POP-in clinic has also afforded flexible day-to-day adaptation to the natural variations that occur in such a high performance work system.[3] The introduction of the clinic has meant that capacity demand matching is possible as there is only one point of entry into the process.[4] The result is reduced waiting times.

### The change process

As with similar changes elsewhere, the introduction of the new clinic posed its challenges. From the occasion the whole team involved in care of the patient gathered to map the patient pathway, professional rivalry surfaced as functional domains vied to ensure that their view prevailed, and initiatives were met with scepticism and resistance.[5] However, the emphasis on communication, participation and learning and adapting created a gradual momentum for growth, self-perpetuation and the sharing of both positive and negative experiences.[6] The self became a team, doing led to learning and survival transformed to growth as the stakeholders consciously or subconsciously extended their roles.

Schein argues that a learning culture must be built on a system of clear information and communication that connects all aspects of an organisation frequently, accurately and consistently.[7] Such communication does not depend just on computerised information technologies; on the contrary POP-in clinic is successful because the key people coordinating the patient care pathway have been (1) the consultant's secretary, (2) the outpatient scheduler and (3) the theatre scheduler. They are literally Mobile, Retrieval, and Notification Administrators (mRNA) that provide the 'connectors' for the 'patient pathway'.[8]

The design of the process was undertaken by those that do the work in order to confer a greater sense of ownership. The momentum for growth and self-perpetuation was established in the POP-in clinic as experiences were shared by the team with a common purpose. Furthermore, each and every team member is central to the whole process.[9]

Although the author could be regarded as the 'improvement champion', the process continues to thrive and adapt, committed to delivering service that has been developed by the team.[10] The process now integrates with the pharmaceutical services and ensures that we strive to meet the American Heart Association Guidelines with respect to treatment of high blood pressure and cholesterol. It is just a segment of a much larger process that includes, for example, the consideration of any social circumstances that may necessitate intervention to facilitate the patient's discharge.

Backward integration has recruited cardiologists to the process by encouraging them to invite patients that require surgical intervention, to make the

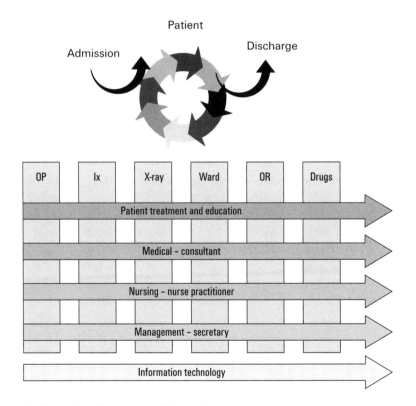

Key: OP = outpatients; Ix = investigations; OR = operating room

**FIGURE 8.7** The patient's journey through each clinical area

short walk from the diagnostic clinic to the surgical clinic. This simple concept not only saves a great deal of administration but eliminates the 13 week wait for an appointment to see the surgeon. (This principle of a diagnostic clinic in the morning with the option of an intervention clinical in the afternoon may apply to many other specialities in the hospital.)

The patient's journey in each clinical area through the POP-in clinic is supported by the named consultant and a named nurse in accordance with clinical governance. The whole process is coordinated by extending the role of the secretary to that of a Patient Care Coordinator who communicates with the outpatient scheduler, theatre coordinator and ward clerk. The hand-offs between the functional silos has improved and efficiency is realised. Each and every patient is thus supported by a tripod of people all centred on the needs of the patient as seen in Figure 8.7.

## A plan-do-check-act (PDCA) cycle

The arrangement of the outpatient clinic alternating between a new patient clinic and POP-in clinic with investigations prior to admission is essentially following a generic process that could be applied across the organisation. This process is made up of six steps.

1 **Identify and follow up need:** initial consultation with a patient identifies and/or follows up a need.
2 **Educate and plan:** education regarding risk factors can be initiated in step one and more importantly a 'script' is agreed with the patient detailing their expected 'journey'.
3 **Investigation:** all pre-operative investigations are obtained prior to consent in the pre-op clinic; if, for any reason, history, clinical examination or investigations highlight any anomaly, admission is delayed to allow rectification prior to admission.
4 **Document and prescribe:** the needs, planning and investigations are documented and the drug charts are written in the POP-in clinic; this reduces transcription errors and omissions as five drug charts were previously completed for any one admission; it follows the patient and heralds the beginnings of integrated notes.
5 **Admitting and treating:** this may apply to any admission requiring specific treatment of intervention.
6 **Discharge:** which cannot be assumed but rather planned and anticipated including getting all the medication ready and educating the patient.

A plan-do-check-act cycle comprises steps 1–4. The POP-in clinic succeeds because the PDCA cycle is completed prior to steps 5 and 6. Documenting and prescribing completes a figure of eight, reinforcing the fact that patients are regularly followed up as part of a continual cycle of audit and assessment (*see* Figure 8.8).

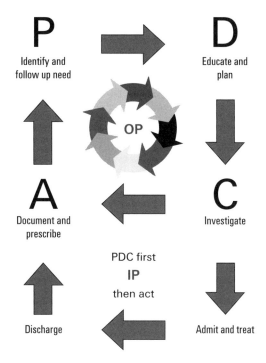

**FIGURE 8.8** The figure of eight: PDCA + Pop-in clinic

## CONCLUSION: RE-ENGINEERING CLINICAL PROCESSES

Re-engineering programmes may have failed because the patient care pathway has not been generic enough to make sense to all stakeholders in a complex high performance work system.[11] It is sometimes very difficult to identify the processes but, more often than not, the types of problems are generic. Nevertheless a few individuals, some teams and sporadic groups have succeeded in developing a process change but not the organisation as a whole. The processes that succeeded in this study were very disease specific and involved dedicated and enthusiastic champions. The same could be said for the results achieved with the introduction of the POP-in clinic.

For a hospital, the process is the patient care pathway – each word a focus of attention for the clinician, the nurse and the operations manager respectively. The labelling of the process, however, infers different typologies, signifiers and understandings that have to be balanced for all stakeholders.[12] The four critical success factors for process re-engineering are communication, learning, power and politics.[13]

The generic rubric that is proposed has been identified by professional colleagues as a 'microsystem' that can be easily translated into other specialities. It has the potential to carry meaning throughout the organisation, defining the function of the hospital and acting as the agreed pathway of interaction and interdependence for the diverse group of stakeholders involved in patient care.[14] Although the POP-in clinic has challenged and continues to challenge the values of medical and professional staff, there is a clear sense of ownership for the process as the participants have the opportunity to self-design the system and thereby build in commitment. POP specific socialisation has overcome the individualism of professional attitude.[15]

The change in outpatient practice has resulted in several benefits for patients and their healthcare professionals and trainees, and thus the NHS. Collaboration has improved efficiency. The continuum of care that has been established is a significant step forward in our attempts to deliver an efficient and effective service while at the same time ensuring appropriate utilisation of resources and maximising the time available for training.

The POP-in clinic has proven to be very versatile. It is this flexibility and adaptability that is enabling the people who are doing the work to actively participate in the process. The team continues to learn and grow as individuals are empowered and realise self-actualisation. If the resulting cultural buzz is an expression of collective worth, it is not a management 'tool' that can be taken out of the 'tool box' and used to fix the organisation. The answer to process change lies in the way we do things. Analysis of the POP-in process identified the fact that 'needs' are realised for the individual, professional and the team resulting in a new culture.[16]

## APPENDIX: METHOD FOR IDENTIFYING THE IMPACT OF CHANGE

Patient grouping was enabled by the Dendrite Clinical Management System.

For each set of data a mean, standard deviation (SD), and 95% confidence limits (CI) were calculated.

Data were analysed statistically using Microsoft Excel XP and SPSS for Windows (version 10; SPSS Inc; Chicago, IL) software.

Length of hospital stay before and after the introduction of consultant led pre-op assessment clinics were compared using Student's t-test.

Multivariate linear regression was used to study the correlation of independent variables with the total hospital stay. The following independent variables were included: type of pre-op assessment clinics, gender, age (under and above 70 years old), Euroscore (below and above 5), and development of post-operative incidences. Binary logistic regression was used to examine the effect of different factors (type of pre-op assessment clinics, gender, age, and Euroscore on the prevalence of post-operative incidences. Significance was determined by p-values less than 0.05.

Post-operative clinical incidents were determined from the Clinical Management System and are represented by a runs analysis using the Dendrite Clinical System before and after the introduction of consultant-led POP clinics.

All the staff involved, directly or indirectly, in the clinic were asked for written testimonies.

## REFERENCES

1 Smith-Love J, Carter C. Collaboration, problem solving, re-evaluation: foundation for the Heart Center of Excellence. *Progress in Cardiovascular Nursing*. 1999; **14**(4): 143–9. Zingone B, Dreas L, Pappalardo A, *et al.* [A quality improvement program in cardiac surgery. Four-year experience from the Ospedali Riuniti of Trieste] [Italian]. *Italian Heart Journal Supplement*. 2004; **5**(2): 119–27. Gobran SR, Goldman S, Ferdinand F, *et al.* Outcomes after usage of a quality initiative program for off-pump coronary artery bypass surgery: a comparison with on-pump surgery. *The Society of Thoracic Surgeons*. 2004; **78**: 2015–21. Holman WL, Allman RM, Sansom M, *et al.* Alabama coronary artery bypass grafting project: results of a statewide quality improvement initiative. *JAMA*. 2001; **285**(23): 3003–10.

2 Jenkins M, Pasternak K, West R. *Performance at the Limit: business lessons from Formula 1 Motor Racing*. Cambridge: Cambridge University Press; 2005.

3 Deming WE. *Out of the Crisis*. Cambridge, MA: Massachusetts Institute of Technology; 1982.

4 Silvester K, Lendon R, Bevan H, *et al.* Reducing waiting times in the NHS: is lack of capacity the problem? *Clinician in Management*. 2004; **12**(3): 105–11.

5 Atkinson P. Managing resistance to change. *Management Services*. 2005; **49**(1): 14.

6 Milgrom P, Qian Y, Roberts J. Complementarities, momentum, and the evolution of modern manufacturing. *The American Economic Review*. 1991; **81**(2): 84. Weick WE, Roberts KH. Collective mind in organizations: heedful interrelating on flight decks. *Administrative Science Quarterly*. 1993; **38**: 357–81.

7 Schein EH. How can organizations learn faster? The challenge of entering the green room. *Sloan Management Review*. 1993; **34**(2): 85.

8 Gladwell M. *The Tipping Point: how little things can make a big difference*. London: Little, Brown and Company; 2000.

9 Davenport TH, Stoddard DB. Reengineering: business change of mythic proportions? *MIS Quarterly*. 1994; **18**(2): 121. Weick, Roberts, op. cit. Katzenbach JR, Smith DK. The wisdom of teams. *Small Business Reports*. 1993; **18**(7): 68.

10 Gutierrez B, Culler SD, Freund DA. Does hospital procedure-specific volume affect treatment costs? A national study of knee replacement surgery. *Health Services Research*. 1998; **33**(3): 489. Uche N. In and out of vogue: the case of BPR in the NHS. *Managerial Auditing Journal*. 2000; **15**(9): 459.

11 McNulty T, Ferlie E. *Reengineering Health Care: the complexities of organisational transformation*. Oxford: Oxford University Press; 2002. McNulty T, Ferlie E. Process transformation: limitations to radical organizational change within public service organizations. *Organization Studies*. 2004; **25**(8): 1389.

12 Mintzberg H. Toward healthier hospitals. *Health Care Management Review*. 1997; **22**(4): 9–18.

13 McAdam R, Leonard D. The contribution of learning organization principles to large-scale business process re-engineering. *Knowledge and Process Management*. 1999; **6**(3): 176–83.

14 Batalden P, Splaine M. What will it take to lead the continual improvement and innovation of health care in the twenty-first century? *Quality Management in Health Care.* 2002; **11**(1): 45.

15 Schein EH. Organizational socialization and the profession of management. *Sloan Management Review.* 1988; **30**(1): 53.

16 O'Regan DJ. Why can't dinosaurs boogie? MBA Dissertation, Leeds University, 2005.

# CHAPTER 9

# Systematising the care of long-term conditions: the Year of Care model

*Pieter Degeling, Helen Close and Deidre Degeling*

The World Health Organization defines long-term conditions as 'health problems that require ongoing management over a period of years or decades'.[1] Long-term conditions have significant deleterious effects on the lives of patients and their carers, the health care system, and society at large.[2] In the UK over 17 million people, including perhaps two thirds of those over 65, have one or more of these conditions.[3]

Specific impacts of long-term conditions are registered on the lives and bodies of people with the conditions and their families, carers and the health and social care system itself. Conditions are associated with physical discomfort, disability and uncertainty, reduced earning capacity, poor quality of life, and a high risk of developing comorbidities including in mental health.[4]

Many people with long-term conditions depend on the support of family members and other informal carers. These informal carers suffer proportionately more health problems than other people of the same age, particularly in regard to back problems and long-term mental health problems such as depression. In such complex situations crisis management becomes the norm, resulting in poor quality of life and clinical outcomes and high health service utilisation by the initial care recipient and the informal caregiver.[5]

The size and complexity of the problems needing to be addressed by the health and social care system have only recently been recognised. The evidence suggests that up to 80% of primary care consultations and 66% of emergency hospital admissions in Britain involve people with long-term conditions.[6] Our recent analysis of Hospital Episode Statistics (HES), suggests that in England 18 of the top 40 HRGs, accounting for 45% of accident and emergency admissions, reference long-term conditions with a high risk of repeat emergency admission.[7] Within Wales, over the past 10 years, 'two thirds of patients admitted as medical emergencies have a chronic condition or have a worsening chronic condition'.[8]

Thus, the quality, effectiveness, appropriateness and efficiency of service provision to people with long-term conditions has become a major challenge for health and welfare systems in the developed world. Despite accumulating evidence about service shortcoming and a procession of government initiatives for service improvement, our understanding of systematic ways of meeting the care needs of people with long-term conditions remains inadequate. This chapter critically examines some proposals to overcome gaps between promise and performance and outlines the essential features of a Year of Care (YoC) programme. We discuss how this might be applied in systematising the design, commissioning and delivery of services to people with long-term conditions as well as informing the 'time specified' care plan that they have negotiated with primary care-based service providers.

## CHARACTERISTICS OF LONG-TERM CONDITIONS AND THEIR IMPLICATIONS FOR SERVICE REDESIGN

Three underlying attributes characterise long-term conditions. First they are deteriorative; thus the aetiology and prognosis of a person with a long-term condition indicates how far the condition has progressed at a given point in time.[9] This characteristic implies that for any individual with such a condition the composition of the service will change as the physical and psychological manifestations of the condition deteriorates and/or as the personal priorities change.

Second, while a long-term condition affects an individual's life, it does not define them, particularly in how they see and project themselves in their work, their relationships with loved ones, and other aspects of their lives. Thus, people with these conditions place continuing emphasis on maintaining control over what is significant in their daily lives.[10] This emphasis signifies the importance of devising and implementing service models that are structured to underwrite the voice and volition of people with long-term conditions and

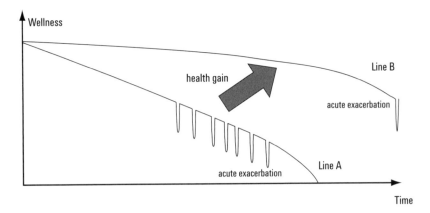

**FIGURE 9.1** Wellness trajectory

hints at the shortcomings that arise when services are construed primarily in clinical terms.

Third, within an individual's genetic predispositions, the onset and subsequent rate of progression of some long-term conditions (such as heart disease, COPD, diabetes) are to a significant degree outcomes of how risks inherent in an individual's personal, social and economic circumstances as well as lifestyle impact on that person's health.[11] Possible clinical effects of this characteristic are displayed in Figure 9.1 which depicts two possible trajectories of wellness over time: rapid decline (Line A) and delayed decline (Line B). The differences between A and B are important for the lives of people and how services are designed and implemented. In very direct and immediate ways the differences underline the individual's position as self-manager of health and thus of the onset and rate of progression of a condition. However the differences also imply personal and socioeconomic factors that affect an individual's capacity to reduce lifestyle and related risks and which service modalities may need to accommodate.

## MODELS OF LONG-TERM CARE

Several models have been proposed to meet these challenges. The aim has been to devise structures and methods that meet the defining features of primary care (continuity, coordination, and comprehensiveness)[12] and provide guidance on how services should be configured to the benefit of improved quality of care, improved quality of life, and increased cost-effectiveness.

One much cited model is Wagner's Chronic Care Model depicted in Figure 9.2 below (also shown in Figure 2.1). Its strengths lie in its identification of the range of factors to be taken into account in designing a service that is appropriate to people with long-term conditions (such as the centrality of informed and active patients, responsive community resources, and proactive primary care teams). Its shortcomings are its lack of guidance on how these design features might be realised on the ground that is, the features to bring together complex clinical treatment regimes, the support that will enable individuals (located at different points of the downward progression of their condition) to take an active role in managing their own care, and the commissioning, monitoring and management requirements of the care services.

A starting point for filling these gaps is the NHS and Social Care Long-term Conditions Model, promulgated in January 2005, along lines displayed in Figure 9.3. Adapting aspects of a model first used by Kaiser Permanente in the USA, the model proposes three levels of need and care: (1) self-management, (2) care management and (3) complex case management.[14] It provides for a more systematised approach to service provision, specifically detailed descriptions of care modalities that, for each identified level of need, are:

▶ prospectively designed with a proactive rather than an emergent and reactive orientation

▸ explicitly defined, planned and coordinated rather than implicit and unplanned
▸ capable of focusing on the health risks of identified populations and the changing wishes and priorities of people with long-term conditions
▸ capable of being collaboratively designed and implemented rather than imposed
▸ structured to facilitate routine review in ways that will engender improved experiences of people with long-term conditions and improved service quality, outcomes and cost.

Enunciating a set of desired attributes, however, does not guarantee their attainment. In the case of service to people with long-term conditions, successful implementation will depend on the presence or absence of a range of integrating structures and methods, specifically:
▸ *explicit methodologies* for (1) stratifying the populations of people that fall within the ambit of specified long-term conditions and (2) for identifying their health risks as well as their wants and priorities as they see these to be
▸ a *person* who is both *authorised* to integrate service provision and *accountable* for its occurrence or non-occurrence

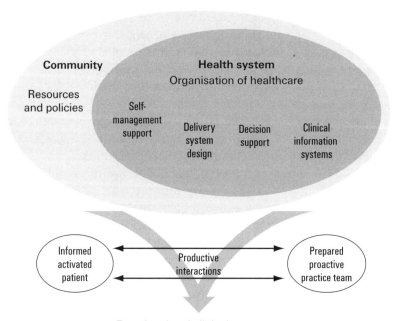

Functional and clinical outcomes

**FIGURE 9.2** The model for improvement of chronic illness care[13]

▶ an integrating *methodology* that specifies how the identified risks and priorities of an individual will be linked with a specified menu of services from within the health service but also from other sources such as social services, the voluntary sector, community sources and informal carers
▶ an integrating *artefact* such as, for example, a care plan or pathway that (1) specifies who will do what, why, when and where, and (2) records the responsibilities and rights of all parties (an individual with a long-term condition, carers and service providers, etc.) can expect from each other
▶ an integrating *performance management and review process* that (1) routinely and systematically examines service performance in respect of its appropriateness for meeting the specific needs and wants of each population stratum and (2) sets the agenda for ongoing service improvement as defined above.

The extent to which these conditions are met in Department of Health pronouncements is set out in Table 9.1. Noteworthy is the variability of the Department's advice on the defining elements of the model in respect of both day-to-day clinical practice as well as how services will be commissioned and managed. In summary, the table illustrates shortcomings at three levels.

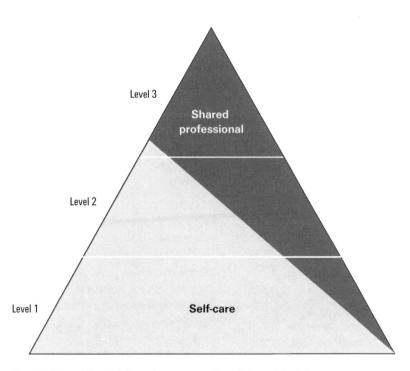

**FIGURE 9.3** The NHS and Social Care Long-term Conditions Model

**TABLE 9.1** Summary of prevailing NHS service models for long-term conditions

| | Level 3 Case management | Level 2 Care management | Level 1 Self-management |
|---|---|---|---|
| Population criteria | *Highly specific*<br><br>Patient population identified using specific clinical indicators such as:<br><br>• two or more hospital admissions<br>• length of stay longer than 40 days<br>• presence of comorbidities<br>• in the top 3% of GP attendees<br>• significant functional impairment<br>• scope and stability of informal care. | *No detailed specification*<br><br>A general statement that the population comprises patients with a single condition or range of problems who would benefit from care management. | *Not specified*<br><br>The boundary criterion for differentiating between the Level 1 population and the total population is not defined; rather, the self-care population is construed as an undifferentiated group traversing all three levels. |
| Identified primary integrator | *Community matron*<br><br>• with authority to order clinical investigations, make referrals and arrange admissions to hospital<br>• who is the fixed point of contact for the patient<br>• coordinates contributions of other professionals and agencies. | *A primary care clinician*<br><br>Any nominated member of a multidisciplinary team who:<br><br>• acts as a point of contact between the patient and team<br>• helps patient to navigate services. | *Not specified*<br><br>No clear statements about who will do what, when and where. |
| Service aim | To reduce repeat admissions and improve quality of life. | To slow down disease progression, reduce disability, ensure better management of deteriorations, reduce need for hospital admission and improve quality of life. | *Not specified*<br><br>Rather, attention is given to specifying the tasks of self-managing patients across all levels of care. |
| Method | *Case management*<br><br>• planned to occur along lines that explicitly recognise current need and anticipates future need on a patient by patient basis<br>• emergent variations managed by the community matron as case manager. | *Care management*<br><br>• Stratified, condition specific registers.<br>• Time specified recall and review process.<br>• Condition specific networks that span primary and acute settings.<br>• Daily service provision in primary care; acute clinicians act as *knowledge node*. | *Not specified*<br><br>Broad discussion of a range of issues and tools relating to:<br><br>• information<br>• skills and training<br>• tools and devices<br>• support networks. |

|  | Level 3 Case management | Level 2 Care management | Level 1 Self-management |
|---|---|---|---|
| Artefact | *An individual care plan that is held and owned by patients that specifies*<br><br>• details of the care to be provided<br><br>• regular reviews to assess need<br><br>• self-care to be undertaken by the patient and informal carers<br><br>• what each professional and agency will do to meet need, manage risk and/or support self-management. | *Single assessment document – some mention of the use of individualised patient care plans.* | *Not specified* |
| Performance management and review | *Not specified* | *Not specified* | *Not specified* |

We attribute these shortcomings, first, to the way long-term conditions are construed largely in clinical terms. Through such construction illness is taken outside the domain of the subjective experience and volition of the persons affected and they become bearers of discrete pathologies and patient dependents rather than co-producing self-managers of their health within the context of a wider life. Such clinically determined needs assessment processes more often than not exclude the voice of the individual labelled as 'patient' and the list of 'patient needs' is then, by definition, nothing more than a composite of clinical bio-physical models and understandings of what services are available.[15] Such constriction often leads clinicians to conspire with a 'patient' to mask the deteriorative character of the condition.[16] It also flies in the face of evidence about how an individual's desire and/or ability to be directly involved in managing their condition and behaviour to the benefit of secondary prevention is influenced by a range of personal, psychological and socioeconomic characteristics.[17]

Second, the variable and limited definitions and specificities of target undermine the commissioning, evaluation and improvement of aspects of service provision for those with long-term conditions. For example, the highly detailed criteria nominated for case management (level 3) services stand in stark contrast to the broad non-specific criteria nominated for care management (level 2) and the absence of any criteria for self-management (level 1). This gradation of specificity (from highly to not specified) is also found in the structures and methods central to service integration, namely the identification of an *authorised integrator*, the specification of an integrating *methodology* and use of an *integrating artefact* that specifies who will do what, why, when and where. Again, while for case management we are given details about the case management responsibilities of community matrons and individual care plans, the same level of detail is not evident for care management and is absent altogether for self-management. Indeed, the absence of detailed advice on the co-production aspects of what, in the model, is termed 'self-care' is a systemic weakness.

## PRINCIPLES OF AN ALTERNATIVE MODEL

We seek here to formulate a model for the care of those with long-term conditions that builds on the systematising developments of the models elaborated above but which first, as a matter of right, maintains the sociality of people with long-term conditions and underwrites their voice and volition, and second, clarifies the why and how of their irreducible personal responsibility for their own health.

In respect of rights, the model construes people with a long-term condition as sentient beings with aspirations, priorities and perspectives that reflect their personal histories as well as ongoing relations with significant others. Equally, the model underwrites the right and ability of these people to exercise control over what happens to them both in the here and the future. In other words we are formulating a model whose use underwrites the inherent sociality of people with a long-term condition, that recognises the web of relations in which they are embedded, that preserves their personal identities and that validates their meanings, priorities and life choices in the terms in which they make these.

On responsibility, by way of its refusal to separate the body and the self, our model explicitly recognises causal interconnections between any individual's health and their behaviour in respect of, for example, diet, smoking and other risk behaviours such as maintaining a work-life balance. We hasten to add that inclusion of this design attribute does not mean that we believe that an individual's health is solely explainable in these terms; as we have recognised above, it may be the product of genetic predispositions, or social and economic circumstances. That said, however, it is also the case that while these added factors have significant effects, they are of themselves not sufficient. Put simply, the fact that the self and the body cannot be other than coterminous it necessarily follows that an individual retains, firstly, ultimate responsibility for maintaining his or her health and, secondly, the right to be the final arbiter of what is done for and to them by others in this regard.

Viewed from this perspective it is apparent that relationships between people with long-term conditions and clinicians are appropriately construed in principal-agent terms. Within this model, people with long-term conditions retain ultimate responsibility for their health, a responsibility inscribed in their relationship (as principal) with carers (as agents) with whom they co-produce their health. Accordingly the process through which services are designed and delivered should be structured along lines that enshrine the rights and responsibilities of people with long-term conditions to be informed, to be consulted and involved in decision making and to enter agreements with agents (clinicians and other carers) that specify what they (as principal) can expect from others and what others can expect from them.

The foregoing does not mean that the concepts of co-production, principal and agent are self-recommending. We recognise the limits set by an individual's genetic predispositions, by socioeconomic processes and circumstances and by other factors on a principal's ability to manage his or her health including by changing behaviour or complying with medication and other regimes. The standing we accord to questions such as these, however, depends on what we regard as appropriate for testing the conceptual, practical and ethical utility of models of care. By its nature, an individual's genetic and socioeconomic inheritance is very largely a personal given outside that individual's direct control. What matters is whether in enactment our proposed model restructures relations, such that people 'dealt a bad hand' by genetics and/or their socio-economic antecedents are more empowered to exercise volition and voice in responding to the circumstances in which they find themselves.

Crucial here are the modes of structuring. As demonstrated earlier, prevailing approaches to service provision construct people with long-term conditions primarily in clinical terms. In contrast, we require a model that casts people with a long-term condition in ways that both legitimise their voices and requires that these will be not only *heard* but also *heeded* by clinicians as their agents. Within a principal-agent conception of service provision the providers (as agents) are responsible for (1) meeting the principal's right to be fully informed about the options from which they might choose and the health consequences that follow from each of these and (2) to provide support within the limits of available knowledge and resources that will enable the principal to overcome limits imposed by personal, social and economic circumstances that an individual's choice (as the principal) is one that will promote his or her health, service providers (as agents) are bounded (within the limits of available resources). Thirdly, in keeping with the underlying logic of their standing as agent, it is incumbent on service providers that they accept the validity of the choices and priorities of an individual, even when these may be counter-productive to 'good' health.

The last of these injunctions, on the agent role of service providers, will raise questions about how we construe the responsibilities of individuals whose lifestyle, habits or behaviours put them at risk of either exacerbating a long-term condition or of triggering the onset of a long-term condition. The matters at issue here swing largely on what is seen as falling within the scope of an individual's responsibility in different contexts. In the personal context, the coterminous nature of the body and the self means that, on both logical and clinical grounds, individuals necessarily retain their personal responsibility for what they do or do not do to their bodies. Equally, in an interpersonal context (i.e. depending on the level of connectedness with family and others), individuals carry some responsibility for what they do about their personal health. At a societal level the collective interest in social and political solidarity has arranged for aspects of social care and illness treatment to be provided by the state. Under these arrangements all individuals, including those who deny their personal responsibility for acting in ways that will promote their health, retain the right to both clinical treatment and support. But we observe an increasing recognition that this right does not absolve them of responsibilities to themselves arising from the coterminosity between the body and the self.

We are well aware that the enactment of a principal/agent conception (of relationships between individuals with a long-term condition and service providers) will be much messier than our statement suggests, a result in part at least from addressing aspects of a condition's downward progression that clinically dominated models mask. Thus, the starting point for constructing the type of partnership we envisage lies with service providers addressing the whole story of what it means to live with a long-term condition; that is, not only to *look at* people with a long-term condition but also to *look with* them as well.[18] This will inform joint assessments of the risks that confront both individuals with long-term conditions and service providers. The reference to **risks faced by both parties** rather than **patient need** is intentional. Patient need assessment processes are self-defining mediums by which clinical and other professionals construct both 'patients' and their 'needs' in terms that fit both clinical deficits and available interventions. Accordingly, along with Reed and Clarke[19] we propose that what used to be termed 'needs assessment' should be broadened to identify actual and potential risks as these are construed not merely by service providers but also by the individual with a long-term condition and their informal carers.

One existing effort of this kind is the Expert Patient Program (EPP). Following principles first enunciated by Lorig, *et al.* in their Chronic Disease Self-Management programme,[20] EPP is a lay-led, generic programme for those with long-term conditions. It is based on the view that such people encounter similar problems whose management, when on the terms of the individual with a long-term condition rather than of service providers, will lead to improved quality of life and health status as well as reduced use of health services. Thus, in addition to strategies for clinically oriented problems such as recognising and acting on symptoms, using medication correctly, EPP also addresses psycho-social problems such as stress management and managing psychological responses to illness and, most importantly, ways in which individuals can ensure their voices are heard and heeded in interactions with clinicians. However, while EPP has been assessed as increasing self-efficacy, reducing GP visits, reducing symptoms and reducing costs, there appear to be no evaluations of how the programme has extended the voice of people with long-term conditions in its design and delivery.[21]

## ELEMENTS OF A YEAR OF CARE MODEL FOR LONG-TERM CONDITIONS

The constituent elements of an alternative model are illustrated in Figure 9.4. The model differs from the original Department of Health model in five ways.

1  In the interest of clearly delineating between people at each stage of downward progression we distinguish between three populations: those who are at risk of developing a long-term condition, those who already have a long-term condition, and those with complex (co-) morbidities.

2  In recognition of the way that co-production by people with a long-term condition (as principals) and carers (as agents) changes at each level of downward progression, the model proposes three service modalities (self-management for health, care management, and case management) each with a distinct profile of the expectations and responsibilities of the parties involved in service provision.

3  For each of these modalities, the model invites consideration of what can and needs to be done in planning and negotiating service provision at both population and individual levels.

4  The model extends the constituent elements of the Department of Health service model beyond *clinical* and *self-management* to also include *support* and invites detailed consideration of the types of support that will be provided at each level.

5  The model invites consideration of the process and outcome measures that will be used (for each service modality) to evaluate and improve its service modality.


In essence the model exhibits three systemic dimensions. First, it focuses on three populations. At the level of self-management are those people who have been identified as exhibiting risk factors that if not addressed would lead to a long-term condition and hence who would benefit from interventions that would support them in co-producing their health. Identification of this group of people will rely on GP practice-based condition specific registers that are designed to highlight individuals at high risk of developing a long-term condition. Such a system is already in existence in which GPs and other primary care staff record interventions under the Quality and Outcomes Framework which offers financial incentives for regular monitoring of blood pressure, for example. However, a system designed along lines of co-production will also need to incentivise the recording and monitoring of psycho-social assessments.

At the level of care management are those people who have been identified as having a long-term condition and hence require specified clinical management, but who do not exhibit the full range of clinical morbidities requiring specific case management, and whose psycho-social circumstances are such that, with

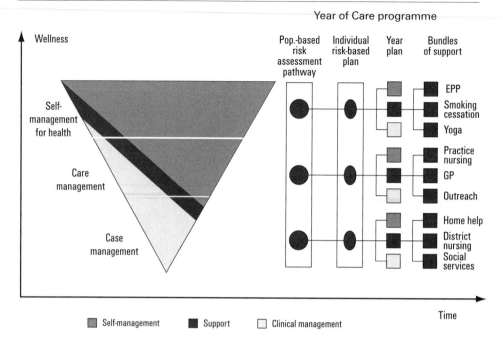

**FIGURE 9.4** A Year of Care model for long-term conditions (showing bundles of support)

the appropriately targeted support are able to self-manage their symptoms and, in many cases, mitigate the rate of downward progression of their condition. Again, assessment and disease specific service provision will rely on NICE and NSF related criteria, in addition to psycho-social assessment.

At the level of case management are those people with complex needs who either exhibit clinical signs and symptoms specified in the existing DoH model or whose psycho-social circumstances are such that they require enhanced support. Identification of people most likely to benefit from case management would rely on guidelines already specified in the Patients At Risk of Readmission (PARR) tool, such as two or more comorbidities, two or more hospital admissions, and length of stay longer than 40 days, as well as disease specific. As important, however, will be assessment based on psycho-social factors such as health literacy, living circumstances, and environmental factors.

Figure 9.5 depicts the cycles of risk assessment, planning, commissioning, enactment and evaluation that will characterise year pathways at the levels of case management, care management and self-management for health. Similarly, Figure 9.6 depicts the same cycle of activities for the case plan, care plan or a health plan that will be co-produced with nominated individuals.

The second systemic dimension of the model distinguishes between the risk assessment and service planning processes that will take place at different

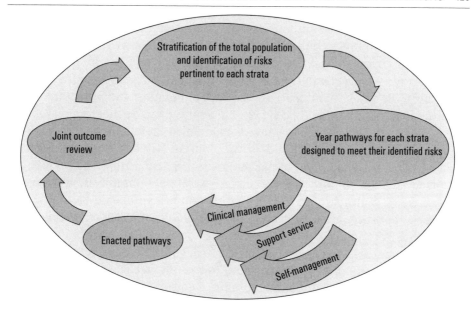

**FIGURE 9.5**  Population-based year pathway cycle

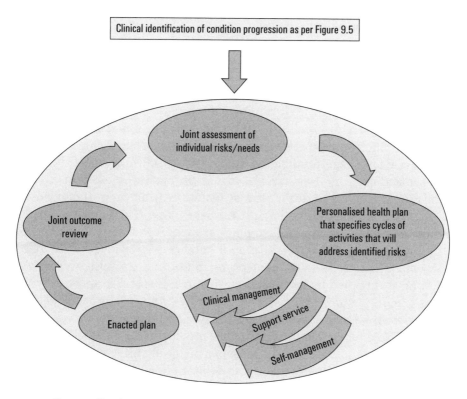

**FIGURE 9.6**  Personalised year plan cycle

levels. The focus on risk rather than need is intentional. It signals that the issues involved in this stage are more to do with process rather than technical criteria. Moreover, the principles of co-production and the injunction that service planners and providers look 'with' rather that 'at' people with long-term conditions, the assessment processes at both population and individual levels are structured to ensure that their view of what is at risk is heard and heeded. The focus is not merely on clinical factors but also on what is at risk from the perspective of the individual and/or their carers. Thus, the risk assessment includes not merely factors that determine the clinical profile of a population or individual but also other factors such as social or economic circumstances, environmental factors, living circumstances and health related factors whose presence or absence (either singularly or in combination) 'prevent people from achieving the optimum of physical, mental and social well-being'.[22]

The foregoing is not to suggest that the focus of risk assessment will be the same at both population and individual levels, or that it is straightforward. The aggregated nature of population oriented assessments means that they will depend more on normative and comparative criteria that have been derived by experts whether clinical, epidemiological or sociological. Consistent with the design features of our model, individual focused risk assessment will place a weight on personal experiences and feelings. This characteristic, in turn, is likely to introduce complications that are 'masked' at population level.

Service planning will occur at two levels. *Population-based service planning* will occur as primary care trusts or local health boards, on the basis of the risk assessment processes outlined above, act to develop year-based pathways that for each level of service provision (self-management of health, care management and case management) specify the cycles (daily, weekly, monthly, yearly) of sequences of activities that will be undertaken by people with a long-term condition, informal carers, service providers, and support services, whose occurrence or non-occurrence (according to the best available evidence, NICE advice and 'expert patient advisers) will significantly affect the quality, outcomes and cost of service provision. On the basis of these year plans the commissioner will act to ensure the availability of the support services that will be incorporated into individualised year plans. These services include condition specific education and support groups, expert patient programmes, routine reviews by nurse practitioners with expertise in chronic disease management, health enhancement programmes (e.g. exercise and smoking cessation), and pooled budgets between health and social services.

*Individualised year (case, care and/or health) plans* will be developed as an individual with a long-term condition as principal) negotiates an agreed year plan (case, care and/or health) with service providers (the agents). These plans (case, care or health) will take the form of a comprehensive written statement that specifies the agreed risks that a plan is meant to address and the outcomes that it is designed to produce; that is, the cycles of activities (daily, weekly, monthly) that will be undertaken by the individual, clinical staff and support service staff at specified times within a cycle and whose occurrence or non-occurrence (in the light of the jointly conducted risk analysis) will significantly affect quality, outcomes and cost. Individual plans thus comprise elements of self-management, care support and clinical management and they are the property of the person with a long-term condition and a means for recording the performance of each party to the plan.

Finally, the third systemic dimension is the improvement oriented evaluation, performance management and clinical governance. Consistent with the centrality we have given to risks as perceived by both the person with the long-term condition and service providers, evaluation processes will focus on the extent to which co-production in the course of a specified time period by way of self-management, support services and clinical services as described in the pathways and individual plans meet identified risks. The methodology (*see* Figure 9.7) thereby provides means for translating expressed wants and priorities of the person with a long-term condition into a time-based pathway which, once described, can be monitored and then managed. It also enables the identification of the extent to which there has been health gain from Line A to Line B in Figure 9.1.

That said we are left with questions about 'what we do about a hospital admission'. First, we need to be clear that a hospital admission is not part of either a care plan or a Year of Care pathway. One of the main reasons for having a year plan is to engender and support a co-production process

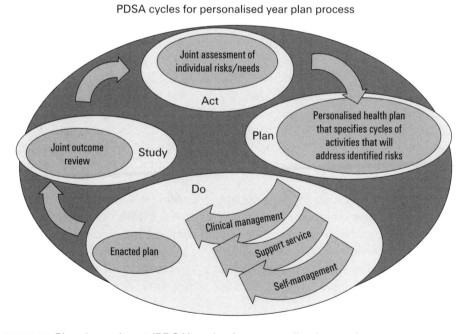

**FIGURE 9.7** Plan-do-study-act (PDSA) cycles for personalised year plan process

that in the interest of quality of life, clinical efficacy and resource efficiency keeps people out of hospital. That being the case, the occurrence of an acute admission has the status of a significant variation to an individual's plan and, as with other outcome variations, the reasons for this should be investigated in the 'study' of the plan or pathway PDSA cycle, particularly where there is evidence a significant number of admissions for health/care/case plans for a nominated condition.

## CONCLUSION

Our analysis of current models of service provision to people with long-term conditions demonstrates how provision is undermined by clinically dominated constructions of such persons as dependent patients whose individuality is buried by the clinical deficits and needs that are ascribed to them by clinicians. In contrast, we argue that the inherent link between the body and the self calls for a model, within which people with long-term conditions are recognised as sentient beings who retain ultimate responsibility for their health as well as the right to exercise their voice and volition in constructing and determining their lives. These rights and responsibilities, in turn, are inscribed in their relationship (as principal) with carers (as agents) with whom they co-produce their health. Accordingly, the process through which services are designed and delivered should be structured along lines that enshrine the rights and responsibilities of people with long-term conditions to be informed, to be consulted and involved in decision making and to enter agreements with agents (clinicians and other carers) that specify what they (as principal) can expect from others and what others can expect from them.

These characteristics (illustrated in Table 9.2 and elaborated further in Degeling, *et al.*[23]) provide the basis for systematising service provision in respect of:

▶ the existence of *explicit methodologies* for (1) stratifying the populations that fall within the ambit of specified long-term conditions and (2) identifying both their clinical risks as well as their risks, wants and priorities as they see these to be

▶ a *person authorised and accountable for* integrating services at a personal level

▶ integrating *methodology* specifying how identified risks and priorities will be linked with a specified menu of services from within the health service but also from other sources such as social services, the voluntary sector, community sources and informal carers

▶ a care plan as an *integrating artefact* that (1) specifies who will do what, why, when and where, and (2) records the responsibilities and rights of all parties

▶ an improvement oriented *performance management and review process* that (1) routinely and systematically examines service performance in respect of its appropriateness for meeting the specific needs and wants of each population strata and (2) sets the agenda for ongoing service improvement as defined above.

In summary, the Year of Care model encourages specificity and clarity along four dimensions. First, it distinguishes between three levels of the population. Second, by recognising the coterminosity of the self and the body, the model provides means for integrating both the personal health responsibilities of individuals and their rights to have their voices heard and heeded in the co-production processes. Third, it provides a basis for risk assessment and service planning to take place at a population level and an individual level. Finally, it provides a framework for making fully explicit (in contrast with existing models; *see* Table 9.1) both what comprises each of the elements of care (self-management, support and clinical), and how they will be related to each other on a person by person basis in ways that enable service provision to be prospectively and proactively designed, explicitly defined, planned and coordinated.

**TABLE 9.2** Summary of Year of Care programme stratified service provision

| | Level 3 Case management | Level 2 Care management | Level 1 Self-management |
|---|---|---|---|
| **Population criteria** | Population identified using both clinical indicators and personal indicators such as:<br>• high score on Hospital Anxiety and Depression scale<br>• nature of family dynamics/dependants<br>• health literacy<br>• self-efficacy. | Population comprises persons with a single condition or range of clinical problems, and personal indicators such as those shown in level 3, who would benefit from care management. | Population defined as those at high risk of developing a long-term condition, due to a combination of clinical risk factors (high BMI, family history) and personal psycho-social risk behaviours (smoking, alcohol etc). |
| **Identified primary integrator** | *Individual as principal and community matron as agent.*<br>• with authority to order clinical investigations, make referrals and arrange admissions to hospital<br>• who is the fixed point of contact for the patient<br>• coordinates contributions of other professionals and agencies. | *Individual as principal and primary care clinician as agent who:*<br>• acts as a point of contact between the individual and team<br>• support individual to navigate services. | *Individual as principal:*<br>with support by primary care clinicians responsible for linking individual with secondary prevention support. |

*cont.*

| | Level 3 Case management | Level 2 Care management | Level 1 Self-management |
|---|---|---|---|
| Service aim | To improve quality of life and reduce repeat admissions. | To improve quality of life, extend active life, slow down disease progression, reduce disability, ensure better management of sudden deteriorations, reduce need for hospital admission and improve quality of life. | To improve quality of life and reduce risks of developing a long-term condition, and if diagnosed to reduce its severity. |
| Method | *Case management*<br><br>• Joint negotiation of individualised case plans that are based on a trade-off of the different constructions of the risks that are in play on an individual by individual basis.<br><br>• Emergent variations, managed by the community matron as case manager. | *Care management*<br><br>• Stratified, condition specific registers.<br><br>• Time specified recall and review process.<br><br>• Condition specific networks that span primary and acute settings.<br><br>• Negotiation of individualised care plans based on a trade-off of the constructions of risk that are in play as these are perceived by the individual and clinicians. | *Health management*<br><br>• Stratified registers identifying those at high risk of developing a long-term condition.<br><br>• Time specified recall and review process.<br><br>• Joint negotiation of an individualised health plan that registers trade-offs between risks as these are seen by individual and clinicians.<br><br>• Provision of secondary prevention support. |
| Artefact | *An individual case plan that is held and owned by individual which specifies*<br><br>• the details of the care to be provided<br><br>• regular reviews to re-assess risk<br><br>• the self-care to be undertaken by the patient and informal carers<br><br>• what each professional and agency will do to meet need, manage risk and/or support self-management. | *An individual care plan that is held and owned by individual which specifies*<br><br>• the details of the clinical care to be provided<br><br>• regular reviews to reassess risk<br><br>• the self-care to be undertaken by the patient and informal carers<br><br>• what each professional and agency will do to meet need, manage risk and/or support self management. | An individual health plan, held and owned by the person and specifies:<br><br>• the health objectives that the individual will pursue<br><br>• the activities that will be undertaken in this regard<br><br>• the support services that can be drawn on<br><br>• regular reviews to reassess risk. |
| Performance management and review | *Time specified application of PDSA methodology* | *Time specified application of PDSA methodology* | *Time specified application of PDSA methodology* |

# REFERENCES

1 World Health Organization. *Chronic Conditions: the global burden.* Geneva: WHO; 2004.

2 Olsson M, Lexell J, Soderberg S. The meaning of fatigue for women with multiple sclerosis. *J Advanced Nursing.* 2005; **49**(1): 7–15. Callery P. Paying to participate; financial, social and personal costs to parents of involvement in their children's care in hospital. *J Advanced Nursing.* 1997; **26**: 992–8. Wilson T, Buck D, Ham C. Rising to the challenge: will the NHS support people with long term conditions? *BMJ.* 2005; **330**: 657–61. Wagner EH, Glasgow RE, Davis C. Quality improvement in chronic illness care: a collaborative approach. *J Qual Improv.* 2001; **27**(2): 63–80. Department of Work and Pensions. *Incapacity Benefit and Severe Disablement Allowance: quarterly summary statistics.* London: Department for Work and Pensions; 2003. McIntyre D, Thiede M, Dahlgren G, *et al.* What are the economic consequences for households of illness and of paying for health care in low- and middle-income country contexts? *Social Science & Medicine.* 2006; **62**(4): 858–65.

3 Department of Health. *Improving Chronic Disease Management. A note for PCT, NHS Trust and SHA management teams.* London: Department of Health; 2004. National Public Health Service for Wales. *A Profile of Long-Term and Chronic Conditions in Wales.* Cardiff: National Public Health Service for Wales; 2005.

4 Penrod J. Refinement of the concept of uncertainty. *J Advanced Nursing.* 2001; **34**(2): 238–45. Lorig K. Partnerships between expert patients and physicians. *The Lancet.* 2002; **359**: 814–15. Close H. Roles and responsibilities in understanding, accepting and adapting in the chronic illness trajectory. PhD thesis, Northumbria University; 2005. Wilson, *et al.*, op. cit. Young KW. Quality of life of people with long-term psychiatric illness living in a residential home. *Int J Psychosocial Rehabilitation.* 2004; **9**(1): 133–45. Department of Health. *National Service Framework for Mental Health.* London: Department of Health; 1999.

5 Henwood M. *Ignored and Invisible? Carers' experiences of the NHS.* London: Carers National Association; 1988. Clarke C. Family care-giving for people with dementia: some implications for policy and professional practice. *J Advanced Nursing.* 1999; **29**(3): 712–20. Atkin K, Ahmad WIU. Family care-giving and chronic illness: how parents cope with a child with a sickle cell disorder or thalasaemia. *Health and Social Care in the Community,* 2000; **8**: 57–69. Payne S, Ellis-Hill C, eds. *Chronic and Terminal Illness: new perspectives on caring and carers.* Oxford: Oxford University Press; 2001.

6 Singh D. Transforming chronic care: a systematic review of the evidence. *Evidence-Based Cardiovascular Medicine.* 2005; **9**(2): 91–4. Wilson, *et al.*, op. cit. Department of Health, 2004, op. cit.

7 Degeling PJ, Close HJ, Degeling D. *A Report on the Development and Implementation of Co-produced, Year Based Integrated Care Pathways to Improve Service Provision to People with Long Term Conditions.* Durham: University of Durham; 2006.

8 National Public Health Service for Wales, op. cit.

9 Murray SA, Kendall M, Boyd K, Sheikh A. Illness trajectories and palliative care. *BMJ.* 2005; **330**: 1007–11.

10 Hevey D. The tragedy principle: strategies for change in the representation of disabled people. In: Swain J, Finkelstein V, French S, *et al.*, eds. *Disabling Barriers*

– *Enabling Environments*. London: Sage; 1993. Reed J, Clarke CL. Nursing older people: constructing need and care. *Nursing Inquiry*. 1999; **6**(3): 208. Thorne SE, Paterson BL. Two decades of insider research: what we know and don't know about chronic illness experience. *Annual Review of Nursing Research*. 2000; **18**: 3–25.

11 Lorig, op. cit.

12 Bodenheimer T, Wagner EH, Grumbach K. Improving primary care for patients with chronic illness: the chronic care model Part 2. *JAMA*. 2002; **288**(15): 1909–14.

13 Wagner EH. Chronic disease management: what will it take to improve care for chronic illness? *Eff Clin Pract*. 1998; **1**: 2–4.

14 Department of Health. *Supporting People with Long Term Conditions*. London: Stationery Office; 2005.

15 Vernon S, Ross F, Gould MA. Assessment of older people: politics and practice in primary care. *J Advanced Nursing*. 2000; **31**(2): 282–7. Reed, Clarke, op. cit.

16 Fox RC. Medical uncertainty revisited. In: Albrecht GL, Fitzpatrick R, Scrimshaw SC, eds. *Handbook of Social Studies and Medicine*. Sage: London; 2000.

17 Woodward M, Oliphant J, Lowe G, *et al*. Contribution of contemporaneous risk factors to social inequality in coronary heart disease and all causes mortality. *Preventive Medicine*. 2003; **36**: 561–8. Pooley CG, Briggs J, Gatrell T, *et al*. Contacting your GP when the surgery is closed: issues of location and access. *Health & Place*. 2003; **9**: 230–2. Rabinowitz E. When patients don't understand. *Managed Healthcare*. 2001; **April**: 3–4. Gillis A. Determinants of a health-promoting lifestyle: an integrative review. *J Advanced Nursing*. 1993; **18**: 345–53. Sherer M, Maddux JE. The self-efficacy scale: construction and validation. *Psychological Reports*. 1982; **51**: 663–71. Thorne, Paterson, op. cit.

18 Bynum CW. *Women's Stories, Women's Symbols: fragmentation and redemption*. London: Macmillan; 1991, p. 3.

19 Reed, Clarke, op. cit.

20 Lorig, op. cit.

21 Barlow JH, Turner AP, Wright C. Instilling the strength to fight the pain and get on with life. *Health Education Research: theory & practice*. 1999; **14**: 533–44. Liljas B, Lahdensuo A. Is asthma self-management cost-effective? *Patient Education and Counselling*. 1997; **32**(1 supp): S97–104. Lorig K, *et al*. Evidence suggests that a chronic disease self-management programme can improve health status while reducing hospitalization: a randomized trial. *Medical Care*. 1999; **1**(37): 5–14.

22 Hawe P, Degeling D, Hall J. *Evaluating Health Promotion*. Australia: Elsevier; 1990.

23 Degeling, Close, Degeling, op. cit.

# CHAPTER 10

# A Year of Care pathway for COPD: problems, pitfalls and solutions from practice

*Jane Robinson and Helen Close*

In May 2005, North East Yorkshire and North Lincolnshire Strategic Health Authority (NEYNL) challenged its PCTs to adopt Professor Degeling's Year of Care model in an attempt to reduce avoidable emergency hospital admissions. One of the PCTs, Hambleton and Richmondshire, attended a workshop presented by Professor Degeling and decided to reduce admissions in three separate areas including chronic obstructive pulmonary disease (COPD). Within 12 months a multidisciplinary, multi-agency project group implemented the first Year of Care pathway in the country for COPD.

This paper analyses this application of the Year of Care concept. The pathway is at an early stage of implementation and many of the problems and solutions described are generic to any disease specific pathway. We will show how the Year of Care concept has been imaginatively and creatively taken up by champions in PCTs because it offers a method for resolving so many of the paradoxes and problems in practice that arise from, and sustain, the current 'silo' approach to performance management, clinical quality and self-management issues. We will also critically discuss the extent to which the Year of Care pathway has been funded, incentivised, clinically agreed, implemented and evaluated and conclude by offering guiding principles, suggestions and solutions for practical implementation.

## CONTEXT

At the time of the initiative, Hambleton and Richmondshire PCT (HRPCT) had a population of 116 000 almost exclusively rural and relatively affluent. The health indicators show the population to have a longer than average life expectancy and a lower incidence of disease than some of the neighbouring, more industrial areas. Accessibility to services is a major problem, although utilisation of services appears high. Pockets of significant disadvantage do exist within the area, most notably around the military base in Catterick Garrison and Colburn.

The PCT itself operated three community hospitals. The Friarage Hospital in Northallerton, operated by the South Tees Hospitals NHS Trust, was the area's main provider of general acute services. More specialist services such as cardiothoracic surgery, neurosurgery and radiotherapy were provided at the James Cook University Hospital in Middlesbrough, although some of the population in the south of the area travel to Leeds for these services. A small but significant proportion received their hospital services from hospitals in York, Darlington, Harrogate, Kendal and Lancaster. There were 20 general practices (18 NHS and two military) in the area, ranging from large group practices to a single-handed practice in the Dales.

The PCT had identified over 1250 people on GP registers with COPD in the Hambleton and Richmondshire area. An analysis of local hospital episode statistics carried out by the Centre for Clinical Management Development at the University of Durham showed high numbers of COPD admissions and multiple emergency admissions (i.e. more than one admission in one year). For example, in 2004/05, exacerbation of COPD was among the top 10 reasons for admission, and an estimated 33.39% of bed day savings could be made if the actual rate of multiple emergency admissions was reduced to expected rates. Thus, COPD appeared to be the type of high volume condition that could benefit from systematised care.

The illness is strongly associated with smoking and long-term exposure to coal dust, and is characterised by a progressive loss of lung capacity and associated physical functionality.[1] Medical treatments draw from a limited range of options designed to maximise lung function and the six month period at the end of life is often characterised by multiple unplanned hospital admissions made in response to attacks of severe breathlessness and infection.[1,2] Despite this gloomy prognosis, sufferers report that gains in quality of life *can* be made in such non-medical treatments as smoking cessation, nutritional interventions, exercise, social support and cognitive therapy to deal with the debilitating panic attacks often associated with breathlessness.

On this basis, GPs were engaged to provide proactive, non-medical management (i.e. focusing on social and psychological factors as well as clinical) and to support patients in self-management. The resultant pathway, implemented in April 2006, goes beyond the usual medical, reactive response to an exacerbation (secondary care focused drugs, stabilisation and discharge) to a proactive, holistic approach in primary and community care with long-term management of the patients to include self-management. The project group is outcome focused and aims to achieve a cost neutral 15% reduction in COPD emergency admissions in 2006/07 and a further 15% in 2007/08.

## GUIDING PRINCIPLES

A Project Team was set up and was governed by a number of explicit and implicit principles. First, from its inception, the development of the Year of Care pathway was outcome driven: to reduce COPD unplanned admissions by 30% by March 2008. This clearly measurable outcome helped the team to be focused and enabled it to quantify the cost savings so vital to securing invest-to-save funding. The cost saving was to prove crucial as the financial climate deteriorated (as with all PCTs at this uncertain time). The team distinguished between the measurable *outcome* of reducing emergency COPD admissions and the *process* of using the Year of Care model to achieve this aim. But while the measurable outcome was fewer hospital admissions, it was always understood that this clearly translated into far better quality of care for patients.

The figure of 30% was set as a stretch target. The team adopted the philosophy behind the Modernisation Agency's Pursuing Perfection programme that only by setting radical goals would a new radically innovative approach emerge.[3] The team did not wish to merely tweak the existing system, but overhaul it. However, neither was the figure plucked from thin air: the data from Durham University had indicated that the observed rates of readmission for COPD in Hambleton and Richmondshire were well over 30% greater than expected rates of readmission.

Second, the pathway had to be cost neutral. At the inauguration of the project, the requirement was to shift resources from secondary to primary care. The recently introduced Payment by Results would allow the savings made from reduced hospital admissions to be invested in primary or community care. The Project Team initially planned a 30% reduction in admissions over two years. However, within two months of the start of the project the economic climate changed: Hambleton and Richmondshire PCT, like so many others, began fighting to prevent a deficit. All investment ceased. The Project's only hope was to make the pathway cost neutral *in one year*.

Third, based on the Project Manager and Clinical Lead attendance at Year of Care workshops run by Pieter Degeling, self-management and a holistic approach to patient care became central to the pathway development. It is very easy to see the impact of non-medical factors on COPD patients, so the emphasis on psychological, social and economic elements within the pathway was always understood. Not only did research evidence back this up (e.g. among older people with COPD, prevalence rates for mild depression are 25% and for major depression reports range from 6% to 42%[4]) but the first hand experience of the specialist respiratory nurses and the practice nurse on the team reinforced the view that people were often admitted to hospital due to factors other than the purely clinical. Once this holistic approach becomes central, a paternalistic model of care is untenable: in other words, unless the person is fully engaged as a co-producer of their own health outcomes, they will not be able to impact on these psychological, social and economic factors.

Fourth, the Year of Care model posits three stages of care for people with long-term conditions: Stage 1, self-management, Stage 2, care management and Stage 3, case management. In effect each stage has its own Year of Care pathway. Any such stratification has an inherent tension between providing collective equity of access to services and individualised care. While the Project Team acknowledged the need to stratify patients, this was simply to determine the frequency of review and the clinician in charge of their support. Thus patients in Stage 3 would receive reviews by the Specialist Respiratory Outreach Nurses at least every three months whereas those in Stage 1 would receive an annual review by their practice nurse. Stratification was based on the perceived likelihood of an emergency hospital admission, with the aim of providing targeted support to those deemed most at risk.

The team agreed that all patients would have access to the same type of management no matter which stage they were in. All are assessed for all 10 aspects of the management plan (shown in Box 10.1) and their care determined by their need. For example, a patient in Stage 1 may need advice and support for nutrition in just the same way as a patient at Stage 3. It quickly became apparent within the team that a key principle was to systematise the good practice carried out by the specialist nurses, and ensure that all patients, at whatever stage, received the same standard of care. Thus patients who have only mild COPD will receive high quality support which will better enable their self-management and thereby keep them at that stage for much longer.

---

**BOX 10.1  Aspects of the COPD Management Plan**

 1  Carers
 2  Drugs
 3  Exercise
 4  Mental health
 5  Nutrition
 6  Patient education
 7  Physiotherapy
 8  Self-management
 9  Smoking cessation
10  Social

---

Fifth, the primacy of primary care was not only a high priority for the Department of Health but also was a significant part of the PCT's vision. Hambleton and Richmondshire is a very rural area, so providing care closer to a person's home really does make a significant difference. As stated above, the pathway was systematising existing good practice and ensuring that all people with COPD received this from the time of their diagnosis. The GP surgery was the obvious place to receive this care for all but those whose illness made them housebound.

But the pathway was not developed in isolation from the acute trust. The respiratory consultant and the two specialist respiratory outreach nurses employed by the acute trust were all members of the Project Group and key contributors. Rather than see the development of the pathway as a threat, they were confident that it would reduce the frustration of avoidable hospital admissions, and ensure that their excellent work was not unravelled once patients were discharged.

Finally, while the motto 'the best is the enemy of the good' was not often spoken, the team was happy to accept that a less than perfect pathway was better than no pathway at all. There was a shared agreement that the pathway would be operationalised when it was deemed to be 'good enough' and that it would then be improved from feedback which was only attainable from usage. The collection of variance data has not yet been systematised; however, feedback is obtained at training sessions and at regular one-to-one meetings between the new community respiratory nurse and practice nurses. Furthermore, because the pathway was not seen as an 'all or nothing' affair, aspects of it were implemented early as quick gains; for example, reminding GPs of the correct drugs to use for exacerbations.

## PROJECT MANAGEMENT

In May 2005 the PCT's Modernisation Manager proposed to the PCT's Professional Executive Committee (PEC) the development of three Year of Care pathways, one of which was COPD. In June a presentation was made to the PCT's Respiratory Local Implementation Team (LIT) and it was agreed that the Year of Care project should become the main focus of the LIT, and that the LIT should re-form as a specific Project Team. This group's first meeting was in July 2005.

From inception, the team was accountable and reported to the Long Term Conditions Steering Group, the PEC and the Modernisation Delivery Group to ensure widespread understanding of and involvement in the project. The Project Team was set up to include representation from all key stakeholders. These included representatives of service users, primary, secondary and community care, the ambulance trust, social services and the voluntary sector. The Team's Chair and clinical lead was a GP and member of the PEC. The patient representative who was initially involved felt she could not contribute adequately and asked a colleague from the PPI Forum to take her place: her input was very useful (although limited due to illness) particularly in challenging the jargon-ridden language of the team.

The team explicitly utilised a project management methodology. At the initial meeting a Project Initiation Document (PID) was agreed setting out the team membership, the aim and scope of the project. Key milestones and the accountability and reporting arrangements were also agreed. The PID acted as a contract that provided focus for the team.

In the early stages of the project, four sub-groups worked on (1) data and costings, (2) drugs and diagnostics, (3) support, and (4) self-management. Each reported to the full team every month. However, as work progressed the issues were so cross-cutting that this structure ended, although sub-group leads retained responsibilities for their areas.

The pathway was launched in April 2006 at an educational event attended by 60 delegates with 17 out of 18 GP surgeries being represented by both a GP and a practice nurse. The GPs' involvement was secured with a Local Enhanced Service (LES) that recognised the additional work they would need to undertake beyond their nGMS contract. At the launch, GP and practice nurse COPD leads from each practice were given an A4 Pathway File. These were also circulated to district nurse case managers, nursing home staff, physiotherapists and others. The files consisted of clear advice on diagnosis and assessment, the flowcharts for all the management plans, a flowchart for COPD palliative care, plus selected examples of patient literature with re-ordering details. Follow-up educational sessions were held in autumn 2006.

## PATHWAY DEVELOPMENT

The Project Manager's initial plan was to benchmark best practice, process map the existing service and then to identify the ideal local service specification. However, just prior to the planned process mapping session in October 2005, the Clinical Lead attended a Year of Care Workshop and became so enthused that he sketched out an outline Year of Care pathway, arguing that process mapping the existing services would not contribute a great deal because the project was not setting out to tweak what existed but to implement something completely new. Yet there is a paradox here: the pathway would be systematising existing local best practice, and yet the approach was innovative. The novelty of the approach was fourfold.

1  All patients diagnosed with COPD would receive the same proactive support, even if their condition was still mild.
2  Primary care would deliver this support, using acute care clinicians as 'knowledge nodes'.
3  The focus would be on the provision of targeted self-management support that was intended to enable people with COPD to self-manage in a way that gave them greater choice and improve their quality of life.
4  Simple written guidelines were collaboratively produced for all parts of the pathway which enabled the systematisation and made transparent the contributions of each stakeholder at each stage of the pathway, including that of the person with COPD.

The outline pathway was so well received by the team that it only changed slightly in the ensuing months. At that meeting in October, the main framework of the stratification model and the elements of the management plans were discussed and agreed.

The Clinical Lead wrote to his GP colleagues at regular intervals in the early days of the project to raise the profile of COPD. The secondary care team informed the team that patients were frequently admitted after being given inadequate medication to prevent an exacerbation worsening. Thus one letter to GPs included detailed advice on the correct medical treatment of exacerbations. GP practices were also sent details of the number of admissions as a proportion of their list size and COPD register size: this encouraged one practice to analyse its admissions and to give feedback to the team that most of their admissions occurred out of hours. Thus out of hours doctors were given education about the correct treatment of exacerbations.

The pathway details the ideal care any patient with COPD should receive in primary and community care in any year. This includes diagnosis, assessment and stratification, management and review. All patients, independent of the stratification, are given an assessment and subsequent management plan covering the areas shown in Table 8.1. The pathway documentation gives simple flowcharts to enable clinicians to follow systematised mini-pathways for all these areas. Some of these mini-pathways are generic and have been included in a Heart Failure Year of Care Pathway that is being developed along the same lines.

The development of the pathway also entailed collaboration with colleagues in social services, voluntary carers' groups, mental health, palliative care, public health, dietetics and physiotherapy. The aim of this collaboration was to establish what best practice was in order to document it to ensure its systematisation across the whole PCT.

## FUNDING AND COMMISSIONING

It was clear that the implementation of the new pathway would not be successful without some additional investment in primary and community care, an investment to be financed from the savings produced by the reduction in admissions. A simple formula was used to calculate the potential savings: the number of spells in the preceding year for the relevant HRGs was multiplied by the predicted percentage reduction (15%) to give an absolute number of predicted admissions saved. This figure was then multiplied by the tariff price for the HRGs to give a total saving.

The project team decided on four main priorities for the new investment.

1 A Local Enhanced Service (LES) payment for GPs to incentivise and compensate them for the additional workload (the payment was based on attendance at the educational launch event (April 2006), attainment of specified Quality and Outcomes Framework targets related to the pathway, and a reduction in admissions of 15% in each locality).

2 A full-time community respiratory nurse (from August 2006) to support the practices and district nurses in the implementation of the pathway.
3 Some part-time community physiotherapy support.
4 Equipment: nebulisers for long-term loan and pulse oximeters for the out of hours teams.

The PCT's Board and Finance Committee had to be persuaded of the benefits of the pathway, both in terms of patient care and of cost. While the Board gave the go-ahead for the pathway in March 2006, the Finance Committee was less happy with the perceived risk. The financial climate had changed from the time of the project's inception; the focus now was on the short-term financial goal of breaking even. Further lobbying was undertaken and a cash flow forecast written to enable close performance management of the financial aspects of the pathway. The Finance Committee was due to make its decision on the morning of the launch of the pathway (with 60 delegates present). Fortunately, the decision was positive, perhaps influenced by the fact that the PCT's Chief Executive and Chair – both members of the Finance Committee – were due to attend the launch later that same day.

## KEY SUCCESS FACTORS

It is too early at the time of writing to report other than impressionistically on the clinical and other patient outcomes of the use of the Year of Care pathway. The project is subject to continuing performance management; thus, unplanned admissions are being recorded monthly but the normal significant monthly variance in admissions means that conclusions cannot be drawn for several months. However, figures for the first eight months of 2006–07 show at least 10 fewer admissions than in the same period in 2005–06 using a limited set of ICD codes: these in themselves have generated a saving of over £20000. As part of the evaluation of the project, feedback is being sought from service users on their views on the improved service. At the time of writing, all those asked to comment have rated the new service as excellent. However, the novelty of such a multidisciplinary project is significant; it is thus worth reflecting on the factors that contributed to its successful implementation.

First, the project had a clinical champion who had passion and enthusiasm for the concept and a desire to improve practice. Furthermore, as a much respected GP, PEC member and GP vocational training tutor, he had the credibility, wisdom and experience to effect change among his colleagues.

Second, the specialist respiratory outreach nurses who were employed by the acute trust were very open to the Year of Care concept, and were valuable members of the project team. Rather than feeling threatened by the project's drive to shift emphasis to primary and community care, they appreciated its value to patients and the positive role they could play in this development, and they worked to break down some of the traditional barriers between secondary and primary care. One of the nurses had previous experience in primary care, which gave her understanding of the role of the practice nurse and thus the benefits they could offer; it also provided insight into the pressures they face – often a lack of time and autonomy.

Third, the wide stakeholder involvement in the project team smoothed the way for implementation. While links with operational managers could have been better, the involvement of key clinical opinion leaders was invaluable. GP engagement was critical for the success of the pathway as the main focus was to be the active management and review of patients in primary care. The setting up of Locality Commissioning Groups (LCGs) in early 2006 gave a useful forum to present the project to GPs, and the LCGs effectively sponsored the project through the PCT's Local Delivery Plan process.

Fourth, the development and implementation of the pathway in such a relatively short time was due in part to the allocation of a project manager to the project. The benefit of this was not only some dedicated time (on average 7–10 hours per week) but also the utilisation of a project management methodology. This avoided some of the pitfalls of committee work and focused on the achievement of milestones and outcomes. The project manager acted as facilitator to the clinicians on the team, providing encouragement as well as practical support, underpinned by assured confidence that the team would achieve its goals. The team members responded well to this, and an energy and momentum was created in which everyone worked hard to ensure that they did not let the others down.

Finally, the effective implementation of the pathway depended on the training and education of those who will deliver it. This was not imposed but shared and led by the clinical champion using a variety of media: letters, e-mails and events. An initial educational event in April was followed up in September, with the latter bringing the pathway to the wider multidisciplinary teams (including district nurses, physiotherapists and community psychiatric nurses).

## CHALLENGES AND SOLUTIONS

The main challenge was securing the funding for the project during a time of significant financial difficulty for the PCT. As we have seen, in the end the case had to rest robustly on the project being cost neutral in one year. The whole pathway could not be prospectively costed and commissioned before implementation because of the lack of clear financial data on separate elements of primary and community care. Only the new elements of the pathway were costed and commissioned. However, as the pathway is fully operationalised, audit data will be collected to enable an understanding of the proportions of patients accessing each part of the pathway. This retrospective costing will enable future prospective commissioning.

An information challenge was provided by the poor quality of the admissions data from the acute trust. The HRG data on which the predictions were based required 'cleaning' to remove duplications and other erroneous entries. This enabled a realistic number – and hence cost – of saved admissions to be calculated. However, performance management of the pathway has to be undertaken with raw data: therefore savings have to be shown by the reduction in the *number* of admissions and not the *percentage* reduction. A key task now is to obtain clinical Read Codes to enable the recording of the stratification of patients on GPs' clinical IT systems. The existing codes only allow the recording of the clinical severity of the condition. Once obtained and practices have coded all the patients on their registers, it will be possible to perform data analysis to understand the proportions of patients accessing different aspects of the pathway. This will then form the basis for prospective commissioning.

A systematised approach to the stratification of patients also proved challenging. Initially the team tried to include all the factors that seemed to affect the likelihood of an exacerbation resulting in an admission. They also endeavoured to completely standardise the process. A realisation that only the frequency of review would be affected by the stratification enabled a solution: only factors that could be improved by increased review frequency needed to be included in the process. The outcome provides a simple model that acknowledges the need for clinical judgement.

Improving both the self-management process and outcomes for people with COPD was another key challenge not least as it was linked to the need for other professionals (especially ambulance and out of hours staff) to access information about the patients' normal condition and their normal and stand-by medication. A Self-Management Plan was produced for patients to keep at home. This told patients how to recognise and react to the early signs of an exacerbation and when to take stand-by medication. Information was produced about the general effects of the disease and also how to deal with the cold of winter or the heat of summer. Also a holistic approach was emphasised because often patients' self-management is thwarted by depression. Clinicians required improved skills in motivational interviewing and this factor is addressed in our educational sessions.

## CONCLUSIONS

The challenge laid down by the strategic health authority to adopt the Year of Care model is one that could easily be ignored, given the local climate of financial concerns and organisational change, coupled with wider concerns about the future for acute services and professional silos. And yet key people working in Hambleton and Richmondshire PCT had the vision to recognise an opportunity to improve the level of control, visibility and influence that clinicians have over the process of delivering good quality patient-centred care, thereby addressing the barriers to improving the patient experience that so often conspire against us.

The development of a Year of Care for people with COPD has taken time, resources, multidisciplinary cooperation and, above all, an understanding of the importance of non-medical, non-acute aspects of patient care. The financial gains of this process will be proven later in the year; there is no doubt that the net effect will be so much more than a drop in avoidable admissions. The value to individual patients is immeasurable; the value to the wider community and for staff working within the organisations is a cultural change which enables the enactment of co-production. This is surely why we joined the NHS in the first place: to care for people in ways that take into account their lives, experiences and ability to make their own decisions. At a time when clinicians often feel exhausted by exhortations to improve the 'patient' experience, this case study shows that collective, multidisciplinary, planned action can indeed make a positive difference.

## ACKNOWLEDGMENTS

We pay special tribute here to the late Dr Bruce Davies, the Project Group's Clinical Lead, who was so instrumental in the development of our COPD Year of Care pathway. Bruce contributed his amazing knowledge and enthusiasm with characteristic wit and humility, and was supportive and encouraging of all team members.

## REFERENCES

1 National Institute for Clinical Effectiveness (NICE). *Chronic Obstructive Pulmonary Disease: management of chronic obstructive pulmonary disease in adults in primary and secondary care*. London: National Institute for Clinical Effectiveness; 2004.
2 Healthcare Commission. *Clearing the Air: a national study of chronic obstructive pulmonary disease*. London: Commission for Healthcare Audit and Inspection; 2006.
3 Department of Health. NHS Modernisation Agency Collaboration Tools. http://www.wise.nhs.uk/sites/crosscutting/pursuingperfection/default.aspx (accessed September 2006).
4 Lamers F, Jonkers CCM, Bosma H, *et al*. Effectiveness and cost-effectiveness of a minimal psychological intervention to reduce non-severe depression in chronically ill elderly patients: the design of a randomised controlled trial. *BMC Public Health*. 2006; **6**: 161.

# CHAPTER 11

# Making primary care systematic: successful cardiac care

*Graham Archard*

Primary care has changed beyond recognition over the last few decades. There has been a systematic move from the one-to-one consultation with a doctor to more complex patterns of treatment involving a number of different professionals with specialised skills and with patients actively involved in framing and managing their programme of care. This has called for a change in the way we do our work.

Historically primary care was delivered essentially as a hierarchical relationship between a GP and the patient. Nurses, pharmacists, physiotherapists and even junior partners knew their place. Only 20 years ago I employed the first practice nurse my practice had ever seen, so much against the views of my senior partner that I had to pay her salary from my own partnership share. The senior partner of one of my local practices did not even know his district nurse who had worked for him for three years. The few practice managers dealt primarily with personnel and employment matters and were usually a promoted receptionist or the spouse of the senior partner with no knowledge of management skills.

The model was hierarchy not teamwork. Staff and patients did what the GP told them to do – and the GP felt safe in his ivory tower. We did not recognise the skills of others, nor use them. Patients were not involved in their own care and it was not felt they should be. Now we recognise that this model is no longer appropriate; we talk about the need for teamwork, but we are still working out what this means in terms of clinical practice. This chapter is concerned with how we can do this and describes one initiative in caring for people with heart disease in Dorset.

## APPROACHES TO SYSTEMATISING CARE

The development of a more systematic approach to clinical care has been pursued in part through the development and circulation of NICE Guidelines.

When each tome of such guidance falls upon the surgery mat, it is carefully placed on a consulting room shelf to be read – at a later date. Guidelines are a bit like appraisal; if you think you are already practising good medicine then why do you need guidance? NICE guidance might fit into appraisal and professional development plans if we do not know enough about a subject but if I knew what I didn't know I would know it! For many of us, NICE guidelines do not connect with our own clinical experience: they are 'what they are telling us' rather than 'what we know from experience' instruments. Perhaps this explains in part at least why NICE guidelines have not been adopted as widely as originally hoped.[1]

What we *do* know is that the increasing shift of clinical care from secondary to primary care environments, the increasing complexities of care and the appropriate demand for higher quality care all lead to the need for additional primary care resources. But the growth in the number of GPs has been relatively small in comparison with the expansion of secondary care doctors[2] and at the same time there are areas of the country where it is difficult or impossible to recruit doctors to take on this additional workload.[3]

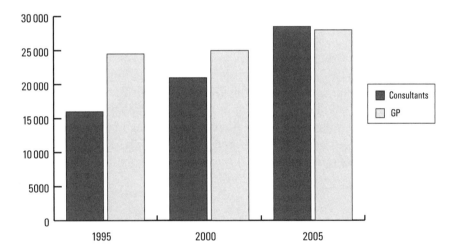

**FIGURE 11.1** Full-time equivalent consultants and general practitioners in England, 1995–2005

Rather than simply hoping for an increase in the supply of GPs, we should be making better use of the staff we now have and, in particular, making better use of nurses and support staff. This means thinking of the practice as a comprehensive team, and getting the best value out of each member of the team, using the skill of all in the team to maximise our potential in the care of our patients. As traditional secondary care conditions have been moved into primary care, so traditional GP roles may be safely conducted by others with the appropriate skill.[4] We have recognised for decades, for example, the specialist skills of midwives in managing non-complicated obstetrics, and the role of nurses in the provision of dressings and immunisations is rarely questioned. It is now increasingly common for healthcare workers to operate across traditional boundaries: for GPs with special interests to link up with secondary care or a pharmacist to contribute additional knowledge to a primary care team. This shift of skills and work between different professionals has led to increased workload pressures within primary care and to give more explicit attention to the development and maintenance of the team, the recognition of each other's skills and of the need to work together as extended teams to accommodate these pressures.

Team working is all about communication in which all members participate. We all need to know what we are each doing, where our skills and responsibilities lie and in what way we can best work together to the benefit of our patients. We have to prioritise the areas of work which we undertake together and form an opinion as to how best to implement our work as a team. The whole team, including GPs, nurses, patients and managers, must agree the priorities, aims and implementation methods (whether *de novo* or drawn from accepted practice such as NICE guidance). Team members can then collectively determine and offer the skills they have to populate the work plan.

This collective involvement not only recognises the value and worth of the team as a whole but also those of each member and the skills that members have and indeed may have not been aware of in themselves and each other. But there has to be a shared sense of purpose. This may be to implement the Quality and Outcomes Framework of the new GP contract or the action plan arising from an audit of a significant event or complaint. The purpose, whatever it is, must have a value to the team or the plan will not be willingly implemented, if at all. Unfortunately, the purposes of many primary care trust initiatives have often not been understood or agreed by those who have to implement them and, as a result, they never really get off the ground.

## HOW DID WE SUCCEED?

SUCCEED (*see* Figure 11.2) is a patient led care pathway in secondary prevention of ischaemic heart disease (IHD). It was introduced in anticipation of the cardiovascular National Service Framework as a means of replacing the old Health Promotion Initiative of the Health Authority that was seen by many as an exercise in collecting data for data's sake. Although SUCCEED was funded through the Health Promotion Initiative, the project was seen to be particularly attractive to primary care teams. Thus over half of the Dorset practices attended a series of evening meetings to design a patient held care pathway to implement best practice in the management of patient post myocardial infarction or post coronary artery bypass grafting. Following a Delphi method, the participating doctors, nurses and managers examined existing pathways and the available evidence, and modified an initial proposed pathway to generate a new, usable, pathway understood and valued by all participants.

SUCCEED

Successful
Cardiac Care
based on
Evidence for
Effectiveness
in Dorset

**FIGURE 11.2** The SUCCEED Project

After short piloting of the pathway, the practices were circulated with questionnaires and the pathway modified. Eleven drafts and two meetings later the pathway had changed from an initial 11 page A4 document to a double-sided A4 card designed to be folded into an A6 wallet for patients to carry with them between primary and secondary care and which served as a record of the time taken at each attendance (against a standard of 30 minutes). Attendance times were recorded on the card. The pathways were run by a care manager; in all but one very small single-handed practice this was a practice nurse.

Patients became involved in the agreement of their goals. For example, although patients were informed of the need to exercise, diet and lose weight and stop smoking where appropriate, they had to agree their own goals with the care manager. Thus, if a patient felt unable to stop smoking but wished to cut down to 10 a day, this goal was noted on the record card and signed by the patient. The practice then supported the patient in any way it could in the achievement of the agreed goal. At subsequent attendances, the goals would be reviewed and renegotiated with the aim of gradually decreasing risk factors and improving outcomes. The patients admitted their commitment to this negotiated process and to feeling more likely to succeed.

Getting secondary care involved was, initially, difficult. Although they were invited to contribute to the pathways, our secondary care colleagues had seen unsuccessful primary care projects in the past and were reluctant to spend more time on similar projects. At every stage, though, secondary care was informed of what the primary care project was doing and they were sent the latest version of the care pathway and reports of the meetings held so that they did not feel excluded, even though they were not at the time attending the meetings.

As the project gained momentum, however, secondary care colleagues not only expressed an interest but also suggested changes to the pathway to improve it. The great breakthrough for working with secondary care came with funding for a cardiac rehabilitation nurse to work in the community. Funded by a pharmaceutical company, the nurse was seconded from secondary care half time to work with practices and patients to provide the link between primary and secondary care. As part of this link the record cards were introduced into secondary care and patients were discharged with the care pathway following admission for acute cardiac events. Thus the introduction of systematised working into primary care led to closer cooperation with secondary care and an integrated pathway from an acute event back into primary care.

The systematisation development did not end with the initial production of a pathway. Newsletters were written on a bi-monthly basis; you might think that there would be little to write, but feedback from practices was communicated through the newsletter so that the care pathway continued to evolve. A new group emerged through the newsletter to include those with existing, stable ischaemic heart disease into the project and volunteers were quickly found to pilot this Stage Two of the project. All those with acute cardiac disease (Stage One) would move into Stage Two after a year. Soon after this, Stage Three was piloted to look at primary prevention in patients with family history of IHD, those with diabetes and hypertension. Through all these changes there was new information to impart, new medications to be considered and pathways to be modified to achieve a single care pathway to incorporate both Stage One and Stage Two of the project. Thus through these stages a comprehensive cardiac care programme developed.

The developmental process reached out even to those who had not initially agreed to take part in the project. Newsletters were sent to all practices whether or not they were involved so that they were fully informed of what was going on. The advantages of the project were obvious and any new practice joining the project was offered nurse (and GP) training where needed and nurse support, both on a mobile telephone and also through regular practice visits. There were also four-monthly evening meetings to discuss the project and to introduce agreed changes to the pathway. We even started to get patients involved through feedback to the practice teams that was in turn fed back to the review meetings. Similarly, patient feedback was actively sought through secondary care and their opinions fed into the developing pathway. However, few patients actually joined the evening meetings. Today, they would, of course, but at the time the patient was not seen to be a member of the clinical team. Although the project missed an important opportunity with this oversight, the patient input into the developing project became important and valued.

After a year, all but two of the 120 practices in Dorset were involved in the project. The Health Authority gave further support in the form of prescribing initiative money and similar funding to practices to promote the project. Thus when the Cardiovascular NSF was published,[5] most of what was to be achieved was already being achieved. It was thus that the project was included as a methodology of implementation within the NSF.

## WHAT DOES THIS TELL US ABOUT SYSTEMATISATION?

Bandolier wrote up the project in September 2000[6] and confirmed, from predicting outcomes, that 22 deaths, 39 re-infarctions and one non-fatal stroke were being prevented on an annual basis in Dorset. It concluded, however, that the success of the project came at a price:

> SUCCEED has shown that common standards can be agreed and implemented but those improvements have a price. People must be in place to coordinate the work, to provide necessary training and provide hands on help at practice level.
>   Specific points that merit attention are:

- ▶ Don't expect everyone to be enthusiastic. Maintain a regular flow of information about progress to all those involved. Avoid the question: 'Is that project still going?'
- ▶ Find ways to present the impact of the work on GPs and practices. How many of their patients are likely to be involved? What does it mean for them?
- ▶ Explore funding opportunities with pharmaceutical companies who may be willing to fund work in ways acceptable to clinicians.
- ▶ Create realistic expectations of practices and do the homework. Which office procedures and systems do they use? Do they have the staff time to get involved?
- ▶ Get hospital staff involved in the work from the beginning. Use of a patient held record used in primary and secondary care might help.
- ▶ Don't let continuing staff turnover undermine your efforts. Create a training package to help ensure new staff adopt the approach you have striven to introduce.
- ▶ Explore ways to talk through your plans with patients. They may have helpful ideas about how to get the messages over.

This brings out several lessons for systematisation. First, it is possible to introduce systematised team working, and as care becomes more process orientated (particularly in the provision of chronic care management), morbidity and mortality can be reduced. But this requires the development of **shared understandings** among the team, not simply the delivery of advice, no matter how sound it may be. The whole purpose of what is being done (in this case not just filling out a care pathway record but reducing post event morbidity and mortality) has to be understood by all, from the most junior receptionist to the senior partner. The shared sense of purpose provides understanding of the importance of the patient as a member of the team, making appointments at convenient times to patients, and ensuring that all patients with post cardiac events were invited to join the project. It also helps to protect the time involved in successful implementation of the project and to appreciate the skills of the care managers so that the nurses could use their new skills with confidence.

Second, for any significant change in work practice to take hold, all those involved need to see the **value and importance** of what they are doing, whether measured in efficiency, professional satisfaction, monetary gain or reduced workload. In the case of SUCCEED, although there was monetary gain in the form of Health Promotion Payments, these were already being made to all practices for far less work. At the same time there was additional expense in the time taken by practice nurses in the care of these patients. Value here was seen primarily in improving the morbidity and mortality of a group of patients. Collectively, as a team, we were stopping heart attacks and saving lives and we all valued that.

Third, NICE and similar bodies should consider the approach it should take. Specifically, it needs to pay more attention to the **meaning and significance of guidance** for the audience to which it is addressed. If guidance has no clear benefit for the primary care team, it will be unlikely to give it priority, whereas something of obvious relevance will be adopted much more quickly. Thus, the impact of the guidance on the implementer is as important as its scientific correctness. There should be some more joined-up thinking not only on what is important as seen clinically by NICE but also from the deliverers' perspective.

Fourth, systematised working can generate **new resources** by developing new capacities among existing staff. The practice nurses gained a great deal: they were trained by GPs and cardiac rehabilitation nurses in physiology, pathology, therapeutics and rehabilitation of patients with cardiac disease, they were empowered to change treatment management in accordance with protocol, and they effectively took over the management of these patients, adding a new dimension to their responsibilities. The GP stepped in only if the care manager had a problem and so their workload was reduced. The nursing team worked much more closely than ever before with the administrative staff to develop recall mechanisms and to identify the timely access of these patients through the project which needed further restructuring of appointment times and availability. The new workload of the nurses resulted in a downloading of some more simple tasks on to others with fewer qualifications and skills thus upskilling their clinical juniors. The new relationships resulted in far-reaching consequences in the future in many practices, including my own, so that many administrative functions were automatically taken over by a more appropriate member of the team rather than being undertaken by a doctor or manager.

The project had a life of its own, controlled not by a single person but by all practices that had any part in the project. Perhaps this is why it still runs in the way it was intended. Patients are still discharged with the care pathway and patients have an active input into their management of post cardiac events. I have suggested more than once that the project should end: it seems now to be 'low key' but it remains as popular as ever.

## AND WHAT DOES SUCCEED TELL US ABOUT THE CHALLENGE OF CHANGE?

In the past GPs were very reasonably concerned about devaluation of the GP role and the threat of others who might be inadequately or inappropriately trained taking over some of their responsibilities. Behind these concerns was a fear of the unknown and of the risks for patient care and profession. This was not prejudice; this was sense.

However, behind all the government initiatives as well as clinical and patient demand the challenges to primary care have been expanding rapidly as (a) care spreads outside the GP's consulting room and the practice becomes more of a team with a diversity of skills, (b) secondary care is pushed out of the hospital and into the community with primary care looked to for support, and (c) patients, especially those with long-term conditions, are expected to become active co-producers of their own treatment, particularly through care pathways and the expert patient intiative.[7] Initially seen as a methodology for patients to *cope* with a long-term condition, the expert patient programme has now becoming far more focused towards knowledge and management of specific conditions. Patients with diabetes have long been trusted to change the dose of insulin they self-administer according to measured clinical parameters. Now there are several projects in which patients change their own dose of medication for hypertensive therapies consequent on the self-monitoring of blood pressure. Asthmatic patients are trusted to increase the dose of their medications at the first signs of rising pollen count or of a viral infection. Patients, it seems, are becoming real clinicians and team members in the management of their own conditions.

Even managers in primary care might be becoming part of the clinical team! They are increasingly active in structuring the treatment process to achieve better clinical outcomes through a process orientated approach such as those suggested in the new GP contract. Reciprocally, GPs and other primary care workers are becoming managers in their work in primary care organisations. The boundaries are blurring and all are moving towards a common aim of improving clinical outcomes through a concerted and focused effort no matter what the individual skills, clinical or managerial. What matters is the *team* skill.

This process of change presents a challenge for all those GPs, other staff and patients who have been accustomed to seeing primary care as the exercise of individual artistry by 'the doctor'. It is perhaps as much of a challenge as was faced by the medical profession when Elizabeth Garrett Anderson sought to enter it. With no medical school prepared to admit women she became a nurse at the Middlesex Hospital but was banned from attending the lectures provided for male doctors. She tried to work in the operating theatres of the hospital but in 1863 the hospital issued a statement on the subject of women doctors: 'The presence of a young female in the operating theatre is an outrage to our natural instincts and is calculated to destroy the respect and admiration with which the opposite sex is regarded.'[8]

As we know, of course, she made it via becoming an apothecary in 1865 and then qualifying as a doctor at Paris Medical School in 1870. She also went on to become Britain's first female mayor (of Aldeburgh, where she is now buried) and her daughter became the Chief Surgeon of the Women's Hospital Corps from 1914 to 1919.

**FIGURE 11.3**  Elizabeth Garrett Anderson

The objections to women doctors were grounded in the norms of medical practice at the time. Will the reluctance to reformulate primary care as systematic teamwork look any less strange, 20 years from now? Systematisation in primary care is the key to improving outcomes for patients and improving job satisfaction among healthcare workers. It takes effort to work as a team. Not to do so, however, is not sense; it really is prejudice.

## REFERENCES

1 Sheldon TA, Cullum N, Dawson D, *et al.* What's the evidence that NICE guidance has been implemented? Results from a national evaluation using time series analysis, audit of patients' notes and interviews. *BMJ.* 2004; **329**: 999–1004.
2 http://www.ic.nhs.uk/pubs/nhsstaff/mdbulletintab/file Worksheet 2b (consultants); http://www.ic.nhs.uk/pubs/nhsstaff/gpbulletintab/file Worksheet 1b (general practitioners excluding GP registrars).
3 BMJ News Roundup. England short of 970 GPs. *BMJ.* 2003; **326**: 243.
4 Sutton M, McLean G. Determinants of primary medical care quality measured under the new UK contract: cross sectional study. *BMJ.* 2006; **332**: 389–90.
5 Department of Health. *The National Service Framework for Coronary Heart Disease.* London: Department of Health; 2000.
6 How to 'succeed' with cardiac care in primary care. *Bandolier.* September 2000; **9**: 4.
7 Department of Health. The Expert Patient Programme. http://www.expertpatients.nhs.uk
8 http://en.wikipedia.org/wiki/Elizabeth_Garrett_Anderson

# CHAPTER 12

# Assessing the content and quality of pathways

*Claire Whittle, Linda Dunn, Paul McDonald and Kathryn de Luc*

As earlier chapters have confirmed, integrated care pathways (ICPs) are systematically developed tools that set locally agreed standards of care based on the available evidence for managing a specific group of patients, ensuring that multidisciplinary care can be monitored and outcomes measured.[1] They have been introduced as multi-professional tools to improve the quality of healthcare for a homogeneous group of patients.[2] They are helpful in achieving consensus on the consistency and continuity of care[3] and can improve the documentation of evidence-based and patient-focused care.[4]

Although it has been asserted that the standard of integrated care pathways is variable, they have not been systematically evaluated.[5] Although there are a large number of integrated care pathways listed in the National Library for Health,[6] no 'kite mark' has been used to assure a sound clinical, managerial, ethical and legal footing for them. Failures to identify improvements in care following the introduction of an ICP have been linked to their implementation and variability in content quality.[7] These shortfalls in both evaluation and process have serious implications for clinical governance programmes within the NHS and have stimulated the validation of an Integrated Care Pathways Appraisal Tool (ICPAT).[8]

This chapter reports on studies that applied the validated ICPAT in an assessment of the content and quality of a selection of ICPs currently in use throughout the UK. Our aim is to identify the essential components that should be contained in an ICP, elaborate the validated ICPAT items that can be used to assess the quality of ICPs and, using the appraisal tool, report on current shortfalls in ICP quality.

## METHOD

### The format of the ICPAT

The development, format and validation of the content of the ICPAT have been described elsewhere.[9] The final validated ICPAT had six dimensions (summarised in Table 12.1). Each dimension comprised a number of items that allow appraisers to assess the content of an ICP. A response of 'yes' on each coded item scale indicated the presence of such content. Each dimension also had a number of quality items structured as Likert scales (1 as strongly agree to 5 as strongly disagree) to enable appraisers to reflect upon the quality of the ICP.

**TABLE 12.1** Dimensions, content and quality items contained in the ICPAT

| Dimension | No. of Content items | No. of Quality items |
|---|---|---|
| 1  Is it an integrated care pathway? | 10 | 2 |
| 2  The integrated care pathway documentation | 23 | 2 |
| 3  The development process | 13 | 15 |
| 4  The implementation process | 6 | 1 |
| 5  Maintenance of the integrated care pathway | 4 | 13 |
| 6  The role of the organisation | 3 | 12 |

## APPRAISERS AND APPRAISED ICPS

As in previous work[10] a database consisting of personnel involved in ICP initiatives throughout the UK was available to the authors. There was also a continued awareness of biases within this and previous studies in regards to participants having a particular interest in ICPAT development. A convenience sample was therefore again obtained by contacting those on the database. Ninety-eight participants were recruited from 29 NHS trusts and one private care organisation. Five organisations provided one appraiser, while one organisation provided two, and 24 provided three or more. The appraisers in each organisation used the ICPAT to review one ICP that they had developed and implemented. In total 30 ICPs were reviewed using the appraisal tool. The clinical areas were diverse including orthopaedics, general surgery, maternity and mental health.

### Method of appraisal

Appraisers were sent a pack consisting of background information, a copy of the ICPAT, and guidelines for its use. They were requested to evaluate an ICP they were currently using within their service area. Where applicable, appraisers from the same organisation evaluated the same ICP. Unlike previous studies,[11] it was assumed that appraisers would have access to the relevant documentation that supported an ICP's development and implementation and therefore would be able to assess the role their organisation had played during the course of these processes.

A positive 'yes' (coded as 1) response to each **content** item indicated the presence of a particular attribute or standard in the ICP. All other responses ('no', 'not sure' or 'not applicable') were coded as 2. Simple proportions were calculated for each item. If the proportion of appraisers identifying the presence of an item was less than 50%, this was classified as a low presence. Similarly, 50% to 74% was regarded as moderate and 75% and over as a high presence.

Each **quality** item was coded on a scale of 1 to 5: strongly disagree (1), disagree (2), not sure (3), agree (4) and strongly agree (5). To facilitate analysis, responses reflecting agreement with item statements (i.e. scores 4 and 5) were recoded and grouped into the same category. Responses indicating uncertainty or disagreement (1, 2 and 3) were likewise grouped. Simple proportions were calculated for each of these two categories per item. If the proportion of appraisers agreeing with a quality item statement was 75% and over, this was classified as high and reflected a sense of 'doing well' among appraisers. Similarly, 50% to 74% was regarded as moderate agreement and less than 50% as low, both indicating some degree of 'room for improvement'.

## RESULTS

Of the 59 content items, 22 (37%) were identified as having a high presence in ICPs, 20 (34%) a moderate presence and 17 (29%) a low presence. Of the 49 quality items, 6 (12%) were identified with high agreement, 23 (47%) moderate agreement, and 20 (41%) low agreement. We now break down these results by ICP dimension.

### Dimension 1: Is it an ICP?

Table 12.2 shows the high presence of all 10 content items and high agreement with both quality items within this dimension. This suggests that appraised ICPs were considered to be cohesive and multidisciplinary in nature.

### Dimension 2: The ICP documentation

Table 12.3 shows that of the 23 content items in this dimension, six had a high presence. This represents achievement of high standards of documentation. The eight items indicating a moderate presence concerned service user involvement (three items), punctiliousness (three items, version number, instructions and exclusion criteria) and variance/exception reporting (two items). Of those with a low presence, six concerned punctiliousness (page numbers, abbreviations, review date, storage), one focused on service user involvement, one variance/ exception reporting, and one item related to the evidence base of ICPs. Of the four quality items within this dimension, two reflected moderate agreement with ICP outcomes and punctiliousness and two items identified perceived gaps in service user involvement.

**TABLE 12.2** Dimension 1: Is it an ICP?

| CONTENT ITEMS 1–10: High Presence | Number (%) |
|---|---|
| Does the ICP have an identified start point? | 97 (99%) |
| Does the ICP outline the anticipated process of care/treatment? | 97 (99%) |
| Does the ICP have an identified finish point? | 96 (98%) |
| Does the ICP act as a prompt/reminder for staff at the point of care? | 96 (98%) |
| Does the ICP reflect a service user's journey, i.e. moving along a continuum of days, weeks, months, stages, objectives, programmes, etc? | 95 (97%) |
| Does the ICP form the record of care for an individual service user? | 92 (94%) |
| Can the ICP documentation be individualised to meet the service user's needs? | 90 (92%) |
| Does the ICP act as a decision support tool, prompting consideration of various factors like additional problems, comorbidity, risk factors etc? | 88 (90%) |
| Is there space in the ICP document to record individual service user exceptions or variation from the ICP? | 88 (90%) |
| Does the ICP reflect 24-hour continuous care/treatment (where appropriate) | 86 (88% |
| **QUALITY ITEMS 1–2: High Agreement** | **Number (%)** |
| The ICP is a cohesive document with all of it used in the delivery of care/treatment. | 83 (86%) |
| The ICP reflects the input of those who contribute to the care | 80 (83% |

**TABLE 12.3** Dimension 2: The ICP documentation

| CONTENT ITEMS 11–33 | |
|---|---|
| **High Presence** | **No. (%)** |
| Are the relevant service users clearly identified in the title of the ICP? | 95 (97%) |
| Does documentation meet local and national minimum documentation standards? | 87 (89%) |
| Is there space for the identification of the individual service user on each page? | 83 (85%) |
| Are there individual page numbers on all the pages? | 82 (84%) |
| Does the ICP ask for sample signatures of those completing the document? | 81 (83%) |
| Is the date of development of the document marked on the ICP? | 74 (76%) |
| **Moderate Presence** | |
| Does the variation/exception reporting system collect all of the following: date, time, description of variance, action taken, signature? | 72 (74%) |
| Is there a reminder that says professional judgement must be applied while taking into account the service user's wishes and needs? | 71 (72%) |
| Are there instructions on how to record the variation/exception reporting system? | 64 (65%) |
| Is there a version number on the documentation? | 61 (62%) |
| Are there instructions on how to use the documentation? | 59 (60%) |
| Does the service user have unrestricted access to their ICP? | 54 (55%) |

*cont.*

| **CONTENT ITEMS 11–33** | |
|---|---|
| **Moderate Presence cont.** | |
| Does ICP include service user's consent to treatment/care (where appropriate)? | 53 (54%) |
| Does the documentation indicate the circumstances when a service user should come off or should not be put on (exclusion criteria)? | 49 (50%) |
| **Low Presence** | |
| Is the evidence on which the content is based referenced? | 48 (49%) |
| Are all abbreviations explained in the document? | 45 (46%) |
| Is it clear where the ICP is to be stored while in use? | 38 (39%) |
| Is there a prompt of the importance of completing the variation/exception system? | 34 (35%) |
| Is the date of planned review of the document clearly marked? | 33 (34%) |
| Do the page numbers relate to the total number of pages in the ICP? | 24 (25%) |
| Is there provision for the service user to complete some parts of the ICP? | 20 (20%) |
| Are there prompts to identify whether the service user is on another ICP (where appropriate)? | 20 (20%) |
| Are there instructions where to store additional documentation to the ICP documentation? | 16 (16%) |
| **QUALITY ITEMS 3–6** | |
| **Moderate Agreement** | **No. (%)** |
| The outcomes/goals for the service user are clearly identified. | 68 (72%) |
| The instructions for using the ICP are clear. | 60 (64%) |
| **Low Agreement** | |
| There are prompts within the documentation for service user participation in the ICP. | 36 (38%) |
| The variations are discussed with the service user. | 28 (31%) |

## Dimension 3: The ICP development process

Table 12.4 shows that of the 13 content items of the development process dimension two had a high presence (piloting and literature search evidence) and five a moderate presence (three of the latter relating to review or audit and two to records of the development process). Of the 17 quality items, there was high agreement with two items of the comprehensiveness of ICP content and moderate agreement relating to both staff focus (three items) and the role of audit and evaluation (four items) during the development process. Although there was moderate agreement with the testing of ICPs on an adequate number of service users, there was low agreement with five items concerning other aspects of service user involvement. The assessment of risk during ICP development was also perceived as an issue.

**TABLE 12.4** Dimension 3: The ICP development process

| CONTENT ITEMS 34–46 | No. (%) |
|---|---|
| **High Presence** | |
| Has the ICP been piloted/tested? | 74 (76%) |
| Was a literature search carried out to gather evidence for clinical content of ICP? | 73 (75%) |
| **Moderate Presence** | |
| Was pre-existing practice reviewed prior to development of the ICP as a baseline? | 64 (65%) |
| In the notes or minutes of meetings is there a description or list of the staff involved in the development of the ICP? | 62 (63%) |
| Is there a record of the decisions made concerning the content of the ICP? | 54 (55%) |
| Was the completion of the ICP documentation audited after the pilot? | 53 (54%) |
| In the pilot, were the results of the audit of the ICP fed back to those who completed the documentation? | 50 (51%) |
| **Low Presence** | |
| Were the variations/exceptions audited after the pilot? | 46 (47%) |
| Were the outcomes/goals audited after the pilot? | 40 (41%) |
| Do the notes of the development meetings record the rationale for including pieces of evidence/guidelines? | 31 (32%) |
| Has the person with responsibility for the Data Protection Act reviewed the ICP? | 23 (24%) |
| Do the notes of the development meetings record the rationale for not including pieces of evidence/guidelines? | 22 (22%) |
| Has the Caldicott Guardian reviewed the ICP? | 13 (13%) |
| **QUALITY ITEMS 7–23** | No. (%) |
| **High Agreement** | |
| Clinical risk was considered as part of the content of the ICP. | 68 (80%) |
| The discussion concerning the content of the ICP was comprehensive. | 65 (76%) |
| **Moderate Agreement** | |
| The training, education and competency of staff were considered as part of the content of the ICP. | 64 (74%) |
| The staff opinions about the ICP were collected as part of the pilot/testing procedure. | 58 (72%) |
| There was a significant sample size of service users put onto the ICP to test it. | 56 (69%) |
| All representatives of the staff using the ICP have been involved in its development. | 58 (67%) |
| The appraisal of the clinical evidence/research literature was comprehensive. | 46 (59%) |
| The standard of pre-existing documentation was audited prior to ICP development. | 43 (56%) |
| Any evidence/guideline/protocol referred to in the ICP is readily available for the staff to refer to. | 45 (56%) |
| In the pilot the audit indicated that a satisfactory level of documentation was completed for legal requirements. | 37 (51%) |

*cont.*

**Low Agreement**

| | |
|---|---|
| All staff and service users in the pilot required to complete the ICP did so. | 36 (48%) |
| In the pilot, areas of non-compliance presenting an acceptable risk to the organisation were identified. | 32 (47%) |
| The service users multicultural needs have been taken into account. | 36 (43%) |
| In the pilot, areas of non-use presenting an acceptable risk to the organisation were identified. | 28 (42%) |
| The ICP pilot results/findings have been discussed with the service users. | 18 (23%) |
| The service users have been involved in the development of the ICP. | 18 (22%) |
| The service user opinions about the ICP were collected as part of the pilot/testing procedure | 11 (15%) |

## Dimension 4: The ICP implementation process

Table 12.5 shows that of the six content items in this dimension, a high presence was identified on one (documentation storage) and moderate presence in three (staff training and service user involvement). The two items with a low presence related to risk assessment and service user involvement. There was low agreement with the only quality item – the assessment of risk during the implementation process.

**TABLE 12.5** Dimension 4: The ICP implementation process

| CONTENT ITEMS 47–52 | No. (%) |
|---|---|
| **High Presence** | |
| Has an agreement been reached as to where the ICP documentation will be stored once finished? | 85 (87%) |
| **Moderate Presence** | |
| Is there a system in place to feed back the variations of the ICP to the service users? | 65 (66%) |
| Have resources been identified to undertake the training on how to use the ICP? | 58 (59%) |
| Has an ongoing training programme for the staff been established? | 55 (56%) |
| **Low Presence** | |
| Is there evidence that the organisation carried out an assessment of the risks involved in an ICP development before commencement? | 32 (33%) |
| Is there a system in place to feed back the variations of the ICP to the service users? | 17 (17%) |
| **QUALITY ITEM 24** | **No. (%)** |
| **Low Agreement** | |
| The assessment of risk carried out by the organisation was adequate. | 26 (35%) |

## Dimension 5: Maintenance of the ICP

Table 12.6 shows that one of the four content items in this dimension (a named individual) had a high presence, while the remaining three (associated with staff training and review or audit) had a moderate presence. Of the 13 quality items in this dimension, one item reflected high agreement on the regular review of ICP content and documentation. There was a moderate agreement on four items concerning review, and two relating to staff feedback. There was low agreement for the two items that focused upon the review of variation codes and the four items relating to service user involvement.

**TABLE 12.6** Dimension 5: Maintenance of the ICP

| CONTENT ITEMS 53–56 | No. (%) |
| --- | --- |
| **High Presence** | |
| Is there a named individual responsible for maintaining the ICP? | 84 (86%) |
| **Moderate Presence** | |
| Is regular training provided for new staff that will be using the ICP? | 59 (60%) |
| Is training provided to staff when a change to the ICP content is made? | 58 (59%) |
| Is the review date one year or less? | 52 (53%) |
| **QUALITY ITEMS 25–37** | **No. (%)** |
| **High Agreement** | |
| The ICP content and documentation are regularly reviewed in terms of use/completion of documentation. | 65 (75%) |
| **Moderate Agreement** | |
| The ICP content and documentation are regularly reviewed in terms of staff comments. | 60 (70%) |
| The ICP content and documentation are regularly reviewed in terms of variations. | 60 (69%) |
| The ICP content and documentation are regularly reviewed in terms of achievement of outcomes/goals/objectives. | 57 (68%) |
| There is evidence that staff feedback has changed practice. | 53 (64%) |
| The ICP content and documentation are regularly reviewed in terms of new clinical evidence. | 55 (63%) |
| The variations and achievements of goals/outcomes/objectives have been fed back to the staff. | 48 (57%) |
| **Low Agreement** | |
| The variation codes have been updated in line with organisational/local requirements. | 34 (47%) |
| The variation codes used have been reviewed and checked for use and consistency. | 32 (43%) |
| The ICP content and documentation is regularly reviewed (minimum annually) in terms of service user comments. | 25 (30%) |
| The variations and achievement of goals/outcomes/objectives have been fed back to service users. | 14 (17%) |
| There is evidence service user feedback has changed practice. | 12 (15%) |
| Service users involved in the review of the ICP content. | 9 (11%) |

## Dimension 6: The role of the organisation

Table 12.7 shows two high presence content items in this dimension related to the relationship of ICPs with clinical governance, and one moderate presence (ICP planning). Of the 12 quality items in this dimension, one item enjoyed high agreement with regard to the clinical leadership of ICPs. There was moderate agreement concerning ICP development within the context of organisational strategy, management and links to other organisational systems. There were doubts in response to four items relating to clinical documentation, variation reporting, facilitated time for ICP development, and staff training.

**TABLE 12.7** Dimension 6: The role of the organisation in ICPs

| CONTENT ITEMS 57–59 | No. (%) |
| --- | --- |
| **High Presence** | |
| Are ICPs evident in the organisation's Clinical Governance Strategy? | 78 (80%) |
| Is the ICP development programme endorsed by the Trust Board or Clinical Governance committee? | 74 (76%) |
| **Moderate Presence** | |
| Within the organisation is there a plan specifically for ICP development? | 72 (74%) |
| **QUALITY ITEMS 38–49** | **No. (%)** |
| **High Agreement** | |
| The individual ICP development is clinically led. | 74 (81%) |
| **Moderate Agreement** | |
| There is a strategic group reviewing all the ICP developments within the organisation. | 57 (65%) |
| There is evidence that the ICP has been integrated into other organisational initiatives. | 59 (64%) |
| There are organisation-wide guidelines for the ICP documentation. | 52 (60%) |
| The organisation recognises that ICPs involve long-term programme commitment to change. | 51 (58%) |
| Organisational risk management issues were addressed in the ICP development. | 49 (55%) |
| The ICP development programme is managed. | 49 (54%) |
| Within the organisation targets for ICP development are achievable. | 43 (50%) |
| **Low Agreement** | |
| ICP documentation reflects organisation-wide developments of clinical documentation. | 42 (49%) |
| The variation reporting system reflects the organisation style of variation reporting. | 36 (44%) |
| Dedicated facilitation time is identified for development of ICPs. | 32 (36%) |
| There is a comprehensive training package for staff in ICP use and development. | 26 (29%) |

## DISCUSSION

The results of the above analysis are summarised in Figures 12.1 (content) and 12.2 (quality). The high **content** presence of all essential items within

Dimension 1 indicates that the ICPs reviewed in this study have been developed within accepted definitions of what an ICP should be.[12] The study therefore suggests that the ICPs have content validity. However, beyond the nominal existence of ICPs, as endorsed by their organisations (Dimension 6), there are process weaknesses in contemporary ICPs particularly in their documentation (Dimension 2) and development (Dimension 3), and to a lesser extent their implementation (Dimension 4) and maintenance (Dimension 5).

These shortfalls are essentially those of governance and accountability. There appears insufficient weight given to service user involvement, staff training, risk assessment and ICP planning across organisations. The legal standing of some ICPs will clearly be tainted by their lack of meticulousness. Finally, there are specific inadequacies of accountability including the review and audit of ICPs, the keeping of records in regards to their development, and the consideration of data protection.

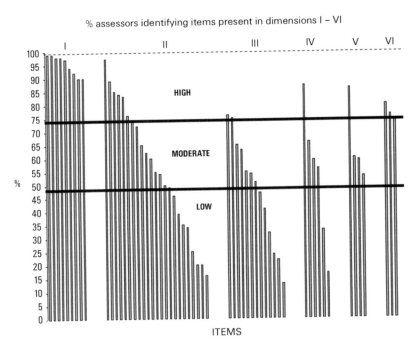

FIGURE 12.1  Gaps in ICP content

These findings have important implications for the many healthcare organisations that have adopted and encouraged ICP approaches in a drive for governed, effective, evidence-based and continuous seamless care. Specifically, they raise pressing issues about the process management of ICP development in the context of their healthcare organisations rather than exclusively for what they contain. First, the identified and perceived shortcomings in accountability, governance and management processes in ICP development could suggest that

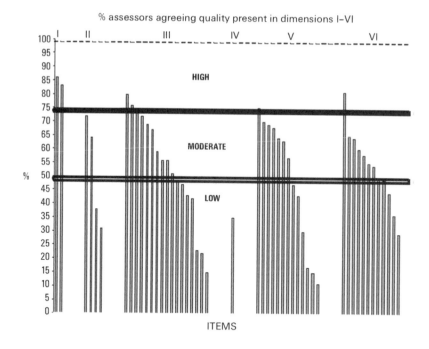

**FIGURE 12.2** Perceived ICP quality

ICP initiatives are often carried out in isolation. Over the past six years the authors have had contact with hundreds of individual champions or committed teams pursuing ICP development in healthcare organisations throughout the UK and abroad. The results presented here concur in many ways with their general sense of 'doing well' in terms of the validity of what they are doing but also substantiate the many frustrations when efforts are made to lock ICP development into wider strategic and organisational structures.

Secondly, shortfalls in user involvement in ICP development may suggest tokenism. This would be a superficial and erroneous conclusion. The results show that most ICPs have a clear focus upon the clinical needs of patients and are able to follow individuals through their care and treatment. The lack of user involvement in ICP development may have alternative explanations. Expectations for more emancipatory input from service users may often overlook the prerequisite knowledge and skill from both the cared for and their carers.[13] It is highly probable that many ICP leaders and service users will not have this expertise without prior training. In addition, users who are eager to be involved in ICP development may themselves face organisational barriers. For example, their access to data during the audit and review of ICPs may raise issues of confidentiality and data protection, and their on-site attendance when engaged in this process raises issues of risk, resource and convenient availability.

The development of quality care pathways is paramount and we have found a high degree of consensus on the content of ICPs as well as some clear areas for improvement in quality. In order that care pathway quality can be evaluated uniformly and confidently the use of the ICPAT should be a priority in order to provide a systematic analysis. We have demonstrated the value of the ICP Appraisal Tool including as an aid in identifying and addressing ICP development needs, which reinforces the view that the ICPAT seems to be the most appropriate care pathways audit tool.[14]

## REFERENCES

1 Riley K. A definition. *National Pathways Association Newsletter.* 1998; Spring: 2.
2 Evans T. An integrated care pathway for leg ulcer management. *Nursing Times.* 2001; **97**: x–ii. Currie V, Harvey G. The use of care pathways as tools to support the implementation of evidence-based practice. *J Inter-professional Care.* 2000; **14**: 311–24. Bayliss V, Cherry M, Locke R. Pathways for continence care: background and audit. *British J Nursing.* 2000; **9**: 590–6.
3 Kitchener D, Davidson C, Bundred P. Integrated care pathways: effective tools of continuous evaluation of clinical practice. *J Evaluation in Clinical Practice.* 1996; **2**: 65–9. Hochkiss R. Integrated care pathways. *Nursing Times Research.* 1997; **2**: 30–6.
4 Campbell H, Hotchkiss R, Bradshaw N, Porteous M. Integrated care pathways. *BMJ.* 1998; **316**: 133–7. Layton A, Moss F, Morgan G. Mapping out the patient's journey: experience of developing pathways of care. *Quality in Health Care.* 1998; **7** (suppl.): S30–6. Overill S. A practical guide to care pathways. *American J Medicine.* 1998; **2**: 93–8.
5 De Luc K. Care pathways – an evaluation of how effective they are. *J Advanced Nursing.* 2000; **32**: 485–95. De Luc K, Whittle C. An integrated care pathway appraisal tool: a 'badge of quality'. *J Integrated Care Pathways.* 2002; **6**: 13–17.
6 National Library for Health. www.library.nhs.uk/pathways/
7 Trowbridge R, Weingarten S. Making healthcare safe. *A Critical Analysis of Patient Safety Practices Evidence Report/Technology Assessment.* Vol. 43 (Chapter 52). 2001. Prepared for the Agency for Healthcare Research & Quality. www.ahcpr. gov/clinic/ptsafety/chap52.htm (February 2004). Sulch D, Kalra L. Integrated care pathways in stroke management. *Age and Ageing.* 2000; **29**: 349–52. Cheah TS. The impact of clinical guidelines and clinical pathways on medical practice: effectiveness and medico-legal aspects. *Annals Academy of Medicine.* 1998; **27**: 533–9. Cannon C, Johnson B, Cermignani M, Scirica BM, Sagarin MJ, Walls RM. Emergency department thrombolysis critical pathway reduces door-to-door times in acute myocardial infarction. *Clinical Cardiology.* 1999; **22**: 17–20. Pitt H, Murray K, Bowman H. Clinical pathway implementation improves outcomes for complex biliary surgery. *Surgery.* 1999; **126**: 751–8.
8 Whittle C, McDonald PS, Dunn L, de Luc K. Developing the Integrated Care Pathways Appraisal Tool (ICPAT): a pilot study. *J Integrated Care Pathways.* 2004; **8**: 77–81.
9 Ibid.

10 McDonald PS, Whittle CL, Dunn L, de Luc K. Shortfalls in integrated care pathways. Part 1: what don't they contain? *J Integrated Care Pathways*. 2006; **10**: 17–22. McDonald PS, Whittle CL, Dunn L, de Luc K. Shortfalls in integrated care pathways. Part 2: how well are we doing? *J Integrated Care Pathways*. 2006; **10**: 23–7.

11 Ibid.

12 Riley, op. cit.

13 Currie, Harvey, op. cit.

14 Vanhaecht K, de Witte K, Depreitere R, Sermeus W. Clinical pathway audit tools: a systematic review. *J Nursing Management*. 2006; **14**(7): 529–37.

# CHAPTER 13

# The executive function in the systematisation of clinical work

*Chris Fokke*

Integrated care pathways tend to be seen as primarily a matter for clinicians. Their general development is attributed to clinical teams giving priority to their own clinical areas and much of the literature on pathways has concentrated on their use and effectiveness in clinical terms.[1] In contrast, not much attention has been paid to the place of senior managers and board members in the systematisation of care and clinical work.

Yet the demands of pathway development (i.e. the need to redesign patient care pathways, to work in partnership with communities and stakeholder groups, to balance labour shortages with the requirement for increased capacity) call for strategy and leadership.[2] Team development, education about integration, and change management are essential if pathways are to foster and be supported by joint working in integrated teams.[3] Moreover, pathways are means for pursuing organisational purposes, such as service development strategy, workforce development, performance and clinical practice management.[4] And at least one recent high profile report has shown how an executive team's confusion of responsibility and authority and its disregard of clinical expertise can result in avoidable harm to patients in severe infectious outbreaks.[5]

Thus, pathway development should be a concern of senior executives and board members, ranking alongside traditional board activities such as organisational performance and financial status. This chapter shows how one hospital's model for the executive function facilitates all systematic clinical practice and innovation in a learning environment.

## THE CARE PATHWAY MODEL IN THE ROYAL NATIONAL HOSPITAL FOR RHEUMATIC DISEASES

Croucher has demonstrated the variability in the current level of knowledge and awareness of the ICP tool developed by Whittle, *et al.* (*see* Chapter 12) and recommends a standard framework for National Health Service staff to follow when developing ICPs.[6] Some guidance is already available, of course, including that from the NHS Modernisation Agency and the National Pathways Association[7] and on which the Royal National Hospital for Rheumatic Diseases (RNHRD) based its organisational framework in 2004 (*see* Figure 13.1).

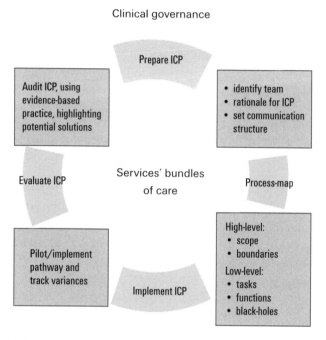

**FIGURE 13.1** The RNHRD care pathway model

The model recognises the need for pathway development to be flexible within different areas of the organisation to enable widespread implementation. Moreover, the whole process sits within a framework of clinical governance which makes NHS organisations accountable for continually improving the quality of their services and safeguarding high standards of care by creating an environment in which excellence in clinical care will develop.[8] But the distinctive feature is the strategic responsibility of the executive function.

How can an executive team promote pathway development? It is usually helpful to have a concise and meaningful mission statement, backed up by a more detailed exposition of how the core work of the organisation will be directed. Bart and Tabone define a mission statement as a 'written, formal document that attempts to capture an organization's unique and enduring purpose and practices'. Bolon urges hospital executives to devote more time to the construction of hospital-specific and comprehensive mission statements that will provide important information for stakeholders. Although healthcare organisations tend to place less emphasis on mission statements than do comparable organisations in other industries, Hewison in her study of NHS values writes that 'the values of an organization are key factors which influence the way it is managed'. Similarly, Soule argues that business leaders need to develop 'adequate moral strategy'; hence there is a requirement for such leaders to formulate management moral principles, consensual agreements and business ethics.[9]

When it became a NHS trust in 1993, the RNHRD adopted the following mission statement: 'We will provide excellent, high quality care supported by research and development, education and the empowerment of patients and staff'. The executive directors operate within this mission statement and have encouraged the development of exciting and new services by the use of the care pathway approach. When the RNHRD became a NHS foundation trust in April 2005, it gained more autonomy through a governance framework including a council of members who represent staff, patients and their families, and the public.[10] In turn this allowed a more focused and appropriate development of clinical practice using care pathway development as a major driver of change.

Such a service development strategy requires an interdisciplinary approach. As Edwards and his colleagues observe, in developing better understanding between clinical teams and managers, policy agencies should ensure that their planning and performance management does not add tensions but allows space for clinical teams and managers to agree on shared objectives – the strategic vision.[11] Clinicians tend to focus on patients' outcomes while senior managers and executives tend to focus on the patients' experience; to ensure cohesive and collaborative interaction between the two groups, the responsibilities of each group need to be broadly defined. In the RNHRD, some executive directors have care pathway and clinical practice systemisation clearly identified in their job descriptions. These job outlines clearly state the requirements and deliverables expected from directors and ensure that clinical models and performance management are supported and monitored.

As Edmonson notes, 'New technologies (clinical practice systemisation) often change work processes in organizations and correspondingly require new roles to enact them. To realise creative new possibilities, group roles (such as for executive directors) must be reframed'.[12] They are responsible for achieving the two basic requirements of clinical governance: standards of care and clinical excellence. As Stanton remarks:

> It is what happens at the clinical coalface which is the hallmark of clinical governance. One acid test for any organisation's governance is therefore the lowest standard of care that is tolerated. Secondly it is the extent to which clinical excellence is relentlessly pursued. Both of these express themselves through the lived culture of an organisation.[13]

This calls for a structured approach to redesigning roles with those executives closely affiliated with clinical governance activities, such as medical directors, nursing directors and performance management directors, ensuring that the clinical function is well addressed and embedded at board level. Systematisation through pathways ensures that senior managers and clinicians at the 'coal-face' have a common language, an integrated vehicle to ensure dialogue and shared decision making. This will be illustrated in the section that follows.

## MAKING SYSTEMATISATION PART OF EXECUTIVE MANAGEMENT: THE VANS CASE

It is important for clinical outcomes that nurses have highly effective prioritisation skills; if equal attention is given to major and minor problems, nurses may not be able to devote the necessary time to resolve the problems that critically affect outcomes.[14] A spate of poor clinical incidents and excess pressure on the nursing function in the neuro-rehabilitation directorate at the RNHRD led to its being selected as a pilot to develop a structured approach to clinical quality. The Vital Aspects of Nursing Safety (VANS) risk assessment information system was created as result.

The poor clinical outcomes had continued without anyone at unit, directorate or board level realising that these were interconnected and needed to be addressed through a systems approach. Using root cause analysis concepts and tools,[15] a close scrutiny of the incidents revealed that prioritisation was not always consistent or embedded and no effective systems were in place to assist nurses to prioritise care and take clinical decisions. The VANS system provided an infrastructure for clinicians, managers and organisational leaders to identify causes of poor clinical quality and excess pressure and supported the prioritisation of resources and activities.

The RNHRD had also wanted to use clinical practice expertise throughout the organisation in a more systematic and quantitative way. We realised that communication often fails because the role of management in assuring the downward and upward flow of information is underestimated.[16] Middle managers in particular have a key role in transforming risk assessment data into meaningful information for clinical teams, and translating the data into quantifiable indicators for the board's overall clinical management function. A local structured process to help managers to achieve this is shown in the process map of VANS (Figure 13.2).

VANS harnessed two new technologies: (1) a change in practice to embed routine and continuous assessment of quality of care, and (2) a new vehicle to transcribe this data into meaningful information for clinicians, operational managers, and the executive board members. However, new technologies or systems such as these can disrupt existing organisational routines and relationships, requiring potential users to re-learn how to work together.[17] Perhaps for this reason it took six months for nursing teams, their manager and the executive manager to provide a systematic platform of communication where the vital core nursing activities and the risk assessments that would quantify the quality and validity of this function were established.

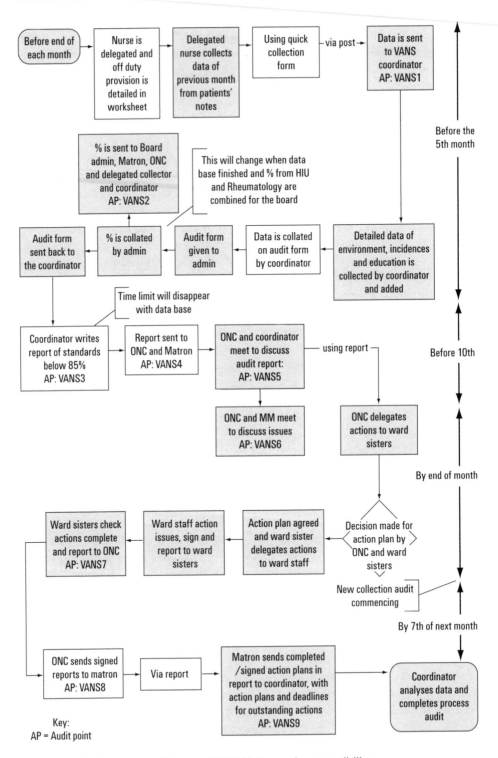

**FIGURE 13.2** Vital Aspects of Nursing (VANS): lines of responsibility

VANS also developed 20 risk assessment tools that covered the vital functions of nursing within the unit. These assessments ranged from checking hazards in the environment to specific clinical observations, difficult behaviour and respiratory care. Each was collected, analysed and reported on a monthly basis. Table 13.1 illustrates one such risk assessment tool, that for *Patient Safety: Poor continuity of care*. The tools provide an audit process that feeds data back to nurses and ward managers. Where individual risk assessments score less than 70%, local action plans and monitoring systems are designed and monitored by the nurse lead of that unit. All the risk assessment scores will aggregate into an overall percentage which will reflect the overall standard of the nursing function on a particular unit. The board receives monthly statistical analysis as part of its organisational assurance framework regarding the overall quality in nursing activity; and if the monthly overall score is below 70%, an action plan report is required for the board.

**TABLE 13.1** Example of vital aspects of nursing care audit sheet

| RISK ASSESSMENT TOOL | | | | |
|---|---|---|---|---|
| **Aspect of safety: Poor continuity of care** | | DATE | | |
| **Indicators** | No. of patients | Yes | No | % Yes |
| Location of patients known to be due for admission in the next 24/48 hours are present in the ward. | A | | | |
| Do the patient records show the signature of the primary nurse within 24 hours of admission/weekly basis? | B | | | |
| Is the primary nurse indicated in the patients records at Band 5/6 or above? | C | | | |
| Do the patient records hold a basic nursing assessment dated within 24 hours of time of admission to the ward? | D | | | |
| Do the patient records hold a full nursing care plan dated within 24 hours of admission to the ward? | E | | | |
| Are the necessary documentation and equipment to implement the care plan recorded as being present within 24 hours of the patient's admission? | F | | | |
| Have the progress records been updated at the end of each shift? | G | | | |
| Are the charts and ongoing documents up to date as required by the care plan at the time of inspection? | H | | | |
| Does observation of the handover report show that the information given is complete and tallies with the written records? | I | | | |

Once this system was established, clinicians felt better supported by managers and the organisation as a whole and nurse leaders within the unit were able to stratify where specific pressure points were emerging, and therefore able to mitigate and eliminate these (through specific prioritisation of areas that scored low) without necessarily needing to change all activities within the whole nursing function.

As with any validated care pathway, the schema has key elements: a clear aim, a set of evidence based practice on which the risk is assessed, and a clear process map with detailed audit points (Figure 13.2). Performing the 20 risk assessments and documenting the deviations produces the variance reports. The auditor's variance analysis is submitted to the unit and triggers action plans to be formulated by the nurse leaders. Where the variance analysis falls below the overall benchmark set by the organisation, a report is submitted to the board. This report alerts the executive management team to the underlying causes of the VANS results and requests board support for measures (e.g. a temporary halt to admissions, increased recruitment drives or funds for additional training to increase competency) that will re-establish nursing care at or above the agreed benchmarks. Thereby, the VANS system allows clinicians, managers and executives to communicate and work together to ensure that clinical practice is within agreed standards.

It could be argued that this amount of continuous auditing requires a disproportionate amount of effort and resources that could be better invested in direct clinical care. But as Currie and Loftus-Hill show,[18] clinical governance must be embedded in routine professional practice, identifying and utilising clinical indicators and embodying an integrated relationship between clinicians, managers and the executive board. And the experience of this pathway has shown that the required audit can easily be incorporated into day-to-day activities. Providing there is sound leadership and a non-blame culture based within a dynamic change management environment, staff will participate.

## THE CORPORATE FUNCTION OF THE ICPS

The ICP approach is not simply a way of organising clinical work; it is a comprehensive strategy for relating clinical practice to the corporate concerns of the organisation. As recent reports have shown,[19] it is not acceptable for executive directors to 'turn a blind eye' to weaknesses in clinical practices. Executives need to support and be involved in the systemisation of clinical practice in order to provide an organisational framework for identifying and remedying such weaknesses. VANS is just one example of how this can be done. Such interdisciplinary approaches to healthcare safety have the advantage of individual risk assessments that are very flexible and tailor-made to the specific activities of a profession or clinical practice. A systematic approach then ensures that accurate interpretation and analysis of clinical practice is transcribed for executive leaders to support the delivery of the organisational objectives.

Systematisation also contributes to financial management. Hospitals with incentive plans built around outcomes indicators such as cost per case and length of stay found clinical pathways with their easily identifiable processes to be an excellent tool for tracking their progress.[20] In addition, multidisciplinary clinical pathways provide a good marketing tool to win managed care contracts.

Defining care in terms of a patient pathway rather than its specialised inputs also facilitates broader staff development. Care pathways allow for healthcare professionals to be trained and work more flexibly and across traditional professional and organisational boundaries.[21] The redesigning of roles delivering the organisational objectives in a healthy working environment is key within the structured approach which is fit for clinical purpose.

## CONCLUSION

This chapter has focused on the importance of clinical practice systemisation in the context of meeting organisational objectives. The key ingredients identified to promote the highest level of success are as follows.

▶ A clear and concise mission statement and strategy for the organisation.
▶ An organisational model of care pathway development that is flexible enough to address the needs of the various directorates within the organisation.
▶ Middle managers who are tasked with interpreting data from frontline staff and transcribing them into information that is usable for executive management.
▶ An executive team that is as focused on clinical practice management as on other more traditional activities such as an organisation's financial status and performance (and recognises that failure to do so can put patients' safety severely at risk).

In this approach to systematisation, we can see a shift from using the *number* of clinical pathways as a measure of clinical practice functions to using care pathway technology as a common *approach* throughout all levels and structures of an organisation. The role of the executive (led by the chief executive) is to provide strong leadership throughout the organisation and ensure openness and effective communication between executive directors, middle managers and clinical teams.[22] Clinical practice systemisation such as VANS provides an approach to fulfil this role. It can also liberate clinical healthcare professionals to contribute to managerial functions such as described in the routine risk assessments. And it also strengthens the corporate capacity of the organisation; the RNHRD has seen an explosion of entrepreneurial innovation and partnerships with other healthcare organisations locally, regionally and nationally through care pathway technology. But, above all, an executive-led application of this approach to local organisational needs and services enhances a safe, effective and efficient patient journey.

## REFERENCES

1 Dykes P, Wheeler K. *Planning, Implementing and Evaluating Critical Pathways: A guide for health care survival into the 21st century.* New York: Springer Publishing Company; 1997. Crump N. *Integrated Care Pathways: re-engineering the NHS for clinical governance.* Lancaster University; 2000. Rees G, Huby G, McDade L, *et al.* Joint working in community mental health teams: implementation of an integrated care pathway. *Health and Social Care in the Community.* 2004; **12**(6): 527–36.

2 Highley K. *Leadership. Primary Care (Special Report).* 17 November 2003; no. 7. Shirey MR. Authentic leaders creating healthy work environments for nursing practice. *Am J Critical Care.* 2006; **15**(3): 256–67.

3 Rees, *et al.,* op. cit.

4 NHS Modernisation Agency. *Toolkit for Local Change.* London: Department of Health; 2003. Edwards N, Marshall M, McLellan A, *et al.* Doctors and managers: a problem without a solution? *BMJ.* 2003; **326**: 609–10.

5 Healthcare Commission. *Investigation into Outbreaks of Clostridium Difficile at Stoke Mandeville Hospital, Buckinghamshire Hospitals NHS Trust.* London: Healthcare Commission; 2006.

6 Croucher M. Evaluation of the current knowledge and awareness of the integrated care pathway tool in a local health community. *J Integrated Care Pathways.* 2005; **9**(2): 51–6.

7 Allen L. *Improvement Leader's Guide to Process Mapping, Analysis and Redesign.* Ipswich: Ancient House Printing Group; 2002. de Luc K. *Developing Care Pathways: the handbook.* Oxford: Radcliffe Medical Press; 2001.

8 Taylor L, Jones S. Clinical governance in practice: closing the loop with integrated audit systems. *J Psychiatric and Mental Health Nursing.* 2006; **13**(2): 228–33.

9 Bart CK, Tabone JC. Mission statement rationales and organizational alignment in the not-for-profit health care sector. *Health Care Management Rev.* 1998; **23**(4): 54–69. Bolon DS. Comparing mission statement content in for-profit and not-for-profit hospitals: does mission really matter? *Hospital Topics.* 2005; **83**(4): 2–9. Carney M. Nursing and healthcare management and policy: positive and negative outcomes from values and beliefs held by healthcare clinician and non-clinician managers. *J Advanced Nursing.* 2005; **54**(1): 111–19. Hewison A. Values in the National Health Service: implications for nurse managers. *J Nursing Management.* 2001; **9**: 253–8. Soule E. Managerial moral strategies – in search of a few good principles. *Academy of Management Review.* 2002; **27**(1): 114–24.

10 Department of Health. *A Short Guide to NHS Foundation Trusts.* London: Stationery Office; 2005.

11 Edwards, *et al.,* op. cit.

12 Edmondson A. Framing for learning: lessons in successful technology implementation. *California Management Review.* 2003; **45**: 35–54.

13 Stanton P. The role of an NHS Board in assuring the quality of clinically governed care. *Clinical Governance.* 2006; **11**: 1.

14 Hendry C, Walker A. Priority setting in clinical nursing practice: literature review. *J Advanced Nursing.* 2004; **47**(4): 427–36. Alfaro-LeFevre R. *Critical Thinking in Nursing: a practical approach.* 2nd ed. Philadelphia: WB Saunders Co.; 1999.

15 Department of Health. *An Organisation with a Memory (Report of an expert group on learning from adverse events in the NHS).* London: Stationery Office;

2001. Ammerman M. *The Root Cause Analysis Handbook: a simplified approach to identifying, correcting and reporting workplace errors.* New York: Quality Resources; 1998. Anderson B, Fagerhaug T. *RCA: simplified tools and techniques.* Milwaukee: ASQ Quality Press; 2000.

16 Adler P, Riley P, Kwon S-W, *et al. Performance Improvement Capability: keys to accelerating performance improvement in hospitals.* Los Angeles: Marshall School of Business, University of Southern California; 2002.

17 Edmondson, op. cit. Smith T. How can healthcare organisations enhance their capacity to learn? *Quality and Safety in Health Care.* 2003; **12**: 313–16.

18 Currie L, Loftus-Hill A. The nursing view of clinical governance. *Nursing Standard.* 2002; **16**(27): 40–4.

19 Healthcare Commission, op. cit. BRI Inquiry Secretariat. (1) *BRI Inquiry Paper on Commissioning, Purchasing, Contracting and Quality of Care in the NHS Internal Market.* London: Stationery Office; 1999. (2) *BRI Inquiry Paper on Medical and Clinical Audit in the NHS.* London: Stationery Office; 1999.

20 Cabello CC. Six stepping stones to better management. *Nursing Management.* 1999; **30**(4): 39–40.

21 Department of Health. *The NHS Plan: a plan for investment, a plan for reform.* London: Stationery Office; 2000. Hewitt-Taylor J, Melling S. Care protocols: rigid rules or useful tools? *Paediatric Nursing.* 2004; **16**(4).

22 Ingersoll GL, Wagner L, Merck SE, *et al.* Patient-focused redesign and employee perception of work environment. *Nursing Economics.* 2002; **20**(4).

# CHAPTER 14

# Organisational lessons from systematisation: the experience of HealthCare Otago

*Allan Cumming and Janine Cochrane*

As we have seen in this book, integrated care pathways (ICPs) have been widely adopted as a way of systematising clinical practice. Fully developed ICPs are seen as desirable in the delivery of cost efficient high quality patient care.[1] But for some 'it is questionable whether care pathways are a universal response to the requirement for modernisation and service redesign in the NHS'.[2] They have been seen by some trust managements as largely irrelevant to the change agenda or, worse, as adding costs in an already difficult financial climate.

Many of the experiences described elsewhere in this volume are concerned with the essential clinical dimensions of systemisation. In this chapter, we consider organisational factors and specifically their importance in the very positive experience of introducing ICPs in Otago, New Zealand.

## BACKGROUND

Between 1994 and 1998 HealthCare Otago, a tertiary teaching hospital serving a small population in the South Island of New Zealand, underwent a major transformation. Using a combination of an unusual management structure, a focus on integrated care pathways, and a commitment to continuous quality improvement, HealthCare Otago transformed an organisation with severe financial challenges into a hospital 'in the black'.

The 1991 health reforms in New Zealand were launched by the green and white paper, *Your health and the public health*.[3] The reforms introduced a split between purchaser and provider: four Regional Health Authorities (RHAs) were set up to purchase services on a competitive basis from 23 Crown Health Enterprises (CHEs). The Crown Health Enterprises were commercial enterprises, with appointed Boards accountable to the Minister of Health and the Minister of Crown Owned Enterprises. HealthCare Otago came into being as a crown owned company operating under commercial finance rules on 1 July 1993.

In early 1995 a new chief executive officer was appointed to HealthCare Otago, and in October 1995 a new senior management structure was introduced. This became fully functional with the appointment of general managers in December 1995. With the exception of the chief financial officer who had been in the post for 12 months, all the senior management posts were filled from outside the organisation. At this time, the organisation was in severe financial difficulties, facing an annual deficit of NZ$24 million, and the Chief Executive was determined to adopt a radical new approach to running the organisation. This approach was based on three main factors: a new management structure that engaged with clinical staff, a commitment to continuous quality improvement, and the use of integrated care pathways to systematise the delivery of care. These, combined with a performance system that provided fully allocated costs to the patient level, assisted the organisation to reach a positive financial position within four years.

This change in fortunes was not achieved without difficulty. Changes to the nursing management structure, and the appointment of some younger consultants to management posts, caused conflict between clinical staff and the new management structure early in the process. There was some resistance to the 'intrusion' of management into clinical care when the ICP programme started. This extended into the relationship between the management of the hospital and management of the medical school, where a number of the consultant staff had joint appointments. Ultimately, a change in the membership of the CHE Board led to the departure of the Chief Executive and the senior management team, and a reversion over the following 12 months to a more traditional style of management.

The story of pathway development in HealthCare Otago does not end with the counter revolutionary arrival of the new management structure in 1999. Although some things changed, what made the HealthCare Otago experience unusual was that the ICP work had become central to the way that clinical staff worked. Pathway work continued without the active encouragement, or even the continued explicit support, of the new senior team.

What led pathways to remain a significant factor in the delivery of efficient healthcare 10 years after their introduction? The three main factors in the change process were the management philosophy, the use of a quality improvement methodology and the widespread use of ICPs. These were not independent strategies. The management structure and philosophy was based on devolvement to Clinical Practice Groups (CPGs) jointly managed with clinical staff. This devolvement meant that accountability for performance was placed with the CPG staff who were given the authority to develop solutions to financial and clinical problems. The quality improvement methodology was central to this devolvement of responsibility, giving both the philosophical basis for devolved authority to 'fix problems' and the analytical tools to enable workplace staff to identify causes of problems, and develop solutions. The ICP programme was the application of the quality improvement methodology to clinical practice: quality improvement methods and tools were used by staff to develop ICPs, and the use of ICPs was seen as the way for the CPGs to achieve their improvement in performance. ICP development would not have occurred without the devolvement of authority to the CPG; neither would the more general quality improvement work. The devolvement of accountability could not have been effective without the tools to deliver change. These interdependencies were telling, as we shall see.

## THE CLINICAL PRACTICE GROUP STRUCTURE

The new management structure introduced in January 1996 had three main features that distinguished it from its predecessor: it denied traditional medical/surgical boundaries, developed dual accountability and leadership, and provided very devolved structures and responsibilities.

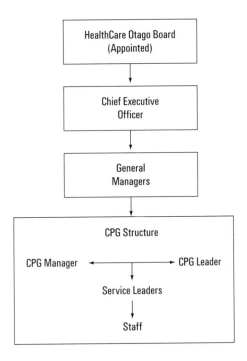

**FIGURE 14.1**  HealthCare Otago management structure

### Overcoming the medical/surgical boundaries

The basic unit of the new structure was the Clinical Practice Group (CPG). Unlike previous structures that followed the traditional division of the hospital into medical specialities and surgical specialties, the CPG structure instead divided the hospital by 'body systems'. Initial CPGs included a Musculoskeletal CPG, containing orthopaedic surgery, rheumatology and physiotherapy, a Cardiothoracic CPG including cardiac surgery, cardiology, thoracic surgery and respiratory medicine, and a Head and Neck CPG including neurology, neurosurgery, ophthalmology, ENT, and maxillofacial surgery.

The CPG structure expressed a belief that the role of the medical consultant was changing and historical boundaries between medicine as diagnostic and surgery as interventional was no longer true. With services such as rheumatology, dermatology and cardiology conducting more interventions and minor procedures, it was apparent to the CEO that services such as cardiology and cardiac surgery had more in common than was previously acknowledged.

Although there was resistance to the structure from some specialities (e.g. neurology was initially reluctant to be combined with neurosurgery), such resistance dissolved. Over time, all clinical support services became part of the CPG that they were most closely aligned to, and CPGs merged and reformed as clinical interests became more clearly integrated. Initially, for example, a number of medical specialities were grouped with General Medicine; however, eventually the specialities grouped with the cardiothoracic group, with General Medicine aligning with Care of the Elderly services, although remaining as a separate CPG.

## Leadership in the CPGs

A key feature of the CPG structure was its management and leadership. The CEO decided at the outset that it was essential to involve the clinical staff, and particularly the medical staff, in the new structure. He also acknowledged that not all doctors were interested in the details of day-to-day management, especially some of the potentially difficult decisions that would have to be made over service configuration. To deal with this dilemma, he introduced dual accountability.

Each CPG was headed by a full-time Clinical Practice Group Manager, full-time but in most cases with responsible for more than one CPG, and a Clinical Practice Group Leader, who devoted 20% of their time to management and retained their clinical duties for the remainder. In most (but not all) cases the CPG Leader was a medical consultant. The job descriptions for the CPG Manager and the CPG Leader were essentially identical, with the two being equally accountable for all clinical, financial and managerial aspects of the service. Both attended meetings together and decisions were made jointly. This meant that the clinical staff were fully involved in all aspects of their services, but had the ability to share the managerial tasks and pain. Equally, the CPG Manager was accountable for clinical quality on an equal footing with the clinicians, avoiding the often seen clinician-manager split of accountabilities.

Another feature in the appointment of staff to these new roles was the selection of relatively junior consultants for a number of posts. A generation of clinical staff was skipped in some areas, leading to some conflict but a fresh approach to many problems.

### Devolving responsibility

The third feature of the structure was a significant devolution of responsibility compared to its predecessors. The intention was to turn each CPG into a self-managing service, a 'hospital within a hospital'; thus it took responsibility for all aspects of the service including the configuration of services and contracts with funders. Over time, nearly all previously centralised support services were devolved into the CPG structure to support this delivery model. Clinical coding, human resources, most financial support and all training, audit, education and quality staff were placed within the CPGs. Central support functions were limited to a small central finance team, management of the case-mix and full-cost allocation accounting system, and the information technology departments, with a small HR support team managing collective staff contracts and recruitment of junior medical staff. Using the problem solving approach set out in the quality improvement training all management staff were required to attend, staff within CPGs were expected to come up with solutions to performance problems rather than have solutions imposed from above. In most cases, as long as the CPG met its targets for delivery of contract volume within agreed budgets, there were few decisions that were routinely required to go to corporate managers.

## FROM QUALITY CONTROL TO QUALITY IMPROVEMENT

The second leg of the tripod supporting the turnaround at HealthCare Otago was the Quality Improvement Programme. The CPG structure placed responsibility for quality firmly with the CPGs and the central quality unit was disbanded and its staff moved into CPGs. The general manager for Medicine and Surgery commissioned the Juran Institute, an American-based consultancy offering training in continuous quality improvement methodologies.

Juran believed that quality improvement and a problem solving approach were important to the management philosophy, that it was the responsibility of all staff to identify and fix performance and quality problems, be they financial or clinical. Senior management set the direction for the organisation, and provided both the authority and the tools to achieve the goals set; but it was the staff within the CPG that had the authority and the knowledge to deliver results. Thus *all* staff with any management responsibility were required to attend a four day training programme, conducted with visible commitment by the CEO and senior management team, and had to deliver quality improvement projects as part of the performance review process. Overall the Juran training programme brought to all levels (including the front line) a higher understanding of the importance of data analysis and the ability to understand and interpret data.

## INTEGRATED CARE PATHWAYS AS A WAY OF DELIVERING CHANGE

The third leg of the HealthCare Otago change process was the widespread introduction of integrated care pathways to systematise the delivery of clinical care. It was the ICP work that outlasted the more structural changes: seven years after it officially ended, nearly all of the pathways developed in the period 1996 to 1998 were still in use, and most were being regularly reviewed and updated.

Integrated care pathways were first introduced under the new management structure in January 1996 when the General Manager of Medicine and Surgery appointed a Care Pathway Coordinator. The ICP Coordinator's role was to facilitate the introduction of pathways within the new CPG structure, and to ensure a common standard and approach to pathways development. The role was one of the very few appointments that sat outside the CPG structure. Pathways were seen as essential to the process of driving down length of stay and costs through the reduction in variation and systemisation of practice. Pathways were also seen as clinical embodiment of the CQI process supported by the Juran approach to data management and interpretation.[4]

There was initial resistance to the pathway approach from both clinical and management staff. Managers could not see the immediate relevance of pathways to achieving cost and length of stay performance targets and clinical staff were concerned about management interference in clinical care. The CPG structure lessened this resistance because, while the freedom to 'not do ICPs' was not an option, the development of the ICPs lay with the clinical team within the CPG. Although the format was mandated (to maintain consistency across the hospital) and the initial conditions were chosen by senior management (on volume-cost basis), all staff within the CPG were involved in the development of pathways in their specialities. At the time the programme was launched, it was supported by experiences in pathway development in Australia and the United States; indeed, American work of pathway development for cardiac surgery appeared to be key in convincing that group of consultants of the value of the work.[5]

The first two pathways were for Coronary Artery Bypass Graft (CABG) within the Cardiothoracic CPG and for Total Knee Replacement (TKR) within the Musculoskeletal CPG. Each took some six months to develop, and the experience of developing these initial pathways eventually led to the development of a Four Meeting Model which would allow a new pathway to be developed in two months.

The introduction of pathways to the organisation took place on a number of different levels. A Pathway Steering Group was set up. This group included medical, nursing, allied health and managers. The Steering Group recommended content of training, agreed the approach for development and oversaw the pace of roll-out. Training in pathways, data analysis and understanding variation was carried out in addition to the monthly hospital-wide CQI training. Training in pathway development was directed mainly at educators, nurse specialists and senior nursing and allied health staff. Medical staff were approached personally and through CQI training. Each professional group was responsible for educating its colleagues. The nursing staff paid particular attention to making sure that each member of staff on day, evening or night shift had an education session. The medical staff education usually took place at a breakfast meeting. It was identified early that pathways needed to be viewed as 'what we do around here'; not using pathways in the day-to-day management of routine care was not an option for any staff, no matter how senior.

In one clinical area use of the pathways was part of the review of the junior house staff. Ongoing training and orientation to the ward was carried out by the staff educators (who were usually from a nursing background, but who covered all staff including medical). It was also recognised that 'pathway police' were required to ensure that they were appropriately and routinely used. This role was usually taken on by senior nursing and educator staff.

The content of the pathway was developed using the CQI approach (and testing theories as to what situations led to poor outcomes or caused patient and system variation). A multidisciplinary team was selected and given the mandate to work with the group and their own professional colleagues. This process of local development, which was seen as important as it led to an understanding of how local micro-systems worked, involved three stages.

1  Identifying the start and finish of the pathway, discharge criteria, all the stages of the pathway as well as a list of anecdotal problems with current care.

2  Testing the suspected problems (e.g. comorbidities, laboratory turnaround, discharge obstacles) and developing theories of what caused them both to address what needed to be incorporated into the new pathway and to dispel myths about the problems contributing to an increased length of stay.

3  Reviewing each discipline's inputs and expectations for each stage of the pathway based on systematised evaluation of evidence to achieve consensus of practice between consultants – a difficult exercise for staff not least as traditional documentation focused upon inputs such as 'taking the patient's temperature' rather than outputs such as 'the patient's temperature was between x and y'.

The development of a common standard and approach meant that each pathway had the same look and feel developed with feedback from staff. Each replaced the traditional progress notes and used exception reporting. The documentation used either a day-by-day progress pathway in which each day's activities and outcomes were described (used primarily for predictable elective procedures) or a staged pathway where in order for a patient to progress through the pathway they had to meet certain criteria (used where there was more variation and less predictability in length of stay; e.g. *many medical* conditions and cardiac surgery). Where daily examinations were carried out (usually by junior medical staff), a pro-forma layout was used. Each pathway document had a graph on the front cover which plotted 'criteria to achieve' on the vertical axis and days (or hours for day surgery) on the horizontal axis. A plot for the expected recovery was printed on the graph. The patient's progress was plotted daily. If the patient was tracking above the pre-printed line, the patient was recovering faster than expected. If the patient was tracking below, the patient's recovery was delayed.

The recording of variations was the most challenging feature of the pathways. Where variations were captured electronically, they were found to be extremely valuable in both ensuring that guidelines were met, and focusing on common problems patients experienced and in which new guidelines were required. Each item signed off on the pathway could generate a variation if the patient did not achieve a particular outcome. At discharge, a patient's inpatient documentation was repatriated to his or her main medical file and the clerical ward staff identified the patient on the pathway database and entered coded variations.

A pathway database to capture variations was developed in Microsoft Access®. Reports could be generated to show the percentage of patients with a particular variation, and the average length of stay for patients that had a variation and those that did not (to see if there was any difference). As patients were expected to have achieved standardised discharge criteria, length of stay was settled on as a reasonable proxy for measuring outcome. The types of variations that appeared to affect length of stay included nausea and vomiting, pain and mobilisation. These activities tended to be the responsibility of the junior doctors and nurses. Prior to the variance analysis from the pathways there was no routine monitoring of guidance compliance. The pathway provided feedback to the entire team. Unlike pathways developed elsewhere, variances were not sent to an audit department but remained part of the chronological patient record. The capture of variances electronically was achieved by training clerical staff to transfer information from the patient documentation.

Some suggest that the language and concepts used when discussing pathways is important in gaining doctor involvement.[6] In Otago the reason for doing pathways was to reduce unwanted, unintended and unnecessary variation. It was important to differentiate between reducing length of stay and reducing unnecessary length of stay (after discharge criteria had been achieved). It was important to focus on improving quality of care as an outcome, not reducing tests or other costs. Only one pathway set out explicitly to reduce length of stay (cardiac surgery). The aim for the other pathways was to improve the quality of care and patient experience. Despite this, all the pathways reduced length of stay within six months of introduction (by approximately one day). Most pathways demonstrated a reduced variability in length of stay post pathway introduction.

The involvement of medical staff in achieving systematisation was important.

This was accomplished using one-to-one meetings with the general manager and consultants, providing peer reviewed articles of other experience with pathways and advertising success in the clinical areas. These strategies support the findings of Mathie about which factors influence doctors' behaviour.[7] As junior medical staff were the most reluctant to engage with pathways, senior consultant involvement was vital. One issue frequently raised by junior medical and nursing staff was the defensibility of the pathway in court. This was dealt with by obtaining a legal opinion from the CHE solicitor which outlined benefits and harm for both the organisation and individual in using pathways. The evidence at the time suggested that if the pathways had been developed in an explicit manner (with staff identified) and outlined a clear plan of care, this was far more defensible than no written plan (which was traditionally often the case).

Systematisation using pathways was integrated into the organisation in an extremely focused way. The role of the general manager in pathway development was key to maintaining this momentum; the pathway remained the way to deliver the latest imperative from the Ministry of Health. Tight delivery constraints meant that the phenomenon of staff attending meetings and then nothing happening or changing was less likely to happen. Staff attendance at meetings was assured, as pathway meetings were seen as the most important non-patient work that clinical staff undertook.

## WHAT RESULTS WERE ACHIEVED, AND HOW HAVE THEY BEEN SUSTAINED?

In preparing this chapter, a number of former and current staff of HealthCare Otago were interviewed. Additionally, length of stay data were analysed for the period 1992 (four years prior to the initiative) through to 2005 (six years after the management abandonment of the initiative). Data were analysed for several of the high volume pathways, as well as speciality level length of stay data to determine the impact on specialities as a whole.

### Coronary artery bypass graft

Selected because of the high cost and high volume of the procedure, pathway work was completed in 1996, and median length of stay reduced from 14 days to 10 days by 1999. Changes to the provision of this surgery in the past three years, with a differentiation between straightforward cases (now done outside Dunedin Hospital) and complex cases (still done within Dunedin Hospital) has led to a halving of the volume of surgery undertaken in Dunedin Hospital. It is unclear whether the changing case-mix or the reduced bed pressure explains the increase in length of stay since 2002. Although the pathway is still in use within both the public hospital and the private facility which manages nearly 50% of the volume of elective cases, the analysis of the variance database and the regular variance review has not been undertaken for some time.

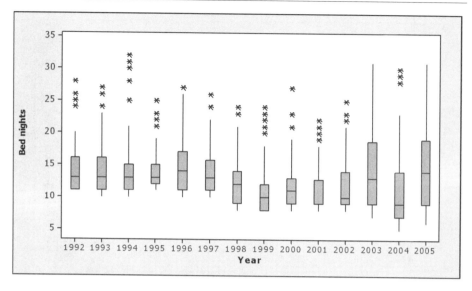

**FIGURE 14.2**  CABG boxplot of bed nights by year

## Elective total hip and knee replacement

The pathways were developed in 1996 and due to the high volume of cases which were undertaken, the impact was seen relatively quickly. These two pathways show reductions in the median length of stay and the inter-quartile range. For the total hip replacement pathway median length of stay reduced from 11 days (1996) to seven days in 2000, and reduction in variation reflected in the inter-quartile range going from five days to two days. For the total knee replacement pathways the reductions in the median were from 11 days to eight days and the inter-quartile range from five days to two days over the same period. This reduction is similar to that found in other studies. Munoz, *et al.* found a reduction from 19.4 days ALOS to 10.1 days ALOS after six years.[8]

The pathways developed within the musculoskeletal CPG are still under review, with annual variance analysis undertaken by the multidisciplinary team and the pathway being modified to reflect subsequent changes in practice. This update of pathways is reflected in the continued improvement in performance for both pathways. The reduction in variation should indicate a tight clinical audit of the variance data to ensure that the majority of patients are maintained on the pathway.

## Transurethral resection of the prostate pathway

Pathways were also developed for General Surgery procedures such as transurethral resection of the prostate. Pathway work commenced in 1997, later than the cardiac and orthopaedic pathways. While the median length of stay did not significantly reduce initially, the impact of the pathway was seen in the short stay patients, with the lower quartile dropping from four days in

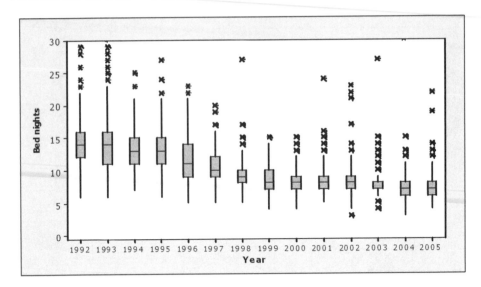

**FIGURE 14.3** Elective total hip replacement boxplot of length of stay by year

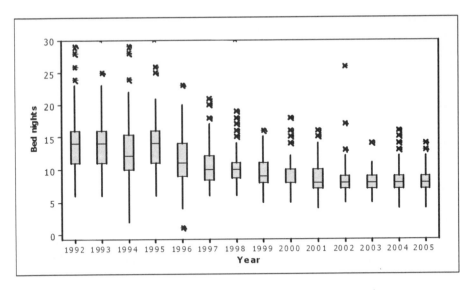

**FIGURE 14.4** Elective total knee replacement boxplot of length of stay by year

1997 to three days in 1998, two days in 2000, and one day in 2003. Although the staff in the area maintain that the pathways are still used and regularly reviewed, analysis of the variance data is not undertaken regularly as in some other specialities, and this may explain the increasing length of stay over the last two years.

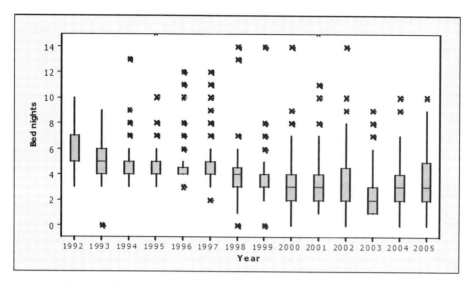

**FIGURE 14.5** Transurethral resection of the prostate pathway boxplot of bed nights by year

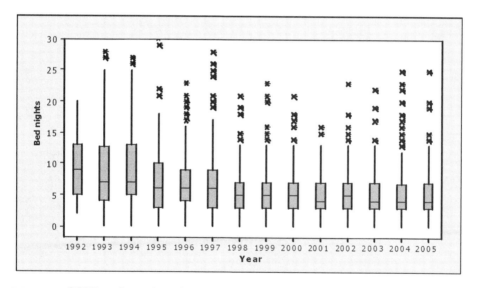

**FIGURE 14.6** COPD pathway boxplot of bed nights by year

## Respiratory medicine: COPD

Pathways in the medical specialities are often seen as more difficult to implement, but pathways developed for respiratory medicine are still in use and reviewed regularly. The chronic obstructive pulmonary disease (COPD) pathway was developed in 1997, and while immediate reductions in the median length of stay were not as apparent as in some pathways due to reductions achieved through improvement in previous years, the variation between patients was reduced and this reduction in variation has been held since 1998.

## Average length of stay (ALOS)

The impact of ICPs and other associated continuous quality improvement work[9] on average length of stay can be seen when ALOS data for whole specialities is analysed. The average length of stay for all patients discharged live, both emergency and elective admissions, is presented for four of the key specialities. While all four specialities show the best performance in 1998, the final year of the CPG management structure, most results have remained lower than the pre-1996 figures through to the present day. These length-of-stay figures include all patients, those included on pathways and those not, indicating that the reductions are significant enough to affect the whole department. For example, if the 2392 patients discharged from orthopaedics in 2000 had stayed the ALOS seen in 1995, an additional 2618 bed days would have been used. At the ALOS of 4.35 days achieved in 2000, this equates to capacity to admit an additional 600 patients.

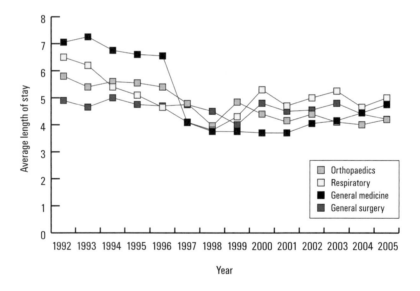

FIGURE 14.7  Average length of stay for four key specialties

## CONCLUSIONS: THE ORGANISATIONAL FACTORS

The pathways introduced into HealthCare Otago were effective in reducing length of stay and therefore cost. These impacts were significant. In the two musculoskeletal pathways described, reductions of length of stay in 2000 compared to 1995 (the last full year before development began) meant that a total of 1386 bed days were saved. In the COPD pathway, if the patients treated in 2000 had experienced the same length of stay as those patients admitted in 1995, an additional 300 bed days would have been used. In the cardiac surgery pathway the saving would have been 334 days; in the TURP pathway, 184 days. The number of bed days saved by pathways at HealthCare Otago has been significant.

The impact of pathways on performance continued long after management moved onto other initiatives. This is largely due to the fact that the clinical staff using the pathways on a daily basis found them to be an improved way of delivering clinical care. In those areas where regular pathway review has continued, pathways continue to be improved, and length of stay continues to reduce.

Yet the pathway success at HealthCare Otago was at least partly due to the position that pathways played in the organisation. And there are at least five organisational lessons for others interested in implementing pathways as part of clinical management improvement. First, they were seen as core to the way the organisation did its business of delivering healthcare. They were supported by senior management, both clinical and non-clinical, and were clearly identified as one way that the organisation would meet its performance objectives. Second, the pathway initiative was led by the senior management team. As core business, the visible support of the executive was central to delivering pathways. Third, the pathway programme was inextricably linked into other strategies pursued by the organisation. In particular, pathway development fitted into the devolved management structure by giving performance tools to clinical staff; it was also the clinical embodiment of the quality improvement programme that affected other areas of the hospital. Fourth, in HealthCare Otago, pathways were developed from the start by multidisciplinary teams, including clerical, medical, allied health profession and nursing staff. No profession dominated this process and none was left to undertake it alone. Finally, and above all, in HealthCare Otago, pathways were seen as a means to deliver better clinical outcomes; they were never ends in themselves.

## ACKNOWLEDGEMENTS

We would like to thank the following current and former HealthCare Otago staff for agreeing to be interviewed for this chapter: J Ayling, C Barker, M Boivin, R Bunton, S Christie, J Hewson, G Martin, A van Rij, J-C Theis, C Wong.

## REFERENCES

1 Schmid K, Conen D. Integrated patient pathways: 'mipp' – a tool for quality improvement and cost management in health care. Pilot study on the pathway Acute Myocardial Infarction. *Int J Health Care Quality Assurance*. 2000; **13**: 87–92.

2 Bragato L, Jacobs K. Care pathways: the road to better health services? *J Health Organ Management*. 2003; **17**: 164–80.

3 Upton S. *Your Health and the Public Health*. Wellington: Ministry of Health; 1991.

4 Juran Institute. *Quality Improvement: health care*. Wilton: Juran Institute Inc; 1993.

5 Bunton R. Personal interview. Dunedin; 2006.

6 Mathie AZ. Doctors and change. *J Management Med*. 1997; **11**: 342–56.

7 Ibid.

8 Munoz A, Garcia M, Perez M, *et al.* Clinical pathway for hip arthroplasty six years after introduction. *Int J Health Care Quality Assurance*. 1997; **19**: 237–45.

9 Rae B, Busby W, Millard P. Fast-tracking acute hospital care: from bed crisis to bed crisis. *Australian Health Review*. 2007; **31**: 50.

# CHAPTER 15

# Clinical networks: systematising communities of practice

*David Walton*

Networks are not new. Based on informal relationships, they have for many years helped to ensure that where the bureaucratic aspect of the English National Health Service fails the patient, clinicians work together to provide the resources which the patient needs. What *is* new, however, is the role of networks as an independent organisational form, with managed structures, memberships and targets.

Managed clinical networks have been evolving over the past few years within the NHS in response to the need for improved delivery and coordination of services across institutional boundaries. In the main, their mandate is determined by national imperatives and the need for clinical engagement in the reforms of clinical practice to which government is committed. Their task is to recognise and then mobilise as part of official practice the informal power of groups of disciplinary practitioners. In effect, they systematise collaboration.

This chapter highlights the experiences and issues of networks. It aims to illustrate the effect such groupings have on the transfer and implementation of innovation and effective performance, the importance of social capital and community of practice as underlying principles for clinical engagement with innovation, and the conditions needed to enable the transfer of knowledge and practice between practitioners. We shall use cancer networks as our illustration.

## NETWORKS AND POLICY INNOVATION

The NHS is in the throes of perhaps the most radical structural reform in its history. But this structural change is only part of the picture. Unlike many previous reforms, the current emphasis is clearly on the clinical services themselves: improving clinical outcomes, acknowledging maximum costs for product-like clinical procedures, responding to patient choices and meeting externally set time scales for locally based treatment. In cancer, these radical changes began in 1995 with the publication of the Calman-Hine Report, *A Policy Framework for Commissioning Cancer Services.*[1]

Aimed at delivering a uniformly high standard of cancer treatment as close to the patient as possible, the report proposed the integration of cancer treatment through a hub and spoke model, where the hub is a (tertiary) cancer centre of excellence and the spokes reach out to the local cancer units in secondary and into primary care. And, in an acknowledgement of the way cancer services involve not only these sectors but also charities, Royal Colleges, university departments and research groups and other healthcare professional bodies, the report proposed the establishment of regional cancer networks, rather than markets or centralised hierarchies. These regional networks were to develop managerial and clinical relationships across and within primary, secondary and tertiary organisational boundaries, with both vertical and horizontal integration. This reflected both the complexity of cancer care and the way clinicians were already working together informally to share ideas and research.

Despite the 'patchy, incoherent and incomplete' way in which those recommendations were implemented in different areas[2] a national web of multidisciplinary networks was established to function alongside primary and secondary trusts. Acceptance of the network role varied, with trusts demonstrating different degrees of commitment to network activity. The relationship between traditional bureaucratic structures and more fluid organisational forms has resulted in some tension, particularly over clinical freedom and resource management. By 1999, there was general agreement that progress towards uniform service development was not moving fast enough and, in 2000, the national Cancer Plan was published.[3] This was a more explicit, strategic plan covering prevention, screening, diagnosis, treatment and care for cancer, as well as the investment needed to deliver services (improved staffing, equipment, drugs, treatments and information systems). It also provided a national and more explicit definition of the tasks and roles which cancer networks were to perform.

Six years on and a decade after the Calman-Hine report, the National Audit Office spelt out the many significant improvements in the management and provision of cancer services since 1995.[4] Overall, cancer mortality for patients under 75 years is beginning to fall and survival rates are improving. New equipment and treatments have been introduced and there is an increased accrual to clinical trials. In specific areas, smoking prevalence is falling, screening programmes have been extended, waiting times targets are more frequently achieved, NICE guidance for multidisciplinary working is increasingly being implemented and the implications for reconfiguring services (establishing specialist centres) are being tackled.

Other aspects of the Report, however, led members of the Public Accounts Committee of the House of Commons to a more critical view.[5] They found a significant number of network failings. There were major variations in cancer mortality and in levels of access to newer drug treatments in different parts of England. From a baseline at which patients suffer more delays and worse survival than those in many other European states, 30% of the networks assessed had no comprehensive plans for providing cancer services in their area. Networks were described as inconsistent in monitoring their performance against the targets in the plan; indeed, no monitoring at all was taking place in five of the networks reviewed. Cancer mortality, particularly from lung cancer, was highest in the most deprived areas. Clinical outcomes data is patchy, pathway and working practice reconfiguration has been slow, radiotherapy capacity is still inadequate and there has been little emphasis on quality or efficiency on inpatient or community based care. It was in this context that the Committee reasserted that networks must reduce inequalities in cancer prevalence and mortality.

In 2007 a national Cancer Reform Strategy is being planned to tackle these issues and new policy imperatives concerning commissioning, prevention and the move to more community based provision. Unsurprisingly, cancer networks have been considering how to respond to suggestions that they have failed to reach the aspirations of Calman-Hine. One line of thinking is on the need for a stronger managerial focus in networks to emphasise their role in the performance management of cancer services provided by trusts. Another is structural reform to distinguish provider networks and commissioner networks. Both approaches bring into question the network as an organisational form.

## NETWORKS AS ORGANISATIONAL FORM

Although there is no single definition of a network,[6] the literature on networks acknowledges that there are a number of types of network within health and social care communities. **Individualistic networks** are often developed by individuals or within single organisations, bringing together a group of affiliates to achieve a certain task, often informally. **Enclave networks** are usually close-knit groups with a flat structure. Members have come together to share information, ideas and new thinking. They may not work within a formal framework but represent coalitions of shared interest and are often voluntary in membership. **Hierarchical networks** are regulated from a central point, such as a steering group, and are often accredited in some way. They may form 'vertically integrated' pathways in NHS trusts, bringing together professionals from different institutions to work on specific care. A subdivision of them might be a care pathway network where specific services are planned across the whole care pathway or a significant part of the care pathway.

Cancer networks are a hybrid of these network forms. They incorporate primary, secondary and tertiary care providers; that is, general practitioners, community health nurses, acute service clinicians (medical and nursing), managers, palliative care representatives, strategic health authority representatives and cancer commissioners from primary care. They are required to respond to national directives and work on inter-hospital transfers and local care provision, work that involves structured decision making and commitments that are characteristic of hierarchical network types. On the other hand, network groups often begin life as a group of individual doctors meeting regionally to review research and matters of common interest. As such they are widely seen by clinicians as a valuable method of sharing research knowledge across professional and organisational boundaries, very much in line with the enclave model.

The networks' development role includes ensuring consistency in the way trusts meet waiting times targets, implement (NICE) Improving Outcomes Guidance (IOG), develop fully integrated patient pathways across organisational boundaries, improve patient information and user involvement, produce guidelines on good clinical practice, implement evidence-based pathway recommendations, and develop strategies for cancer care commissioning and provision across local health economies. Implementing these developments requires ownership and commitment by the clinical teams delivering the service.

To do this, cancer networks are constituted with boards made of representatives from constituent trusts and centrally employed network staff. Each trust has its own lead team for cancer, linking with its wider management structure. The network organisation consists in parallel to trusts with its own lead team and support staff. Some networks also host service improvement staff recruited through a national Cancer Service Collaborative initiative.

Most importantly, the activity of the networks is conducted through Network Site (tumour) Specific Groups (NSSGs). Multidisciplinary groups of doctors, nurses and managers, they are the key mechanism for transacting agreements; they are responsible for establishing protocols, guidelines and integrated care pathways for particular cancers and are also designed to establish arrangements for joint and compatible systems for data collection and audit. Although network guidelines are formulated by groups, however, they invariably acknowledge clinicians' freedom as individuals, to change their practice and determine the way guidelines are applied to specific cases.

In at least one network studied by the author, membership of the tumour site groups is voluntary. As with any social grouping, participants have a variety of motives for attending. Network meetings that address structural issues and resources are well attended. So too are those dealing with controversial therapy and learning events which sometimes accompany the formal meetings. But discussions about individual practice and trust performance tend to be less popular; members are reluctant to challenge or criticise each other. This reluctance has been most marked when the network groups have considered NICE Guidance on Improving Treatment Outcomes for particular types of cancer. Network guidelines have been needed to promote NICE recommendations and some have required structural change to accommodate, for example, the development of tertiary, specialist surgery. Inter-hospital transfers, the development of integrated pathways, the establishment of specialist centres and the standardisation of practice have been difficult and taken much time to progress. In some of these discussions, it appears that individual perspectives, rather than the views of clinicians in general, have been uppermost. Despite board level representation from trusts there is some evidence that clinicians who voluntarily attend network group meetings do so out of personal interest and, in some cases, neither communicate with nor represent colleagues from their trusts. These behaviours are consistent with the enclave model of networks.

But not all networks operate in this way. Cancer networks differ in their approach and tend to reflect the level and aspiration of clinical leadership within the Network Lead Team itself, rather than the wider network membership.[7] Networks with individual eminent clinicians tend to follow a more hierarchical pattern both in structure and functioning. Those with greater teamwork or managerially based leaderships tend to have flatter structures and more inclusive approaches. However, an interesting feature of cancer networks in London is that those with a flatter managerial structure seem to have less strategic clarity. Uncertainty among constituent trusts about network strategy may also have significant implications for the degree to which mutually beneficial outcomes are perceived to be possible and, as a result, responsiveness to network initiatives.

Whatever structural form a network takes, however, there is evidence that its effectiveness is influenced by how its members define what is expected from it. In research into London cancer networks, Ferlie and Addicott report many significant differences in what those involved in networks want them to do.[8] On the whole, policy makers and commissioners prioritise commissioning, leadership and structural reconfiguration, while clinicians emphasise clinical need, capacity, multidisciplinary collaboration, organisational support and research. Such differences can be accommodated but the key problem lies in the priorities which individuals feel should be addressed. Evidence from networks in other fields suggests that mutually beneficial outcomes are achievable when members (and their organisations) agree to forgo their right to pursue individual (professional and organisational) interests. Effective communication, trust between individuals, frequency of contact and consistency of vision and effectiveness of decision making appear to be the critical criteria for reducing the perceived risk inherent in alliances.[9]

## INNOVATION, EVIDENCE AND PROFESSIONAL SUB-CULTURES

Ever since the seminal work of Coleman, et al.[10] networks have been seen as important in the process by which clinicians adopt (or fail to adopt) new innovations in clinical practice. Yet, until recently, very little has actually been known about the dynamics of social networks of clinicians in the modern healthcare setting or their effect on innovation. In a network of equals, clinicians are able to discuss and share professional knowledge through meetings, educational events and other interactions. They can they frame issues, validate information, make decisions, and create management protocols, all of which contribute to learning in practice. A network that works in this way should become more than a loose coalition of professionals; it becomes a trusting cohesive entity in which challenge and criticism are rich and constructive tools enabling the 'un-learning' of existing practice and implementation of new ideas. But there has been less attention paid to the reality of this sharing or to lessons from non-clinical research about the implementation of effective practice; the way in which evidence or knowledge is distributed and applied is less simple than it may appear. And in the clinical field there is debate even on what constitutes evidence.

The current network model asserts that the development of innovation and best practice is more effective when all stakeholders in the service (including service users) work together. Ferlie and Addicott found that, far from the multi-disciplinary groups simply reviewing evidence and then enabling innovation, the reality is that innovation is non-linear and complex.[11] Scientific evidence is a social construction as well as objective data; thus there may be competing bodies of evidence and values available. And the basic assumption, that when networks review evidence and others' practice they trigger innovation in clinical practice, may not be as solidly rooted as it appears; there are significant filters (personal roles, perceptions and experience) which challenge the apparent scientific paradigm of evidence-based practice.[12]

This research also suggests that professionals construct and act within sub-groups and cultures, with each professional grouping having its own knowledge base, behaviour and research culture. In some networks some behaviours indicate exclusive rather than inclusive collaboration. This can arise through the predominance of, for example, secondary care physicians or surgeons. In such circumstances some members of a network may be perceived to be more equal than others and this in turn may impede the capacity to learn from other disciplines and absorb ideas and innovation. Thus, knowledge transfer may take place much less easily when the priorities and value systems of other professional groupings need to be aired.

It is also possible that the transfer is inhibited by the current complex demands on the healthcare system. Recently a large group of clinicians from one network, including chairs of its tumour specific groups and clinical leads, came together to identify a range of issues which they felt contributed to a climate of uncertainty within which they deliver patient care. Specifically, they identified a number of reforms which, however functional for the contexts in which they were set, had begun to inhibit network development of patient pathways and the effectiveness of integrated working in general. They included the following.

▸ The impact of Practice-based Commissioning and Payment by Results (especially its incentives for specific sectors to hold onto patients to secure the revenue stream and consequent disincentives for clinicians to work together.

▶ Changing primary care trust organisation and commissioning responsibilities.
▶ The potential involvement of the private sector in future.
▶ Changing corporate and clinical governance and its role in supporting the implementation and effectiveness of integrated care models.
▶ Difference in perspectives on the quality of care provided, especially the need to link medical and operational perceptions of the cancer agenda to ensure ownership of the need to act.
▶ The need for a greater clarity about the model of care to be provided across primary, secondary and tertiary boundaries and the importance of being explicit about interdependence (how we need to work together).
▶ Administrative, coding and information system weaknesses in support of networks.[13]

The key drivers thus stem from forces for disintegration that at best feed a strong sense of uncertainty and conservatism and at worst threaten to undermine the trust that is the foundation of network effectiveness. These threats (and they are perceived as such, rather than 'challenges') may partly explain the variation of both level and extent to which people participate in network activities. In such high risk settings, the importance of development and mutual learning receive much less attention.

## NETWORKS AND COMMUNITIES OF PRACTICE

Perhaps these threats and their impact obscure the potential benefits of networks in sharing and developing clinical practice. Everyone is committed to the rhetoric of learning and innovation. However, changing practice means both starting new things and stopping others. Most clinicians would consider these risky unless you have trust in the source of advice for change. As providing such advice is part of a network's role, the quality of relationships becomes a key success criterion. And that requires considering a dimension of the way networks operate which, perhaps because of its apparent intangibility, is in danger of being overlooked: the network as a community of practice.

If a cancer network is to have impact on individual practice, a culture of development and change is needed. Bielaczyc and Collins suggest that a key factor in this must be to structure how learning can take place and to test that it is a shared goal. In practice this means clear goals for service improvement, problem definition and learning. Practical ways of sharing knowledge are vital and from their earliest days, good networks have done so as part of a community of practice.[14]

Communities of practice develop around things that matter to those who join them – usually voluntarily. As a result, their practices reflect the members' own understanding of what is important. Obviously, outside constraints or directives can influence this understanding, but, even then, members develop practices that are their own response to these external influences. Even when a community's actions conform to an external mandate, it is the community – not the mandate – that produces the practice. In this sense, communities of practice are fundamentally self-organising systems.

Many writers in the education world have begun to develop the theoretical and practical basis for the functioning of communities of practice. Wenger describes them as an evolutionary arrangement for learning in groups; they stem from a necessity to accomplish new tasks and create avenues for learning that exist within, between and outside traditional organisational boundaries. Liedke emphasises the fluid nature of such communities; they form, evolve and disband according to the needs of the situation, the aspirations of their members and necessities of their environment.[15]

The distinction drawn earlier between enclave and hierarchical forms of network is repeated in the difference between communities of practice models and cancer networks. The former differ from other kinds of groups found in organisations in the way they define their enterprise, membership, evolution and boundaries. In particular, Wenger posits that communities of practice show different degrees of institutional involvement (Table 15.1).

TABLE 15.1 Relationships of communities of practice to networks and healthcare organisations[16]

| Relationship | Definition | Challenges typical of the relationship |
| --- | --- | --- |
| Unrecognised | Invisible to the organisation and sometimes even to members themselves. | Lack of reflexivity, awareness of value and of limitation. |
| Bootlegged | Only visible informally to a circle of people in the know. | Getting resources, having an impact, keeping hidden. |
| Legitimised | Officially sanctioned as a valuable entity. | Scrutiny, over-management, new demands. |
| Strategic | Widely recognised as central to the organisation's success. | Short-term pressures, blindness of success, smugness, elitism, exclusion. |
| Transformative | Capable of redefining its environment and the direction of the organisation. | Relating to the rest of the organisation, acceptance, managing boundaries. |

The roots of communities of practice lie in constructivism, in which control shifts from experts, teachers and others with power to participants, learners and those whose principal task is to practise rather than manage. Constructivism provides clinicians with the opportunity to debate their own experience and thus enables those with less expertise to utilise the knowledge and understanding of others about real practice and the often ill-defined problems it contains in ways that are most appropriate to their own situation and approach.

In traditional authority-led situations, innovation runs the risk of applying oversimplified or abstracted ideas to highly variable and complex situations. The constructivist approach embodied in communities of practice acknowledges that in real life, improvement and problem solving often require good teamwork and tolerance of complexity. The interaction in effective teamwork brings different skills and backgrounds to help solve complex and ill-structured problems. So it is when networks function as communities of practice. Their effectiveness will be dependent upon creating social interdependency.

Communities of practice are by their nature driven by individual freedom to act and learn but they also need leadership and support. Schein points to the need for maturity in such groups, particularly with leadership as an interdependent role being exercised by everyone from time to time and acknowledging its value to the development process.[17] In a group of peers, it is the gift of power to leaders by the followers which acts as a stimulus for cohesion and development.[18]

Wick defines collaborative groups of professionals working on best practice as entities that help solve authentic problems. He defines communities of practice concretely as groups of professionals with similar task responsibilities. With clarity of role and membership, such groups can promote the cross pollination of ideas, enabling interdisciplinary knowledge and practice. He points out that such groups work best when they quickly form (and dissolve), meeting immediate needs. If cancer networks become too bureaucratic, political organisations concerned in the main with structural change or become detached from the real urgency or frontline patient care, the conditions for a community of practice to grow will not be there.[19]

It is here that a conflict arises within the modern world of managed clinical networks and healthcare. The increasing formalisation of roles and accountability in a network may result in membership being necessary, but not voluntary. There may be greater accountability resulting from membership which may not add value for many clinicians. It may ask them to offer their judgement on others' practice in a setting which prizes an individual's own responsibility for practice. It may involve arbitrating mutually exclusive options for service models, structures and resources that arise in part from the competition between trusts. In such an environment there is a risk that network leadership does not place much emphasis on the social and group behaviours necessary for developing sharing practice. If the development of a community of practice is not recognised as a legitimate way for networks being effective, managed clinical networks could become yet another structural form imposed to deliver improvements but with only minimal impact on changing individual practice.

## MANAGING THE SHARING OF PRACTICE

Clinical networks have great potential for transferring evidence-based practices across the network and accelerating learning. But do networks fulfil this knowledge management role? A study of managed NHS cancer networks in London found that networks concentrated on structural reconfiguration; knowledge management remained marginal. In the light of some network activities (e.g. some aspects of NICE Improving Outcomes Guidance) this may be legitimate, irrespective of the social consequences for competition over status and resources. However, emphasis on structural and resource considerations in place of developing a learning environment where challenge to existing practice is the norm may not lead to rapid or significant innovation. In situations such as those in clinical work (where independence of practice is highly valued), it is arguable that communities of practice may be highly appropriate for continuing professional development, improving personal practice and academic research. Participants want to learn and change. However, where the task is to determine how to meet centrally imposed targets, the authority tensions in both identifying and solving problems may diminish that personal wish to learn and change. As Knowles, *et al.* point out, some form of negotiation process over goals is essential for adult learners.[20] Moreover, as Wick observes, knowledge and the staff who hold it are indeed a network's intangible asset[21] but it is the management of that knowledge, and the ability of the network's members both to review ideas and use them, which adds value.

As a result, the limited spread of innovation highlighted in the recent review of cancer services might be considered predictable. The emphasis on the 'performance' agenda appears to have been replicated across England and Wales and its primacy may have been a root cause for the criticism, cited earlier, by the Public Accounts Committee in 2006.

The existence of a knowledge management strategy is also an essential tool for quality assurance. In cancer networks, the frequency of meetings and the capacity for interaction is limited and this suggests that network informatics relating to quality, clinical outcomes and relative cost is very significant. With only one study finding that collaboration is richer because the participants actually know each other,[22] Johnson emphasises the importance of informatics using remote, web-based communication and systems that have common application across trust boundaries.[23]

Within that, however, there are fundamental questions about the way in which the transfer of evidence-based practice works. A core principle of cancer networks' perspective on service development is the assumption that information about others' experience will lead to changes in practice. However, evidence suggests that integrating knowledge is not simply combining, sharing or making data commonly available. It involves understanding by others of the diagnostic and treatment practice in context. Simply hearing about or reading reports of someone else's view of best practice makes little sense without an understanding of the struggles and gaps it was intended to traverse.[24]

Existing professional boundaries, the concomitant distribution of 'knowing' and commitment to 'the way we do things here' as well as different resource climates means that new ideas are sometimes rejected as 'unworkable here'. Within each new context, the various professionals involved may need to generate the same collective knowledge which characterises the situation in which best practice was defined. Otherwise, best practice models can become simply general templates – knowledge which must be legitimated each time in each context and subject to examination of flaws and difference rather than an opportunity for adaptation.[25]

## COMMUNITIES OF PRACTICE AND SOCIAL CAPITAL

Knowledge management and shared learning are not quite the same things. A basic assumption about networks is that when members review evidence and others' practice, they trigger innovation and change to clinical practice. Learning happens because networks are 'communities of practice'. But, as we have seen, there are complex processes at work.

Communities of practice develop around things that matter to those who join them – usually voluntarily. How they work reflect members' own under-standing of what is important. Although external constraints or directives can influence this understanding, members develop reactions that are their own response to these external influences. In this sense, communities of practice as opposed to some network forms are fundamentally self-organising systems and this is greatly valued by many clinicians.

The expectations of cancer networks following Calman-Hine[26] asks clinicians to fulfil nationally defined mandates – in the context of an increasingly product-focused (Payment by Results) and competitive (Patient Choice) health service. But culture, professional values and personal interests play their own part in shaping personal perspectives. In an environment where competition between providers is increasing, the task of cancer networks has been to agree and implement service reconfigurations involving (for some) loss of services and, potentially, professional expertise. The emphasis on performance and management has been difficult for many clinicians, with ideas of cook-book medicine and clinical freedom being wound up within debates about systematising care, reconfiguration and financial transparency.

So the role of network groups has become an issue. For some clinicians the learning and research role (the community of practice element) of network activity is the most important. For others, the business of delivering reconfigured and systematised services is about fighting your corner and demonstrating your trust's capacity or superior skill. Can both roles co-exist in the same network? The tensions which are raised by this role conflict can only be satisfactorily resolved when:

- members have clear goals, norms and standards to base their thinking on, which are explicit
- members must invest sufficient time for networks to build relationships – the derivation of social capital itself – beyond the comfortable; the capacity to challenge and question must be an indicator of the quality of a relationship

- rapport, informatics and a shared sense of value enables knowledge to be shared effectively and improve performance
- a sense of trust flows from their interactions
- members have a common understanding of the issues they share or must face
- they have a sense of achievement and relevance
- they possess the simple social skills of listening without judging and seeking information
- they resolve leadership, power and support issues through shared beliefs and commitments.

So, the concept of social capital can be defined simply as the sum of actual and potential resources embedded within, available through and derived from the network of relationships. Calman-Hine envisaged these relationships influencing organisational performance. Their potential for doing so (by decreasing learning curves, preventing reinvention, increasing cross boundary cooperation) may be limited by the externally mandated role which cancer networks now perform.

## MOVING FORWARD

As we have seen, the task facing those who participate in network activity is a complex one. Networks consist of many layers with the predominant relationship being peer to peer.[27] Within any individual network, the multitude of priorities and agendas makes people who work with them describe them as 'more or less relevant, from time to time', 'messy' and 'frustrating'.[28] The silo views of some clinicians are particularly frustrating for others, who during network activities, seek order, vertical service integration and standardisation of practice.[29] Moreover, if the formalisation of networks increases (described earlier as the move from an enclave to hierarchical form) the conflict of views may intensify. So, perhaps it is legitimate to ask what the role of a cancer network is in the management of these organisational and cultural complexities. How can they function to encourage spreading and sustaining good practice, implementing change more speedily and achieve better results?

The literature is fairly clear that if networks are to work as organisational forms, criteria such as the following provide an infrastructure for effective operation.

- **Constancy of purpose:** clear goals and appropriate measures of their achievement, alignment of objectives with member capacity, role clarity and differentiation authority to act.
- **Structure and strategy:** coherence of individual member (trust) and network service strategies, interlinking of planning, governance and risk processes, facilitators who support and align (rather than determine)

strategy, information management processes and systems which generate real information rather than data summaries.

▶ **Avoidance of anxiety:** the security of knowing that resources are allocated to where real needs lie, and having employees who do not fear to focus on patient experience.

▶ **Leadership:** clear sense of purpose, mutual learning, integration, innovation and the avoidance of fragmented care.

These criteria need to be described in operational terms but are one way of assessing the organisational effectiveness of networks. Clear measures for the success of networks are vital if they are to be fit for purpose. In some cancer networks there is a need to reconcile different views about what the network is for.

Even if we accept that the networks discussed here have impacted positively on service outcomes, there is much to do. By their very nature, networks are highly complex interrelationships of organisations, agencies, professional teams and individuals. Each has its own cause and special interest and the diversity of settings for health communities makes the establishment of owned, inter-organisational goals and strategies extraordinarily difficult. In this setting, managers and health professionals need to have some form of binding mechanism for integration, to learn from each other and to stimulate innovation. But today's healthcare system is more fragmented, political and risk averse than ever. Many argue that networks are the future; some argue that the mammoth, control-based structures of the past have long reached the limits of their capacity to cope with change. We require more flexible organisations and partnerships capable of responding to the continually evolving needs, expectations and resources which are being observed daily, in all health communities. The binding mechanism (and metaphor) for networks is the patient journey, crossing institutional boundaries and providing a focus for the contributions made by multi-professional groups of healthcare workers. As a performance management mechanism, this is less threatening and rooted in those aspects that are actually in the control of the professionals. But it requires a new form of governance.

A number of current national initiatives are now creating a focus for cancer networks on performance monitoring and the delivery of high quality integrated care, within timed patient pathways. Effective governance within the network will require groups to establish those pathways (with appropriate priorities), make high impact changes and audit the extent to which they are being delivered. Where variance is acceptable from a clinical practice or access point of view, the new standards require the rationale to be both explicit and reviewed periodically. But this is not simply performance management. The pathway focus also provides the freedom for clinicians involved in service delivery to focus on what they are good at – patient care. It empowers them to manage the wide range of social phenomena that defines the network's character and norms (the assumptions, beliefs, behaviours and modes of deference and subversion). Most importantly a prospectively costed, quality-measured pathway provides a structure for bridging the cultural gap between the resource and treatment dimensions of care – empowering clinicians to ensure that clinical governance is integrated into debates with financial managers about how services can develop.

In one large cancer network the twin drivers of governance and integrated pathway development are the starting point for reviewing its approach and effectiveness. Discussions have been taking place within that network for some time to develop an effective model by which these drivers create a template for the way in which groups work. The utilisation of the cancer network potential, through the social capital invested in communities of practice, depends upon participants linking new possibilities to practice, innovation to a shared belief about what should be being delivered for patients. The ability to be explicit about agreed models of service, acceptable variation and defined patient path-ways, and the capacity to put learning from others into practice are prerequisites to securing commitment from politicians, commissioners and managers to the decisions needed for a transformation of the existing healthcare system.

The network is currently beginning to develop a work process to clarify some of the issues identified in this chapter and formulate a model for its governance which both permits and encourages a community of practice to flourish within the network functions. Early discussions have raised questions about the nature and function of the Network Board, the membership and participation in network activities, the engagement of commissioners in network group activity and the ownership of the network to stimulate development. Key to it all so far has been the concept of governance, both clinical and corporate, and the engagement of clinicians.

The concept of integrated governance in this context means having structures and processes to answer some key questions, such as the following.

1  Are we doing the right things? (Given assessed health needs and existing resource constraints, are we delivering value for money? For common con-ditions, how appropriate and effective are the services we offer? Do we have the right service model? Are we achieving the best clinical outcomes?)

2  Are we doing things right? (Are we managing clinical performance accord-ing to national codes of clinical practice? For common conditions, how systematised are our care processes and how are we performing on risk, safety, quality, patient evaluation, and clinical outcomes?)

3  Are we keeping up with new developments and what are we doing to extend our capacity to undertake clinical work in these areas? (What strategies are in place for service and professional development for each condition? What are we doing about clinical mentoring, leadership development, and staff appraisal and review? Groups would need to consider data contributed by trusts, on evidence, cost, outcomes, clinical effectiveness, quality, safety, adverse events, variance and complaints.)

4  Is patient experience across the organisations within the network as good as it could be? (The use of evaluated, integrated care pathways for systematising care extends the evidence base, strengthens service integration, and improves clinical effectiveness, quality and technical efficiency. They should also increase patients' satisfaction and the clinicians' experience of providing care.)
5  Do we learn effectively from one another and does our learning add value through implementation in practice?

In the light of the constantly changing setting for healthcare, a network asking these questions may have difficulty in getting busy clinicians to address these questions. But implementing improvement is not a simple affair; it happens when everyone is part of a shared improvement culture – a community of practice in which knowledge management and innovation are recognised as managerial priorities in their own right.

The systematisation of networks means putting structures, language and processes in place to relate clinicians' priorities and interests to those from other cultures; in so doing, to enhance the social capital of networks by fostering communities of practice. In cancer the challenge is to do so in the context of uncertainty about the future and the need for more clarity and coherence in policy making, commissioning and stronger leadership from professional leaders.

## REFERENCES

1  Calman K, Hine D. *A Policy Framework for Commissioning Cancer Services*, London: Department of Health; 2005.
2  Kewell B, Hawkins MA, Ferlie E. Calman-Hine reassessed: a survey of cancer network development in England, 1999–2000. *J Evaluation in Clinical Practice.* 2002; **8**(3): 303–11.
3  Department of Health. *The NHS Cancer Plan: a plan for investment, a plan for reform.* London: Department of Health; 2000.
4  National Audit Office. *Cancer: A Progress Report.* London: National Audit Office; 2005.
5  House of Commons Public Accounts Committee. *The NHS Cancer Plan: a progress report.* HC 791. 2005–06. Kmietowicz Z. England's cancer networks in danger of missing targets. *BMJ.* 2005; **330**: 555.
6  Pettigrew A, Fenton E, editors. *The Innovating Organization.* London: Sage Publications; 2000.
7  Ferlie E, Addicott K. *Determinants of Performance in Cancer Networks: a process evaluation.* Cardiff University; 2004.
8  Ferlie, Addicott, op. cit.
9  Baxter LA, editor. *Dialogue: theorizing difference in communication studies.* London: Sage; 2002. Carr A, Degeling P, Winters M, *et al.* Understanding the psychodynamics of culture and the psychological contract in a period of

organisational change: results from an empirical study. *Proceedings of the 11th European Congress on Work and Organisational Psychology*, Lisbon, Portugal; 2003. Ring PS, van de Ven AH. Developmental processes of cooperative inter-organizational relationships. *Acad Man Review*. 1994; **19**(1): 90–118. Das TK, Teng BS. Resource and risk management in the strategic alliance making process. *J Management*. 1998; **24**(1): 21–42. Das TK, Teng BS. Between trust and control: developing confidence in partner alliances. *Acad Man Review*. 1998; **23**(3): 491–512.

10 Coleman J, Katz E, Menzel H. *Medical Innovation: a diffusion study*. Indianapolis, IN: Bobbs-Merrill; 1996. Coleman JC. *Foundations of Social Theory*. Cambridge, MA: Harvard University Press; 2000. Coleman J. Social capital in the creation of human capital. *Am J Sociology*. 1988; **94**: S95–121.

11 Ferlie, Addicott, op. cit.

12 Miles R, Snow C. Causes of failure in network organisations. *California Management Review*. 1992; **34**(4): 53–72.

13 Yorkshire Cancer Network. *Complexity and Uncertainty: developing a network approach*. 2005. http://www.yorkshire-cancer-net.org.uk.

14 Bielaczyc K, Collins A. *Learning Communities: advancing knowledge for a lifetime*. NASSP Bulletin: Sage; 1999.

15 Wenger E. *Communities of Practice: learning, meaning and identity*. Cambridge: Cambridge University Press; 1999. Lave J, Wenger E. *Situated Learning: legitimate peripheral participation*. Cambridge: Cambridge University Press; 1991. Liedke J. Linking competitive advantage with communities of practice. *J Management Inquiry*. 1999; **8**(1): 5–16.

16 Wenger, op. cit.

17 Schein E. *Process Consultation Revisited: building the helping relationship*. Harlow: Addison-Wesley; 1999.

18 Degeling P, Carr A. Leadership for the systemization of health care: the unaddressed issue in health care reform. *J Health Organization and Management*. 2004; **18**(6): 399–414.

19 Wick C. Knowledge management and leadership opportunities for technical communicators. *Technical Communication*. 2000; **47**(4): 515–29.

20 Knowles MS, Knowles HF. *Introduction to Group Dynamics*. Chicago: Association Press; 1972. Knowles MS, *et al. Andragogy in Action: applying modern principles of adult education*. San Francisco, CA: Jossey Bass; 1984.

21 Wick, op. cit.

22 Oliver R, Herrington J. Using situated learning as a design strategy for Web-based learning. In: Abbey B, editor. *Instructional and Cognitive Impacts of Web-based Education*. Hershey, PA: Idea Publishing Group; 2000. pp. 178–91. Oliver R, Omari A, Herrington J. Exploring interactions in collaborative World Wide Web computer-based learning environments. *J Educational Multimedia and Hypermedia*. 1998; **7**(2/3): 263–87. Storck J, Hill P. Knowledge diffusion through 'strategic communities'. *Sloan Management Review*. 2000; **41**(2): 63–74.

23 Johnson CB, Squire KD. Supporting distributed communities of practice. *Educational Technology Research and Development*. 2001; **48**(1): 23–43.

24 Swan J, Scarbrough H, Robertson M. The construction of Communities of Practice in the management of innovation. *Management Learning*. 2002; **33**(4): 477–96.

Newell S, Edelman L, Scarbrough H, *et al*. 'Best practice' development and transfer in the NHS: the importance of process as well as product knowledge. *Health Services Management Research*. 2003; **16**(1): 1–12.

25 Czarniawska B, Jorges B. Travels of ideas. In: Czarniawska B, Seven G, editors. *Translating Organisational Change*. Berlin: De Gruyter; 1996.

26 Calman, Hine, op. cit.

27 Lipnack J, Stamps J. *The Architecture of Complexity*. The Seybold Series 9. Resources Information Systems Inc; 1990.

28 Walton D. Anxiety and organisational change. *J Psychoanalytic Psychology*. 2005; **22**/1: 212–65.

29 Degeling P, Maxwell S, Iedema R, Hunter D. Making clinical governance work. *BMJ*. 2004; **329**: 679–81.

# PART THREE

# Implications

# CHAPTER 16

# The workforce implications

*Debra Humphris*

At the heart of New Labour's reforms of both the NHS and the public services more generally has been a major drive to expand, and more importantly redesign, the workforce that provides those services. The focus of this chapter is to illustrate some of the educational challenges faced by the NHS if the workforce is to be prepared to deliver a more systematised approach to care delivery along the lines set out elsewhere in this book.

The desire to reform health services and how clinical work is organised is not new.[1] Indeed, as Masterson and Humphris noted, 'There will always be a need for creative change in response to opportunity and demand in the delivery of services.'[2] The government's commitments made in the NHS Plan were thus followed up with the publication of the human resource strategy, 'Working Together, Learning Together' in which the Department of Health made a clear commitment to set out a 'radical agenda for modernising education and training' in support of service and workforce redesign.[3]

In this chapter two real life examples of such modernising reforms are offered to illustrate the challenges faced by health and social care organisations and frontline practitioners in delivering this agenda. The two examples of educational reform that are described illustrate the scale and nature of the challenges faced by both the NHS and Higher Education Institutions in preparing a workforce equipped to deliver flexible, team-based services.

## THE SYSTEMATISATION OF CARE

The systematisation of care requires that service users, health and social care staff and managers are able to work together in multidisciplinary (and increasingly in multi-agency) teams to explore and understand specific clinical production processes.[4] This requires that the staff involved develop the capability and confidence to work and learn together, to critically examine the delivery of and accountability for care. Therefore, attempts to systematise the management of clinical work will necessitate a willingness by various groups of staff not only to work and learn together, but to put the patient experience at the centre of that process. Developing the capacity and capability to work effectively in teams, and for teams to be effectively focused on the needs of patients, has been a consistent message of the recent NHS and social care reforms. The Department of Health has reiterated its commitment to see 'better integration between health and social care, better integrated workforce design and the needs of people who use services and supported by common education frameworks'. The Department has gone as far as to suggest that this will involve 'joint workforce planning across health and social care' and that new 'health and social care multi-skilled teams will be established' whose development is underpinned by a common national framework of competencies and occupational standards.[5]

All of these changes raise fundamental questions about what, who and how care in the future will be delivered, how the care providers will be prepared and the nature of the regulatory framework that will be required to accommodate such changes.

## DEMOGRAPHY

To understand the workforce implications of systemisation in healthcare it is important first to briefly explore the demographic changes occurring in the population. The most recent UK census demonstrated that the population increased by 0.3% from 1991 to 2001, and most importantly that there have been significant structural changes in the population overall. The largest changes were observed in four age groups: the very elderly (85 years plus) due to increased life expectancy; the post World War II baby boomers (45–64 year olds), 30–44 years olds as a result of high birth rates during the sixties and children aged 10–15. The same census data revealed a decrease in the numbers of 16–29 year olds due to low fertility rates during the seventies. Another important trend in relation to population is the falling overall fertility rate (from 117.5 in 1992 to 91.6 in 2002) and the extent to which women are deferring childbirth. Women in their twenties are having fewer babies whereas the fertility rates among women in their 30s and early 40s rose by 4% in 2001–02.[6]

Over the past 40 years life expectancy at birth has continued to increase. The Government Actuary's Department (GAD) estimates that by 2021 the life expectancy at birth for men will be 78.6 and for women 82.9. At present there are estimated to be four people of working age for everyone over 65 in the UK. The GAD predicts that this is likely to fall to between two people of working age for every three over 65 and then two for every six by the middle of the century. As a consequence, the average age of the British workforce will continue to rise. It is predicted that by 2010 the proportion of working age people between 50 and 64 will be greater than at any time since the mid-1970s. Consequently, the productivity of this age group will have an important impact on the performance of the workforce as a whole: 'From 2005 onwards the proportion of prime-aged adults (30–49) will begin to fall, with the proportion of 50–64 year olds rising from around 20% in 2000 to 32% in 2020.'[7]

The retirement intentions and likely decisions of workers aged 50–64 remain one of the major uncertainties in the area of workforce planning. Dixon suggests that policy initiatives which have been actively designed to reduce incentives for early retirement have indeed resulted in a greater proportion of older workers in the workforce.[8] It is likely therefore that as the workforce ages it will force employers to think hard not only about the need to maintain the employability of older workers, but the relevance of their skills, the mobility of the workforce in relation to the location and the composition of jobs.

## THE POLICY CONTEXT

The New Labour reforms of the NHS have encouraged a 'whole systems' perspective in which the traditional demarcations between professions and the compartmentalisation of care have been seen as antithetical to the delivery of person-centred services. In 2000 the intentions and commitments made in the NHS Plan included a wide range of proposals for changes in services and as a consequence the workforce.[9] At an early stage in this process of reform, Her Majesty's Treasury commissioned what was to become a series of important and challenging reports by Derek Wanless into the state funding and delivery of healthcare. The first, *Securing Our Future Health: taking a long term view* explored fundamental questions about models of health and service and the related workforce assumptions. Among the telling observations was the clear need for significant changes in the healthcare workforce, suggesting that:

> It seems likely that there will be major changes in the roles of different groups of workers and considerable scope for the health service to make better use of its most skilled workers. Although the number of healthcare professionals is important for the capacity of the system, arguably the way the workforce is used is even more important [para 11.52].[10]

## PREPARING THE FUTURE WORKFORCE

The government recognised that the initial preparation of future professionals was a key stage in creating a reformed workforce that was appropriately prepared to work in new ways, and specifically in multi-professional team-based approaches.[11] The phrase 'more people working differently', much used in policy documents, emphasised the need not just for change for existing professionals but also for the need to think differently about what health work was and what new and existing roles were needed to undertake it.

The Bristol Inquiry into the deaths of children undergoing cardiac surgery also acted as a major driver for the promotion of more effective team working.

In his final report Professor Sir Ian Kennedy stressed the importance of ensuring that practitioners and managers work together in a culture of mutual respect and understanding of each other's roles, and that they have opportunities to develop such a culture in their initial and continuing education: 'One of the most effective ways to foster an understanding about and respect for various professional roles and the value of multi-professional teams is to expose medical and nursing students, other healthcare professionals and managers to shared education and training.'[12]

## TRANSFORMING PRE-REGISTRATION PROGRAMMES

Historically, the preparation of individuals seeking careers in health and social care professions, as well as health service management training, has been undertaken in silos and yet what the Bristol Inquiry and other studies highlighted was the need in practice for effective multi-professional team working.[13] The Department of Health in its response to the Kennedy Report agreed that there should be 'more opportunities for different healthcare professions to share learning'. The Bristol Inquiry brought into stark relief the challenges and contradictions of training practitioners and managers in silos and then expecting them to work effectively in teams once qualified. A policy commitment had already been made to effective multi-professional team working through a clear emphasis on the principle of learning together in both pre- and post-qualifying professional education. The delivery of this commitment was, however, reliant on engaging the higher education sector, who are responsible for preparing the vast range of health and social care practitioners, and the regulatory bodies and professional associations.

In acknowledging this recommendation from the Bristol Inquiry, the Department of Health committed itself to 'increase and expand interprofessional education, based on key areas of competence' which included mutual understanding and respect for each other's contribution'.[14] This commitment to reform pre-registration education resulted in an open bidding process to fund a number of 'leading edge sites' to take forward common learning.[15]

## THE NEW GENERATION PROJECT

The University of Southampton has a long history of providing innovative pre-registration programmes designed to prepare students for future health and social care roles. It has over 3000 students on a wide range of courses including audiology, medicine, nursing, midwifery, physiotherapy, occupational therapy, podiatry and social work. Since the 1980s the university had been developing small-scale interprofessional initiatives across a range of clusters of professions and practice settings. In response to the shifting policy context described above, in the late 1990s the university at a strategic level made a commitment to capture and build upon the learning from these micro developments in order to make a university-wide macro level change. In so doing the university committed itself at a senior level to expanding and enhancing the interprofessional learning provision for students.

The university was therefore well-placed to take the lead in developing a new generation of undergraduate and post-qualifying and CPD programmes in health and social care. In 1999 the university established an Interprofessional Education Committee which set out a vision of programme design that would fully exploit opportunities for common and shared learning and teaching from entry year to 'internship' and beyond. A critical element of this was cross disciplinary and multi-professional commitment to radical curriculum reform and culture change in order to enhance the delivery of innovative learning approaches. As a result of this long-term vision, the New Generation Project was established in 1999. In 2001 the project expanded and evolved to become a partnership between the University of Southampton, the University of Portsmouth and the former Hampshire and Isle of Wight Workforce Development Confederation. The partnership reaches across the 11 professions, four faculties, two universities and the health, social care and voluntary organisations that supported students learning in practice across Hampshire.

In 2001 a Department of Health undertook a national bidding process to support a small number of leading edge sites to take forward common learning in support of its policy commitment to see 'common learning in all pre-registration programmes by 2004'.[16] As a result of that process in January 2002 the New Generation Project (NGP) was identified as one of the four Department of Health national 'leading edge sites' to reform pre-registration education. The investment enabled the development and delivery of integrated common learning across 11 professional pathways. From October 2003, students were to experience common learning in each year of their programme. This innovation involved significant curriculum revision and culture change. The innovative learning approach involved creating interprofessional small group learning opportunities in university and in practice for the annual cohort of over 1500 students each year. The aim of this was to provide students with opportunities to develop the capability to learn and work in multi-professional teams.

When the NGP started it was seen both within the university and externally as a quantum leap in emphasis away from small-scale micro ventures to addressing the challenges of taking a whole systems approach to integrating interprofessional learning in all pre-registration programmes. A key aim of the NGP was to: 'introduce opportunities for undergraduate students from different health and social care professions to learn together in order to enhance professional collaboration and teamwork skills and so improve the quality of care provided for patients and clients'.[17]

The NGP curriculum reform process placed a clear emphasis on developing multi-professional teamwork and problem solving and encouraged a greater understanding of differing roles and an appreciation of flexibility, while maintaining the integrity of relevant knowledge base acquisition. Based on extensive analysis to inform the curriculum development process it was identified that there were areas where 'students' learning could be enriched by studying the topic in a learning environment where other professional perspectives would be represented and could be appreciated and explored within the learning group'.[18] To date the NGP has resulted in a curriculum that has integrated Inter Professional Learning Units (IPLUs) within programmes that lead to professional qualifications across 11 different professions.

The model of learning which underpins the IPLUs provides students with an opportunity to come together in an interprofessional learning group of 10–12 students, drawn from at least five different professions, with a facilitator. The focus of the IPLUs is on collaborative practice, team working, audit, service development and governance. In essence the learning experiences provided for students reflect many of the areas of development identified for future practitioners that emerged from the Bristol Inquiry and reiterated by more recent inquires into similar critical incidents.[19] It also reflects the Department of Health statement that the integration of common learning is a clear way 'for all health professionals to strengthen team working' (para 15).[20]

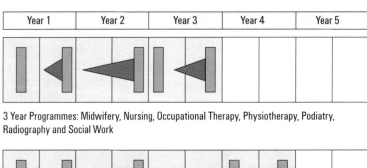

3 Year Programmes: Midwifery, Nursing, Occupational Therapy, Physiotherapy, Podiatry, Radiography and Social Work

4 Year Programmes: Audiology, Medicine (BM4), Pharmacy

5 Year Programmes: Medicine

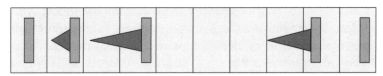

| Key | Profession specific learning | Learning in Common | Inter-professional learning |

**FIGURE 16.1** Common learning: inter-professional learning units

Practice settings often become the 'rate liming' factor in this process of change, providing as they do access to practitioners who exercise a powerful influence as role models upon the socialisation of students.[21] Transforming how students learn in practice has also been a vital part of the NGP. Supporting and developing practitioners who provide practice learning opportunities involved considerable investment in building on and enhancing effective interprofessional team-based learning experiences. For practitioners this has aligned with the overall drive to improve team-based working and service redesign processes including the development of care pathways. It has also served to highlight the vital interdependence between education and service providers in transforming the educational preparation of future practitioners.[22]

While the reform of pre-registration education and the integration of interprofessional learning is at a relatively early stage in terms of becoming 'mainstream', what is apparent is the need for longitudinal studies to investigate the longer term outcomes of these changes in relation to team-based working.[23] As the systemisation of clinical work grows so it will require staff who are able to work effectively together; this in turn must raise questions about how we prepare our future generations of practitioners to work in this way. The NGP is an attempt to transform the preparation of future practitioners for a world of practice in which mutual respect and flexibility will be vital.

## NEW ROLES AND CAPABILITIES

While considerable emphasis has been placed on reforming the preparation of future professional practitioners there remains an equally important need to reform the existing workforce and develop new roles and patterns of care. The workforce changes required to deliver the government's health and social care objectives must stem from a clear understanding and analysis of the 'work'. Initially, much of the transformational work was led by the NHS Modernisation Agency, established in 2001. Its role was to support the NHS and its partner organisations to improve the outcomes and experience for patients by modernising services. In 2005 the agency was superseded by the NHS Institute for Innovation and Improvement. The significant stream of work started by the agency on role redesign logically led to questions about what the work is, how it can be carried out, what skills are required and who can deliver services. The Department of Health was keen to encourage all staff to become involved in reviewing and redesigning roles as part of redesigning care.[24]

The development of intermediate care was identified as a key area of service modernisation within the NHS Plan.[25] As noted earlier, changes in the population profile in the coming 50 years will see a likely increase of almost 300% in the very old – that is those over 85.[26] The very old are heavy users of health and social care services. Therefore, in the face of the likely expansion of health and social care need and its growing complexity, the challenges for health and social care services will be to respond and develop comprehensive, person-centred services that are focused on the needs of people who access services rather than historic patterns of provision. In responding to these demands service providers will by necessity need to develop appropriate workforce models that not only enable the delivery of services but that are also appropriate to local labour market conditions.

While it has been acknowledged that the term 'intermediate care' has no clear agreed definition,[27] in a review of the literature Steiner identified a number of themes that characterise such services: they are seen as 'supportive rather than directive', reflect a model of care more akin to nursing rather than medicine, and care delivery is focused in or near to the patient's home setting. Such services tend to have a core set of features including 'holistic assessment, timely reassessment, flexible input from a multi-professional team and a plan to send the patient home as quickly as possible or to keep the patient out of hospital'.[28]

Intermediate care services vary from setting to setting. A range of service delivery modalities may be involved, including rapid response teams, GP nursing home beds, nurse led units, hospital at home schemes, social service rehabilitation, community hospitals, community care centres and hospital beds. The range and complexity of interrelated services highlights the need to take 'whole systems' approach to the development and provision of such services and development of an appropriate workforce.

The Department of Health was determined to encourage new ways of working in health and social care, in particular to develop new associate and advance practitioner roles including a non-medical consultant role.[29] Indeed this policy also required cross departmental joined up working for its delivery as it was the Department for Education and Skills which enabled universities to offer the award of a Foundation Degree which under the NHS pay reforms is seen as the underpinning education requirement for the new role of an Associate Practitioner in healthcare.[30]

In Hampshire and the Isle of Wight a two-year project to redesign inter-mediate care and create appropriate supportive educational provision brought together the various stakeholders across the area. Underpinning this work was a commitment to multi-professional working and interprofessional learning, encouraging individuals and teams 'to learn with, from and about each other'. Given the varied definitions and manifestations of intermediate care nationally it was essential for this project to provide from the outset a clear definition of intermediate care that was meaningful locally. The following definition was adopted by the project team to relate to adults over the age of 16 and older people with mental health needs: 'A short period (normally no longer than six weeks) of intensive rehabilitation and treatment to enable patients to return home following hospitalisation, or to prevent admission to long term residential care; or intensive care at home to prevent unnecessary hospital admission.'[31]

A key element of the project was to improve patient outcomes by optimising staff interventions and their use of time. There was plenty of anecdotal evidence of well intentioned but fragmented and resource intensive care delivery. In one example a patient discharged to the care of an intermediate care team received 17 visits from various team members in five days, many of which were for single straightforward interventions. When the detail of this example was shared with a wider group of practitioners there was agreement that not only were there significant opportunities for the delivery to be more systemically planned but that the fragmentation of tasks by professions detracted from the ambition to deliver person-centred care.

The scheme adopted is illustrated in Figure 16.2. Its overall aims were as follows.

1  Scoping the nature, demand and provision of intermediate care.
2  Developing an Associate Practitioner role in intermediate care.
3  Designing common learning in intermediate care.
4  Designing a pathway for the future consultant workforce in intermediate care.
5  Evaluation.

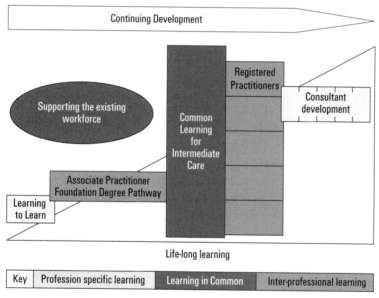

*Source:* HCIU University of Southampton 2005©

**FIGURE 16.2** Intermediate Care Project Scheme

The development process involved bringing together a wide range of staff from different professions and work roles to explore the process of care, how work was undertaken and who actually did it. From these events it quickly became evident that there were areas of learning and skills that were actually or could be shared, or that by being distributed differently could potentially reduce the fragmentation of care. Working with the staff an agreed framework evolved to share specific skills and knowledge between various professions; this led to the development of a single Intermediate Care Course, in effect providing an opportunity for interprofessional learning for the existing staff involved in intermediate care teams (*see* Figure 16.3). The course involved Essential Units and Options, underpinned by a Standard Competency Framework and informed by the Single Assessment Process which was introduced as part of the National Service Framework for Older People.[32]

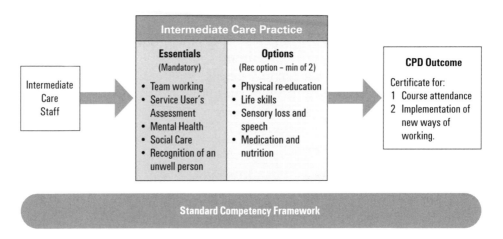

**FIGURE 16.3** Intermediate Care Course

Throughout the development process, Rehabilitation Assistants (RAs) were fully involved, and from this involvement it became evident that with appropriate training there were significant areas of work that could be more appropriately undertaken by them. The project had sought to develop a standard Associate Practitioner role in intermediate care; as a result a specific pathway was created and validated as part of the Foundation Degree in Health and Social Care at the University of Southampton. Partnership working of this nature to create an appropriate curriculum, matched to employer needs, was one of the underpinning principles set out by HEFCE for the development of foundation degrees.[33]

Alongside the educational and process development a research study was undertaken with two Intermediate Care Teams to model the new workforce. The purpose of this study was to look in particular at the work carried out by the two teams in order to examine in detail the types of interventions provided. This study used an operational research design and mathematical modelling to analyse the most effective way to deploy the current staff, project future skill mix, and identify the common skills set required by all staff to optimise contact time with patients. Linked to this the modelling was designed to predict the future workforce requirements for intermediate care teams.

The results are currently being written up but the analysis to date has revealed some telling facts about the reality of care delivery and the workforce implications. The staff that formed the teams were involved in coding the data related to whether they were generic (easier) or specific (harder) interventions. Based on the data drawn from both teams, it emerged that 80% of the time spent by staff carrying out interventions is spent performing generic interventions. Using the existing definition of competences by intervention, a Rehabilitation Assistant could carry out over 60% of the intervention time needed. While the data raises a wide range of questions one immediate reaction could be to see a real terms increase in the number of appropriately trained rehabilitation assistants to deal with the bulk of generic work. It raised also the need to consider that systematisation of clinical work matched to a clear competency framework. Yet at national and local levels workforce planning remains strongly focused on commissioning many of the existing professional roles at a time when, as the two examples cited above illustrate, what is required is a workforce that is flexible, adaptive and innovative.[34]

## CONCLUSION

Throughout this chapter the case studies have been used to demonstrate that systemisation of care calls into question what professions are, what care activities are required, who should undertake them and therefore how individuals should be prepared for health and social care work and careers. Team working is at the heart of the modern health and social care services and higher education providers must make clear how they systematically include opportunities for interprofessional learning and working in both undergraduate and post-qualified levels. If the systemisation of care really does provide an environment in which the needs of patients are uppermost and in which pathways of care are clearly articulated then it will present significant challenges for some of the existing professionals given that for many 'constantly expending energy to keep things the same in the face of change is tremendously wasteful'.[35]

## REFERENCES

1 Degeling P, Maxwell S, Kennedy J, et al. Medicine, management, and modernisation: a 'danse macabre'? BMJ. 2003; **326**: 649–52.
2 Masterson A, Humphris D. New role development: taking a strategic approach. In: Humphris D, Masterson A, eds. Developing New Clinical Roles: a guide for health professionals. London: Churchill Livingstone; 2000. pp. 185–201.
3 Department of Health. The NHS Plan: a plan for investment, a plan for reform. London: Stationery Office. Cm. 4818-I; 2000. Department of Health. Working Together, Learning Together: a framework for lifelong learning for the NHS. London: Department of Health; 2001.

4 Maxwell S, Degeling P, Kennedy J, *et al. Improving Clinical Management: the role of ICP based clinical management systems.* University of Durham; 2005.

5 Department of Health. *Our Health, Our Care, Our Say: a new direction for community services.* Cm. 6737. London: Stationery Office; 2006.

6 Carvel J. Multiple births rise by 20%. *The Guardian.* 18 February 2004.

7 Government Actuary's Department. *Interim Life Tables.* London: Government Actuary's Department; 2006.

8 Dixon S. Implications of population aging for the labour market. *Labour Market Trends.* 2003; **111**(2): 67–76.

9 Department of Health, *The NHS Plan*, op. cit.

10 Wanless D. *Securing Our Future Health: taking a long term view.* London: HM Treasury; 2001.

11 Department of Health, *Working Together*, op. cit.

12 Kennedy IC. *Learning from Bristol: the report of the public inquiry into children's heart surgery at the Bristol Royal Infirmary 1984–1995.* Cm. 5207. London: Department of Health; 2001.

13 Borrill C, Carletta J, Carter A, *et al. The Effectiveness of Health Care Teams in the National Health Service: Report.* Aston University, University of Glasgow, University of Leeds; 2001.

14 Department of Health. *Learning from Bristol: The Department of Health's response to the Report of the Public Inquiry into children's heart surgery at the Bristol Royal Infirmary 1984–1995.* Cm. 5363. London: Department of Health; 2002.

15 Department of Health. *HR in the NHS Plan: more staff working differently.* London: Department of Health; 2002.

16 Department of Health, *Working Together*, op. cit.

17 O'Halloran C, Hean S, Humphris D, *et al.* Developing Common Learning: the New Generation Project undergraduate curriculum model. *J Interprofessional Care.* 2006; **20**(1): 12–28.

18 Ibid.

19 Laming D. *The Victoria Climbié Inquiry: the report of an inquiry by Lord Laming.* Cm. 5730. London: Department of Health; 2003. Smith J. *The Shipman Inquiry Report 5, Safe Guarding Patients: lesson from the past – proposal for the future.* Cm. 6429. London: Department of Health; 2004.

20 Department of Health, *Working Together*, op. cit.

21 Melia K. *Learning & Working: the occupational socialisation of nurses.* London: Tavistock Publications; 1987.

22 Degeling P, Carr A. Leadership for the systematisation of health care: the unaddressed issue in health care reform. *J Health, Organization and Management.* 2004; **18**(6): 399–414.

23 Barr H, Ross F. Mainstreaming interprofessional education in the United Kingdom: a position paper. *J Interprofessional Care.* 2006; **20**(2): 96–104. Humphris D, Hean S. Educating the future workforce: building the evidence about interprofessional learning. *J Health Services Research and Policy.* 2004; **9**(1) Supp: 24–7.

24 Department of Health, *HR in the NHS Plan*, op. cit.

25 Department of Health, *The NHS Plan*, op. cit.

26 The Royal Commission on Long Term Care. *With Respect to Old Age: long term care – rights and responsibilities.* Cm. 41292-I. London: The Stationery Office; 1999.

27 MacMahon D. Intermediate care: a challenge to the specialty of geriatric medicine or its renaissance? *Age and Ageing.* 2001; **30**(Supp 3): 19–23.

28 Steiner A. Intermediate care: a good thing? *Age and Ageing.* 2001; **30**(Supp 3): 33–9 (quotations from p. 33).

29 Workforce Development Confederations' Standing Conference. *A proposal to Develop a National Framework for Assistant Practitioners and Advanced Practitioners: draft report.* WDC Standing Conference, Manchester; 2003.

30 Higher Education Funding Council. *Foundation Degrees: report on funded projects.* Bristol: HEFCE; 2001.

31 Department of Health. *National Service Framework for Older People.* London: Department of Health; 2001.

32 Ibid.

33 Higher Education Funding Council, op. cit.

34 Masterson, Humphris, op. cit.

35 Ibid.

# CHAPTER 17

# Systematisation of clinical care and health capital planning

*Barrie Dowdeswell and Jonathan Erskine*

Despite the continuous renewal of hospital buildings, revitalised in the UK almost beyond recognition by the Private Finance Initiative (PFI), hospitals remain in the main utterly familiar and resonant of the past. The traditional Nightingale ward still exists in principle, but varies somewhat in design according to the fashion style of the moment. Departmental demarcation still defines clinical territories and administrative and support services are rehoused regularly on an opportunistic basis. Even where there is opportunity for new design (e.g. green field sites) there is little evidence of any break with the past or recognition of the more profound changes that are reshaping healthcare.

In the 19th century, hospitals were a place to warehouse the sick and the dying. In the 21st century, they have become warehouses for technology, where patients attend (for the briefest possible time) as part of a regime of treatment that begins before admission and extends beyond it. Hospitals are now just part of a whole systems continuum of care. Yet an apparent lack of awareness of this concept change is evident in not only the healthcare planning processes but also in capital procurement and financing models. The latter may be good for bringing in large scale capital projects (some might say monoliths) on time and on budget, but they are not so effective at sustaining life cycle economic effectiveness.

What is needed is a more efficient interface, one that closely aligns capital investment with both the principles of integrated care and the rapidity of change in clinical modalities. In this context, as we shall see in this chapter, the systematisation of clinical work helps to relate clinical practice to planning the capital stock.

## CAPITAL PLANNING AND SERVICE PROVISION

Common sense suggests that in a national health service hospitals would be built to deliver the care that is needed in a place and a form suitable for the services to be provided. But we rarely start with a clean sheet: hospitals are located where someone once chose to establish them, and their buildings, accumulated over time, reflect the understandings of appropriate medical care at the time of their construction. Even in the PFI era the green field site options are invariably shaped to mirror the predecessor buildings; the justification for relocation is often voiced as lower capital cost rather than clinical appropriateness. Needs and services change, but buildings are long-lived and often difficult to modify to accommodate new requirements. Hospitals of the Victorian era still function tolerably well; modern hospitals have an expected lifespan of 30 to 40 years. Writing off these investments is difficult enough in economic terms, leaving aside the social dimensions.

Hospitals are locations for professionals to collaborate in delivering professional practice that evolves with medical practice. New clinical thinking and competencies are a driving force for change, as are shifts in broad social understandings about health and healthcare. For example, before 1900 babies were generally not born in hospital; expectant mothers were reluctant to take their place with the sick and dying. The 20th century saw 'the medicalisation of childbirth', as doctors asserted their special skill at controlling childbirth risks, maternity wards and delivery rooms were added to hospitals. But by the close of the century, many women demanded greater control over the birth process, less medical intervention and more involvement of those close to them, leading to the creation of 'birthing centres' associated with hospitals but separate from ward structures. Changes in the social construction of medical care call for changes in the physical 'plant' in which it is provided.

Yet history continues to show just how difficult it has been to make these changes. One reason for this is that professionals are attached to their routines and autonomy, and resist attempts to impose changes to their mode of operation – what, how or where they do it. Another is that a hospital is not simply a facility for delivering medical care: it is an icon, a symbolic affirmation of community achievement and government commitment, and it will be vigorously defended by community leaders and politicians as a demonstration of the value invested by government in a local community's healthcare. So capital planning becomes a struggle to overcome the widening gulf between rapid changes in clinical technologies, public expectations, political ideology and economic outlook on one hand, and, on the other, the way that conventional planning and procurement of hospitals and health infrastructure, and the buildings themselves, lock us into existing patterns of practice.

Capital planners, however, are aware of the need for flexibility of thinking:

> We no longer build buildings like we used to, nor do we pay for them in the same way. Buildings today are . . . life support systems, communication terminals, data manufacturing centers, and much more. They are incredibly expensive tools that must be constantly adjusted to function efficiently. The economics of a building has become as complex as its design.[1]

But they are rarely 'plugged in' to the planning of the service that is to be accommodated – the delivery of medical care. And, in any case, service planning is segmented, with facilities being organised around the diversity of professionals who are engaged in delivering care, with the patient moving (as it were) from one waiting room to the next.

The moves for the systematisation of care change the focus from the individual points of care delivery to the total process of treatment – from the stations along the way to the patient's entire journey. Focusing on this journey not only facilitates the integration of the various elements of treatment, it also creates a zone of common understanding where clinical staff and facility planners can understand one another.

## CAPITAL PLANNING IN THE UK

The disjunction between population service needs and the nature, location and design of healthcare facilities has long been recognised. It has informed a series of policy frames and guidelines to ensure the appropriate and effective application of capital investment in healthcare facilities.[2,3] But, have these guidelines proved effective?

If in generic terms the purpose of healthcare planning is to provide services to meet the current and future health needs of a given population, then hospital capital planning guidelines have said much the right thing:

> The *Capital Investment Manual* seeks to reflect and reinforce the important changes that have taken place over recent years . . . with the changing patterns of health care delivery. In doing so, it aims to ensure that local expectations of health care provision are not raised beyond what is realistic within the context of the service as a whole and to bring the demand for NHS capital more into equilibrium with its supply. The new process is intended to reduce unnecessary and often expensive planning work which subsequently proves to be abortive.[2]

And:

> Planning in the past has been done annually and constrained by time pressures and the requirement for multiple plans. For the first time ever health services are now able to plan over a three-year period with, later this autumn, local health services receiving three-year budgets. Following the completion of the Local Government Finance Review, councils will have some confidence about the distribution of resources available over the next three years, including for social services. This will allow organisations to look in depth at their services, plan change with confidence and implement improvements year on year.[3]

Thus the underlying tone and theme of this guidance is straightforward: match facilities to population need but within affordable resources and (implicitly) ensure a greater degree of intersectoral collaboration and resource sharing.

However, current debate about the ability of new hospitals to support changes in clinical technologies and models of care, and to respond to the implications of consumer demand (the patient choice agenda), suggests that there have been problems down the line.

The difficulties can be demonstrated by contrasting just two of the dimensions that shape investment policy: demographic analysis and the management dimension. Population demographic profiles are usually well defined and robust, but less clear and reliable are the formulae adopted to convert these profiles into a capital planning language. The traditional currency has been bed numbers, with the conversion achieved by the outcome of expressed population demand (hospital attendances) × performance efficiency factor (bed utilisation rates). This proved adequate during periods when the hospital system was in a comparatively steady state of linear progression, that is, most of the 1970s, 1980s and to some extent the early 1990s. Periodically, and lately more frequently, leverage was applied to improve operational efficiency, measures driven almost wholly by fiscal necessity and often emerging as a targeted reduction in the ratios of beds per planning population. This reflected the priority given to cutting off supply side cost drivers rather than tackle demand side factors. Although there may have been underlying justification in the trend towards fewer beds (e.g. the impact of day case surgery) there is still no satisfactory way of correlating bed needs to treatment practices rather than population.

In addressing the management dimension the picture is distinctly different. In the context of capital asset provision, the manager serves and is accountable to three constituencies: the Department of Health as the ultimate service pay-master, the internal (hospital) professional groupings, and the local population. This brings into play the issue of tactical budgeting and performance targeting as a feature of capital bidding and planning. The goal is to get the project onto the books. While estimates are in good faith, they are tuned to meet political realities, and thus constitute what the Treasury calls optimism bias. For the government, clinician and local community, what counts is assured delivery of a new hospital. However, the process involves the normalisation of deviance, where project cost and time overruns are anticipated (and in the main accepted), and performance targets marginalised in subsequent capital evaluation. This was turned to good effect by the incoming Labour Government in justifying the Private Finance Initiative, one of the key selling points being the transfer of risk of cost and time overrun to the private sector.

## A LACK OF COMMON LANGUAGE

What is lacking in all this is a common language that unifies the various players and brings into play the clinicians as the interface between responses to the demographics of healthcare need and the impact of management realities. It is the clinician who drives cost, delivers performance and achieves quality.

The conventional measures that determine capital provision seem to relate directly not to clinical processes, but to proxies such as bed numbers. Over time, historical performance assessment has prompted safe parameters of provision, specialty to specialty, but there remain wide variations in individual performance standards. The lack of any clearly defined relationship between clinical process and effective capital resource utilisation has proved the underlying reason why capital planning has usually degenerated into a process of bed transaction.

Within healthcare organisations, the language of facility planning is different for each grouping. For clinicians, effectiveness tends to be defined in terms of the fit between the facility and personal clinical practice. Planners recognise this in the endless discussions about 'room adjacencies' when negotiating architectural design concepts. Nurses, on the other hand, tend towards supporting systemisation,[4] hence the greater acceptance of national standards for ward bed configurations, but even here there are abrupt changes in design fashion, not always with any evidence-based foundation, and often in the primary interest of saving labour costs rather than quality of care and outcome.

Healthcare strategists, both those embedded within government and those who act as independent policy advisors, are in the main impatient for new thinking and change. The recent tendency to look outwards to the private sector to stimulate innovation is indicative of this, notwithstanding that given the right support and freedoms the public sector can arguably do equally as well.

Those concerned with setting and monitoring performance targets, however, seem the more influential short term drivers of the business focus of recent capital investment. All targets are leveraged through the ultimate sanction of Her Majesty's Treasury's financing models conditioned by guarantees to meet short term performance measures. In the latter equity of geographic access has tended to be overlooked in favour of equity of speed of access: witness the waiting time directives as a perfectly natural artefact of the government's need to deliver on its manifesto pledges. Thus we tend to see the hierarchy of criteria for new capital projects dominated by those that have short and effective delivery time scales, preferably coincidental with the electoral lifespan. At the other end of the scale are capital planning strategies that hardly register on the radar for healthcare, such as designing flexibility for long range life cycle changes in the functionality of buildings.

All of the above are in play in the capital planning world. Ultimately, they interact in a manner that recent authoritative reports suggest[5] may inhibit rather than support the translation of new service concepts into capital solutions relevant to progressive healthcare: the organisation of clinical work and the development of new models of care to improve health outcomes. The bottom line is this: the rapidity of change in service dynamics is outstripping and overwhelming the capacity of the current capital models and systems to respond adequately.

## UK CAPITAL INNOVATIONS: THE PRIVATE FINANCE INITIATIVE AND PPP TREATMENT CENTRES

The application of the Private Finance Initiative (PFI) reflects the above analysis. After the cost saving pressures of the 1980s and early 1990s left government capital stock severely run down, the PFI was introduced to regenerate it. PFI is a means of financing public service capital without recourse to creating public debt. It utilises a long-term leasing arrangement to engage the private sector in funding, designing and operating capital projects, with innovation, risk transfer (to the private sector) and sustainable quality (better maintenance standards) implicit in the deal. The government attracts a private firm or more usually a consortium by guaranteeing payment from the public purse, over a 25 to 30 year period, in return for the construction and maintenance of the asset.

If for the NHS the PFI has funded the largest hospital rebuilding plan in Europe, critics have argued that borrowing costs are higher than they would be if financed from government coffers and that the process itself is expensive. Some PFI hospitals have been accused of reducing beds in order to meet increased costs, and even the location of some new hospitals has been said to favour private sector profit. However, despite its many acknowledged shortcomings, PFI is not the root problem. It has simply amplified a deeper failing: the absence of evidence-based strategic planning that links the nature of the healthcare service to the capital investment made to accommodate it.

A more brutal interpretation suggests that long range strategic planning is too difficult given the unpredictable nature of healthcare, and the PFI has provided a timely escape pod. However, other businesses make successful multi-billion pound investments in markets where customer choice is fickle and loyalty has to be earned, and, once built, the infrastructure is fairly static. What has been missing in healthcare is the establishment of capital planning systems, grounded in evidence, that apply strategies to manage the continuous change processes demonstrated by that evidence. Instead, the preoccupation has been PFI process itself.

The more recently introduced public-private-partnership treatment centres may be a tacit acknowledgement of the failure to link clinical process with capital planning. The centres were hailed as a means of achieving two objectives:

▶ creating additional capacity, in an accelerated time scale, to help reduce waiting times for high priority elective surgery, such as cataracts and hip replacements, and

▶ demonstrating innovative working practices to stimulate similar improvement in the public hospital sector.

However, the UK House of Commons Health Select Committee reported that the PPP centres were both largely unnecessary, as public hospitals could have delivered the capacity, and could encourage bed closures and instability in public hospitals by undertaking work that might otherwise have gone to them.[6]

This conclusion overlooks both the intended lessons and the lack of evaluation. The defining anticipated innovation, widely proclaimed but not acknowledged in the report, was the supposed adoption of care pathway service design and in turn its provision of a template for design, build and financing systems. Yet, there has been little evaluation of these relationships between the systemisation of care and capital design.

## EUROPEAN INNOVATIONS
### Rhon Klinikum, Germany

Are matters dealt with differently elsewhere? The German model of healthcare is based on the 'Bismark' insurance fund system. While citizen contributions lie outwith the government taxation system, the hospitals in the main remain in state (regional) ownership, their licence to operate requires them to meet all referral needs, and financing is tariff based through insurance fund contracts. A recent, and growing, characteristic of the hospital sector is the establishment of public-private partnerships (PPP) to provide a vehicle for states to transfer (sell) hospitals into private ownership. A major and rapidly expanding player is Rhon Klinikum, a private healthcare operator specialising in PPPs and with a telling business strategy based on the fundamentally important connections between the systemisation of clinical care, work process control, capitalisation, and quality of clinical outcome.

The company has dispensed with conventional demarcations between departments and their budgets in favour of a multidisciplinary structure based on care pathway organisation of work. The patient progresses through the hospital according to the planned and predicted treatment and care model. This provides the anchor point for:

- hospital design that maximises the effectiveness of the workforce within the multidisciplinary care pathway
- investment decisions (capital and technology) that are aimed at optimising the effectiveness of the pathway
- workforce integration
- work process control, including of costs
- disease-related group pricing and budgeting, and
- quality assurance.

Investment decisions are in essence based on a cost-benefit analysis that measures return on investment, as a balance between quality and cost of outcomes, sustainable future capital investment, shareholder return and commissioner value.

Three criteria drive this model: (1) an application of the principle of systemisation of care, (2) a workforce committed to this framework, and adjusted to the reality of continuous change, and (3) a capital investment strategy aimed at keeping pace with technological change, workforce competence and rising expectation of patients and workforce. Gone is the notion of moving from fixed point to fixed point in its capital planning; it is much more a process of continuous improvement. The impact on service cost is revealing, as shown below. The higher rate of capitalisation is identified by Rhon Klinikum as a factor in developing systemised care programmes to enhance service effectiveness. Capital and service investment synergy is judged by the company to contribute to a 13% cost advantage over corresponding public hospitals.

**TABLE 17.1** The impact of the Rhon Klinikum model on project costs

| Average hospital cost per case | Service cost € | Capital cost € | Total cost € | Capital as % of total cost |
|---|---|---|---|---|
| Public hospital | 3600 | 270 | 3870 | 7% |
| Rhon Klinikum | 2660 | 720 | 3380 | 21% |

There are also two criteria that do not receive quite such high profile coverage. Patients within this progressive care model are mobile within the hospital system: they move through a gradation of levels, each with a scaled intensity of workforce and technological support. Stays in different levels can be short (often hours rather than days) according to patient needs. This is at variance with the more popular notion of patient stability within the hospital.

The company is explicit in its understanding of hospital cultures. One of its primary criteria in assessing whether to buy the licence to operate (it reserves the right to reorganise and restructure the hospital as it thinks appropriate) is the attitude of the workforce. A demonstrable commitment to the company principle of care pathway systemisation and work process control is a prerequisite of purchase: no commitment, no deal. All staff working for Rhon Klinikum are rewarded personally for their ownership of the principle: all workers become shareholders in the hospital and each hospital within the organisation is a stand alone profit centre in its own right.

## Coxa Hospital, Finland

The Coxa Hospital (Tampere, Finland) has also followed similar principles. The hospital provides a specialist joint replacement service, borne out of a desire by clinicians working in this field at Tampere Hospital to improve clinical effectiveness. State (treasury) capital was not readily available to finance new development, so a PPP was established (in the form of a partnership owned, limited company) to provide finance for a new independent hospital (located in the grounds of the parent hospital), create greater flexibility for project design and generate greater flexibility for sustainable capitalisation.

As above, the change capacity of new investment was used to stimulate and define new treatment models: care pathways allied to work process control.

In turn, these informed the design concepts of the new hospital and future capital investment policy. But the pathway model has been extended outside the hospital to interlink the community services and other hospitals in the whole systems care of patients from diagnosis to rehabilitation.

The results have been impressive. Follow-up data indicates that the rate of infection following surgical procedures has fallen dramatically: the percentage of patients acquiring an infection is only 0.3% (1% would be considered good). Also the number of patients requiring renewed surgery has also decreased and Coxa even gives its patients a 10-year guarantee: if a renewed operation is needed during this time the patient gets it at a 50% reduction in price. Moreover, the surgeons now operate on more patients per day, thereby improving effectiveness and efficiency, preparing the operating theatre for a patient now takes only 19 minutes instead of 90 and reported levels of staff satisfaction have also increased.

## Common factors

There are some strikingly similar common factors in the German and Finnish case studies, including the:

- design of hospitals and facilities around the core processes of the hospital
- effective description of core processes through the definition and adoption of clinical pathways
- systemisation of care (pathways) to reduce the complexity of this approach without compromising clinical freedoms while improving quality and productivity
- application of business practices that focus on the life cycle economy of the capital investment.

The business-related element is important here. What seems evident in conventional planning models is the lack of measurable connectivity between the three classic dimensions of hospital service organisation and business structuring. Figure 17.1 represents the principal business drivers and the way they work together.

1 Integrated capital and revenue profiling: capital is no longer a sunk cost to be depreciated, or debt to be written down but represents an ongoing revenue cost to the hospital, and makes a measurable (revenue contribution) to facilitating the service.

2 Work process systemisation converts the full spectrum of clinical and care practices into definable and measurable form in a language that can be understood by planners.

3 Adaptable Design Strategies to provide flexibility to meet changing needs (e.g. clinical technologies, policy shifts, citizen values and safety standards) and meet several different categories of risk triggers that may render conventional, inflexible designs at best restrictive of clinical progress and at worst obsolete.

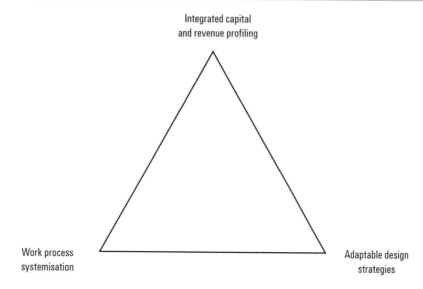

**FIGURE 17.1** Integrating capital planning, work process systematisation, and adaptable design

What the case studies demonstrate (and it is the acid test of true business practice) is the need and the ability to *measure*, and thus place a 'business' value on the relationships between the three core elements, that is:

▶ how various levels and type of capital investment (including a premium for design adaptability) can improve clinical effectiveness
▶ how the improvement in clinical effectiveness can play through to price competitiveness or cost efficiency
▶ how service contract volatility affects the life cycle economy of the hospital, i.e. the ability to meet debt repayment or sustain dynamic future capitalisation strategies.

It could be argued that these hospitals have successfully integrated business and clinical practice: there is a demonstrably high level of mutual confidence (and professional reliance) between the clinicians and managers that reinforces the synergies between capital and service strategy in a manner that transcends sectional interests. It is doubtful this could have been achieved without the bedrock of systemised care processes.

## LESSONS FOR CAPITAL PLANNING

In summary, capital planning for the UK's healthcare infrastructure has historically focused on beds and buildings and largely ignored the links between the processes by which patients are treated and the available models of capital investment. The reasons for this disjunction stem from a number of different forces. Patterns of ingrained professional practice, both clinical and administrative, have tended to encourage repetition of the same service structures, and hence a tendency to (re)construct the old within the new. The iconic status of hospitals within the NHS, exploited by politicians, and publicly embedded as an expectation that every 'local' hospital should provide the full spectrum of acute care, only adds to pressures to maintain the familiar. Where new capital investment models (such as PFI) have been introduced, they have had some limited success in improving the standard of existing hospital stock, but they have introduced their own inflexibilities in terms of contract conditions and repayment commitments. Broadly speaking, the result has been that newly constructed or rebuilt hospitals do not as yet embrace the possibilities inherent in emerging notions of systematised healthcare, and remain strongly resonant of the past.

Contrast this with the European cases which demonstrate an effective correlation between service and capital planning and investment. The critical success factors here seem be the stimulus of competition, evidence-based measurement, and analysis of benefit. (By way of contrast, in the current PFI dominated marketplace in England, the competitive elements are separate, as are the measurements of value.) In the European models the successful organisations are those that regard capital investment, and its life cycle economic profile, as an implicit part of the design and cost structuring of the service model. The glue that binds service and capital in these models is systemised care processes.

European evidence suggests that the closer integration of service and capital planning is widely under way. Three of the highest profile initiatives are as follows.

▸ The whole systems approach to integrated local health economy planning in locales as diverse as Northern Ireland, Skane Region in Sweden and Tuscany, Italy; in each case structural planning has profoundly reshaped the former hospital structures through changes in role delineation or intrinsic change of function.
▸ The 'quality at entry' principles developed by the Norwegian Government which places greater emphasis on the conceptual and qualitative dimensions of capital investment in supporting core business objectives as a preliminary step in the business planning system.
▸ Moving from the current emphasis on life cycle costing for capital projects (which shifts focus towards technical cost efficiency) to life cycle economy strategies (which place emphasis on whole life, whole systems cost effectiveness) as seen in a Netherlands healthcare related project.

Underlying all these models are the principles of transparency and integration: all the activity is seen as part of a single process, the patient journey, and the facilities to be provided are those which best facilitate this journey. Seeing the work of the hospital in this light generates a common language in which clinicians, patients and their representatives, managers, facility planners, architects and others can communicate with one another and understand each other's contribution to the care process. An integrated clinical pathway is not only a tool for clinicians, it is a vehicle for making efficient clinical work the basis for capital investment and business planning.

## REFERENCES

1 Reugg R, Marshall H. *Building Economics: theory and practice*. New York: Van Nostrand Reinhold; 1990.
2 Department of Health. *Capital Investment Manual*. London: Department of Health; 1994.
3 Department of Health. *Improvement, Expansion & Reform: the next three years*. London: Department of Health; 2002.
4 Degeling P, Maxwell S, Kennedy J, *et al.* Medicine, management, and modernisation: a 'danse macabre'? *BMJ*. 2003; **326**: 649–52.
5 Future Health Care Network. *NHS hospitals call for PFI process to be updated*. Press Release 422. London: NHS Confederation; 2005.
6 House of Commons Health Select Committee. *The Role of the Private Sector in the NHS*. London: Stationery Office; 2002, HC 308-I.

# CHAPTER 18

# Systematisation of clinical care and the structuring of public authority

*Hal Colebatch*

The systematisation of healthcare emerged from a recognition that the quality of care has something to do with how it is organised, and with how organisational questions are addressed in a policy context. Care is specialised in order to achieve the highest levels of skill, but this produces discontinuities of care. Because there are many different specialised medical workers involved in the delivery of healthcare, and the treatment of any given patient involves bringing a number of these specialists to bear in a particular sequence, the organisational logic of specialisation and autonomy conflicts with the logic of patient focus and integration. But for the healthcare manager, this specific question of discontinuity of care is located in broader problems:

- costs of care are rising, largely owing to an ageing population, escalating technology and rises in the price of skilled labour
- increases in expenditure are not accompanied by commensurate increases in the level of health (however defined)
- increased specialisation of medical care and the interdependence of specialisations makes the management of care complex
- quality of care varies in treatments, hospital-acquired infections, and errors
- patient and public expectations are rising with waiting times for treatments an iconic indicator of service quality, and
- structures for managing the provision of care seem to be inadequate.

Policy attention has therefore focused on how care can be reorganised to deliver better care, contain the rise in costs, and restore public confidence. Reforms have concentrated on structure, including organisational forms and payment systems. They have been seen as exercises in organisational change, although few have asked if that is appropriate to the diversity of institutions and practices through which care is delivered. Healthcare is not delivered by a single organisation, and its delivery is found in the way that workers exercise their skills and how these are related to those of other workers. The appropriate focus is not 'the organisation', but 'organising'.[1]

## INTEGRATION AS A PROBLEM IN THE MANAGEMENT OF HEALTHCARE

Attention to the organisational dimension of healthcare in the UK, whether of political leaders, policy workers or healthcare managers, has tended to be large scale, and expressed as changes to organisation charts, such as how to locate clinicians in relation to managers. The object of attention is the National Health Service, which is a very diffuse form of organisation. At its establishment, it was primarily oriented to hospital care. General practitioners, who provided the bulk of medical care, were not employees of the NHS, but independent contractors, and both they and consultants retained the right to private practice outside the NHS.

The organisational structure of hospitals tended to be built around specialised practice, and the management function in hospitals was divided between a non-medical person (often called 'administrator' or 'secretary' rather than 'manager'), a medical director, and the leaders of the specialties, perhaps the strongest organisational formations within healthcare. Health workers were recruited, trained and employed by specialty: as anaesthetists, for instance, or intensive-care nurses or physiotherapists. The specialties had their own organisations, the most prestigious being the Royal Colleges which controlled the medical specialists.

This made for a weak pattern of management, focused on keeping the peace among the different providers of specialised care. A succession of reforms sought to strengthen central management and overcome the 'Balkanisation' of medical care. There were three main themes: hierarchy, competition and standards.

Hierarchy was the dominant theme in the early years. It was felt that 'no one was in charge' of the hospitals, and that a strong hand was needed to impose order on the rival clans of specialist care.[1] Job titles were changed, duty statements revised and organisational charts redrawn. There was an early belief in 'generic' management; that is, that healthcare managers did not need to have a background in the field but would apply the managerial skills learned in other fields of practice. This particular belief was later overtaken by a counter-view that the need was not to impose a manager on the specialist health workers, but to involve the latter in management by appointing managers from among the health workers initially from doctors, followed by nursing and the allied health professions.

In the late 1980s, attention swung to competition as the driver of healthcare reform. The Thatcher Government espoused a general faith in market forces, saw the organisational problems of the NHS as the pathologies of an over-large state bureaucracy, and sought to restructure it so that market competition would bring about the desired improvements in quality and cost. As in many areas of government at this time, the purchaser-provider split was seen as a technology for quality assurance and efficiency. Service agencies would determine what service was needed, and would then contract with another organisation to provide it, and the terms of the contract would include the standards of service quality, the mechanisms for enforcing them and the price to be paid. The NHS was to become a quasi-market, a web of contractual relationships between health managers and care providers. Since patients might know little about the sort of service they need or the relative quality of competing providers, it was thought that GPs would become their agents (fundholders), buying the services they needed from the most cost-effective provider. Health managers would not run hospitals, but would buy services from them on specified terms. So hospitals providing high-quality services would flourish and those with low standards would languish, and would be compelled to improve their standards or go out of business.

This meant determining what the appropriate standards might be, and how well particular care providers met them. This third focus for management-driven improvement was a major concern of the centre: to collect data, define standards, and evaluate service providers' compliance with them. Central agencies were established to determine performance measures (often in consultation with stakeholders), monitor performance, and disseminate their findings. By 2006, the government required health authorities to give patients due for elective surgery a choice of four hospitals, and a number of measures of hospital performance (such as waiting times and infection rates) were placed on the world wide web to enable patients to make an informed choice.

These three themes – hierarchy, competition and standards – overlapped, and none of them was entirely absent from the rhetoric of government at any point, though there were different stresses at different times. But they reflected a common theme of the need to strengthen control over the diversity of practice that made up healthcare, and a shared assumption that this was to be done top down; that is by the imposition of tighter control from above through structural change. It was assumed that organisation determines process.

Although much attention which was given to performance-oriented reform (with a massive increase in spending), the issue did not disappear as a policy concern. Reform initiatives impacted upon one another: moves towards market competition, or the creation of specialist bodies for standards, both cut across existing patterns of control.[2] Moves to decentralise decision making did not reduce the perception that the centre was (or ought to be) in control. And the constant drive to manifest concern by making changes meant that changes that had been made were always in danger of being superseded by the next wave of reform, and that reform fatigue, attended by weary cynicism, would set in.

## ORGANISING KNOWLEDGE IN HEALTHCARE

If we focus our attention on how healthcare is delivered rather than the healthcare system, the organisation of healthcare looks rather different. Rather than a systematic whole, we see many hands involved in care, with the relationships between them constructed by social practice rather than defined by constitutional formulations. Healthcare cannot be understood as a single organism, to be shaped at will by persons in positions of authority. Rather, there is a variety of organisational relationships; hierarchical authority is not conclusive and attention needs to be given to how organisation is constructed and maintained; that is, to governance and to its specific application in relations to hospitals, clinical governance.

Healthcare involves more than a diversity of professionals, and consists of much more than clinical interventions in hospitals and surgeries. It can be argued that most healthcare is provided by self and family, and that clinical intervention plays a relatively small part. Certainly, many of the determinants of health, such as diet, smoking and employment, are largely outside the reach of clinical practice. As we shall see in our discussion of the care of long-term conditions, the way in which both informal care and the practice of the person under care are woven into the regime of therapy is a critical question in the governing of care.

The traditional Anglo-Saxon model of healthcare, however, has been based on clinical intervention by an individual skilled artisan – the doctor. With the physicians and surgeons having achieved positions of dominance, all other forms of healthcare having been subordinated to them (e.g. midwifery) or excluded from clinical practice (e.g. herbal medicine). The medical practitioner is seen as an autonomous expert, directly accountable to the patient and indirectly to the collectivity of practitioners, the profession. The assertion of professional status is a claim to the right to make individual judgements about appropriate clinical practice, subject to such modes of peer review, formal or informal, as may have been established. Primary care is the responsibility of an individual doctor, who may choose to also use subordinate health workers like nurses, audiometrists or physiotherapists.

By extension of this model of primary care, the hospital has emerged as the site for advanced care. It is the location where medical specialists can practise their art, and where subordinate staff, such as nurses, technicians and the 'hotel staff' (e.g. cooks, cleaners and porters) are employed to facilitate the work of the specialists. The organisational chart of the hospital is largely built around these specialist forms of work, modified slightly by the recognition of particular conditions around which a clinical team has been developed (e.g. a hand clinic). As more specialised forms of practice are developed, each has something distinct to contribute to the treatment of each patient, who is passed between specialised caregivers in ways which make sense to them. The hospital is not so much an organisation with purposes and practices of its own as a location where rival tribes (the specialist therapists) interact, with the patient as a site for specialised practice.[3]

So the nature of the care administered to a patient is not determined by the hospital as such, but emerges from the interaction of different groups of caregivers. It is structured not by hierarchy and reference to the putative goals of the hospital, but by the perceptions held by these specialists of what constitutes good practice. The hospital is governed by negotiated order.[4] Changing the way in which these practitioners provide their specialised care is a restructuring of this order, involving changes in the dominant structures of meaning, and this calls for attention to the ways in which meaning is generated and sustained, such as to the organisational forms, career trajectories, budgetary practices, even the architecture, in which clinical practice is carried out.

Thus systematisation may be seen as an interrogation and articulation of meaning and a vehicle for renegotiating organisational practice: what do different sorts of clinical specialist regard as good practice in particular conditions? What do they expect to do themselves? What do they expect other clinical workers to do? How long should each part of the process take? By taking part in this sort of discussion, clinical workers could see their work as the collective production of a known outcome (the product), such as a hip replacement, rather than simply as the performance of a particular specialised skill. And it is the outcome for the patient, rather than their own part in it, which becomes the focus of attention.

## PATHWAYS AND PROFESSION

The systematisation agenda can be seen as a threat to professional autonomy. Healthcare is delivered through a wide range of specialised occupations, each of which claims a distinct expertise and the right to judge how it can be appropriately brought to bear in a particular case: this is professional judgement. What is good practice at any point is a matter for autonomous judgement by the specialist, subject to the collective wisdom of fellow-specialists. Moves to standardise practice can be seen as a challenge to the expert judgement of the specialists, and appeals for teamwork as a threat to professional autonomy, an attempt to establish bureaucratic control over specialist expertise.

Systematising reformers, especially those developing integrated care pathways (ICPs), sought to head off this potential response by stressing that the development of a pathway was built on the expression of professional expertise; that is, what members of any given specialty do (and what would they expect others to do). In the locations which were constituted for members of clinical teams to define (for instance) 'how we do a hip replacement', the judgement of any specialist is not being challenged, but is being articulated and recorded as a guide to practice, to inform other members of the team and the person being treated. Making these statements might be quite challenging for team members who have not previously been asked to define their practice, but the request did not contest their autonomy. Rather, it redefined the collectivity: the 'we' in 'this is the way we do it'. While clinical specialisations have traditionally defined themselves in terms of their specialised knowledge, that knowledge can only be brought to bear in a team made up of a number of different specialists. Clinicians are accustomed to being accountable to their peers, but with ICPs, the peers are the fellow members of the multidisciplinary team rather than other members of the discipline in other locations.

But the moves to define ICPs were, in most cases, not seeking to standardise behaviour which had previously been random, but to make the standardisation of practice explicit and shared. In one area where a systematic attempt to introduce ICPs was made, analysis showed that of more than 500 Health Resource Groups (HRGs) 30 accounted for 45% of all emergency episodes and 39% of all emergency bed days.[5] Attention was therefore focused on high volume procedures in which the practice of clinicians was likely to be already, to a considerable degree, standardised. What is distinctive about ICPs is, first, that the clinicians articulate their standard practice so that it is known by other clinicians, and by the patients, and, second, that the model which integrates these specialised standard practices becomes the basis for organising the flow of work. The path of each patient is reviewed, and variations from the model pathway are scrutinised and analysed. Clinicians are not bound by the ICP, but they know that when they depart from it, they will be expected to explain their judgement to their professional colleagues.

The introduction of ICPs also signals a significant change in the nature of professional accountability. The traditional individual clinical professional was seen as being responsible for the skilful performance of a specialist function. But how was accountability provided for the way in which these different specialised forms of care were combined in a particular case, and for the outcome for the patient? With ICPs, good clinical care is defined in terms of the outcome for the patient, and the lines of accountability run from individual clinicians to the team, and from the team to the institution and the patient. Professional autonomy and accountability has been redefined in a way which reflects the multidisciplinary nature of care.

What we see here is a reconstitution of the nature of professional work. Concepts of professional autonomy in medicine originated in a perception of care as an individual relationship between the clinician and the patient and, more indirectly, between the clinician and the collective of fellow-specialists. As care moved into hospitals, the forms of this individualised relationship were maintained, with specific identification with patients (the name at the foot of the bed) and the maintenance of boundaries between professional specialisations. As Giddens points out, what we see as organisational structure is in fact a process of structuring, in which structure informs practice, and practice recreates structure.[6] But structure does not control practice, and actors can re-interpret their situation, and act in ways which amend structure. As clinicians came to see themselves (and were seen by patients and by managers) as members of a team rather than as solo players, they adopted different modes of practice, so that the structure of professional work came to look rather different.

The transformation of clinical practice involves organisational change as the pathways are codified and new management structures and practices emerge to hold practice to the pathways. But the process does not begin with the creation of new organisational forms; these develop in interplay with the changes in perceptions and practice. ICPs, and other forms of systematised care, can be seen as the expression of autonomous professional judgement within context of accountability *to* other clinical workers and *for* the outcome for the patient.

## ICPS AS POLICY CHANGE

It may be argued that the moves to introduce ICPs cannot be considered health policy; that is, something made by the government, expressed as a decision, and usually regulated, resourced and even provided by government. But policy is more than this narrow understanding.[7] Firstly, it can be seen as *authoritative choice*, with the process of government seen as a series of strategic choices by the authorities ('anything the government chooses to do or not to do'[8]) preferably aimed at a specific and known outcome. Health policy, in this account, is the choices made by governments to achieve their objectives in relation to health.

But policy participants often find it hard to identify a significant actor called the government which has specific objectives in relation to healthcare. Rather, they see a process of struggle and negotiation among a range of participants, some of them holding official positions (and therefore part of government in one sense), others being clearly outside government (e.g. private hospitals, health funds and patient groups). This generates an account of policy as a process of *structured interaction* between a diversity of organised participants. What can be considered health policy will be the outcome, at any particular time, of this struggle and negotiation.

But policy is not simply the outcome of conscious struggle between recognised stakeholders, but reflects a much deeper layer of understanding about what is normal and what is problematic, who is expert, and what action is appropriate; it is a process of *social construction*. Thus:

> To speak of health policy is to draw on a body of shared understanding and practice about what constitutes 'health' and whose action contributes to it. And this body of shared knowledge is fluid and subject to change – e.g. whether such matters as diet, road safety and drug-taking are health matters. In this perspective, health policy is a particular way of interpreting social practice which makes some outcomes, and some forms of social action, problematic, which validates action by particular experts and authority figures to combat the 'problems' which are disclosed by this account of governing.[9]

These different accounts will be appropriate at different times. Announcing a national diabetes strategy, for example, would be operating in the authoritative choice account: this is happening because the government wants it. We might find, though, that the government (in the sense of the elected leaders) had no particular interest in the area. Rather, it was endorsing initiatives taken by a coalition of clinical specialists, nutritionists, epidemiologists and private health funds who are under no illusions about the interest of the politicians in the project, but find the national strategy a useful lever in their dealings with their superiors, other organisations, and funding bodies. In their dealing with one another, they will be operating in a structured interaction account. But participants may also recognise that there is not a great deal that governments can do directly to reduce the incidence of diabetes, that it reflects popular understandings and framings of the problem, changes in lifestyle, diet and the pattern of physical activity; that is, they may locate the question (at least in their own professional discussions) in a 'social construction' account of policy.

In an authoritative choice account of policy, ICP development would not be seen as terribly significant. Authority figures were not involved (and in fact the ICPs are attempting to deal with the effects of perverse incentives which have been authorised), and there was no consideration of options or announcement of decisions (although savvy practitioners could see advantage of describing their activities in the language used by politicians and senior managers). But while ICP developments were consistent with the expressed wishes of authorised leaders, they did not come from them.

ICP development looks much more like health policy in a structured interaction account. It recognises the negotiated order of the hospital, and the concerns of a diversity of workers in the process of care, and constitutes locations and processes where the nature of care can be negotiated in ways that reflect these different values. But, distinctively, in ICP development the negotiation is not conducted in the national capital by associations representing the different specialisations, but in the workplace, by the workers themselves. And it is beginning to involve those outside the workplace, incorporating the patients and their support teams in the structuring of practice.

In a social construction account of policy, ICP development becomes significant because of its impact on the understanding of health and the technologies (including organisational forms) through which it is pursued: who can talk, what can be discussed, what are appropriate forms of knowledge and responses to illness. Within the hospital, the focus shifts from the autonomy of the specialist to the collective commitment to the pathway. As the field of vision is widened to take in participants outside the hospital, quite significant changes in the understandings and practices that make up healthcare become possible.

So the argument about whether the ICP reforms constituted policy making takes us back to our conceptual base. If policy is seen as the intentions of government, the ICP reforms might not be regarded as policy. But if policy is seen in terms of interactions between stakeholders, or of the framework of ideas and practices within which healthcare is interpreted, they clearly are moves to change the policy settings. The ICP innovators were not consciously making policy, nor were they trying to transform the healthcare system; rather they were reforming the elements of healthcare in which they were involved, and in this way making policy.

## ORGANISATION CHARTS AND REFLEXIVE DISCOURSE AS SOURCES OF CHANGE

In this context, much of the significance of the ICP approach to change lies in its stress on understandings of good practice, reflexivity among practitioners, and attention to the development of shared meaning, and, from this, the construction of collective commitment. The focus is not on redrawing the organisation chart, but on expanding participants' understandings of their existing positions. There are changes to the organisation chart in many cases (e.g. the creation of a position of Nurse Navigator, a specific concern for the movement of patients through the pathway), but these are the outcomes of the process of organisational change rather than the source of it. It is an exercise in social construction and structured interaction.

The ICP approach and focus on developing self-awareness and collective commitment can be contrasted with roughly simultaneous reforms aimed at improving public involvement in the NHS as an exercise in authoritative choice and focused on the organisation chart. Between 1991 and 2004 there was a succession of organisational changes that aimed to give patients and the public more voice in healthcare.[10] There had for some time been Community Health Councils to channel community input. The Conservative Government, strongly committed to introducing market principles in healthcare, introduced a Patients' Charter that set out the rights of the individual patient and a Patient Partnership Strategy to facilitate patient involvement in their own care. After 1997, the Labour Government, committed to democratic renewal and facing widespread public criticism of the state of the NHS, required each of the 572 NHS Trusts to set up a Patient Involvement Forum (later renamed the Public and Patient Involvement Forum), which was paralleled in each trust by a Patient Advisory and Liaison Service, and crowned at the national level by a Commission for Patient and Public Involvement in Health.

The authoritative choice nature of the exercise was reflected in the succession of announcements of changes to the organisation chart. The national CPPIH was announced in 2000, created by statute in 2002, commenced operations in 2003, and was reviewed and then abolished in 2004. The forums were reviewed in 2005 and are to be replaced by local involvement networks, but this change was announced ahead (and independently) of a white paper on local government, which increased the scope of its overview and scrutiny committees of healthcare.

The result of this expansion of formal organisation, however, was to stretch limited resources of people and skills over a wider framework, the knowledge acquired by the existing Community Health Councils was not transferred to the new bodies, and achieving change on organisation charts seemed to take precedence over securing change on the ground. The forums and the advocacy services tended to operate in isolation from one another and from the systems for quality assurance and performance management in healthcare, and the new structures have been criticised for failing to recognise the competing legitimacies in healthcare. Baggott concludes:

> Small-scale institutional changes may achieve more than completely new structures, particularly if existing institutions can be modified to involve and engage with patients, users and carers more effectively . . . democracy in health might be more effectively promoted by focusing attention on improved decision-making, accountability, transparency, choice, and the right of redress within existing procedures rather than pursuing a 'holy grail of community control'.[11]

The lesson seems to be that changing the pattern of healthcare calls for attention to the structured interaction of participants, and to their constructions of the nature of care, as well as to announcements of authoritative choice.

## WIDER IMPLICATIONS FOR HEALTHCARE

The introduction of ICPs is significant not only for the differences that they make to healthcare in these specific instances, but also for their wider implications for the structuring of healthcare. There are lessons in the ICP story about structure in healthcare and the appropriate approach to change. It suggests that reforms which begin with clinical therapists' ideas about what constitutes good clinical practice are likely to have more impact that those which begin with some outsider's idea of a desirable outcome. Introducing ICPs calls for practitioners to think about process (how therapy is understood, organised and practised) rather than structure (organisational forms and lines of accountability). The focus is, therefore, more on the organisation and practice of care, rather than on the problems faced or the putative intentions of government, and this cuts across the dominant rhetoric in UK healthcare that what is needed is firmer management and more central control. We see in the ICP cases a recognition of multiple sources of legitimacy in the structuring of care, negotiation among the participants over practice, with legitimate authority being mobilised as part of the interaction and, in particular, in the presentation of the outcomes – all the elements of the original application of governance in the analysis of the practices of governing.

The ICP reforms seek to develop a sense of collective responsibility among care providers, which requires determining who is in the team and, ultimately, what we regard as healthcare. The ICP cases so far have been negotiated among professionals in organised care settings, mainly hospitals; but to an increasing extent healthcare is recognised as taking place outside these organised settings. How will this process of systematisation be applied to the care provided by non-processionals, such as in the treatment of long-term conditions? The Year of Care model (an integrated pathway to long-term conditions, *see* Chapter 9) makes non-professionals part of the negotiation of the pattern of care. As health comes to be seen as involving lifestyle and self-care, the perception of healthcare is shifting from the delivery of an expert service to a broader pattern of caring, involving not only professionals but also the work of carers and the governing of the self.

The ICP also signals a shift from prescription to negotiation in healthcare. In a world of multiple legitimacies, with diverse and overlapping sources of knowledge, the ICP is not a final and authoritative statement of the best practice, but a manifestation of the commitment of the clinical team to base their practice on the best possible model, and to be accountable to one another for compliance with the model or variations from it. It is a template in a continuing process of negotiation, and we can ask how this approach might be used in the broader engagement of professional carers with their patients, how templates might be used in the renegotiation of the work of patients as healthcare seeks to move beyond the delivery of services to the management of social practice.

## IMPLICATIONS BEYOND HEALTHCARE

There are many other occupations where there is pressure for the exercise of professional judgement to be subject to a systematic code: for example, social workers considering whether to remove an abused child from its home, or police having to decide whether to engage in the high-speed pursuit of a suspected offender. It is no longer sufficient for the specialist to say that he or she had to make a professional judgement; there is a demand that this judgement be reviewed. Governing calls for the codification of practice, and the use of this codification to control the behaviour of government officials and their relationship with their clientele.[12] This demand for the review of practice reflects the multiplication of the values applied in judgement. If the police have the right to stop and search people suspected of carrying prohibited drugs, do they choose to search black people more than white, young people more than old, and the scruffily clad more than the well-dressed? Is this a reasonable exercise of judgement, given what is known about the characteristics of drug dealers and users, or the victimisation of unpopular groups? Should policy be required to keep records of those they search so that the statistics over time can be reviewed?

The question is how this demand for systematisation is responded to. Advances in information technologies have made it much easier to collect data and to compare practitioners or groups of practitioners with one another.

Is this then used as the basis for framing norms of practice, which are then imposed on the specialist practitioners by control functions such as financial allocation? In the ICP case, the specialists moved to codify their own practice in order to retain their autonomy, and in so doing, managed to overcome the traditional barriers between specialist occupations. But this means that the nature of professional autonomy is changing, and we need to ask how the practice of occupational specialists is structured in terms of the organisational forms through which it is accomplished (the work group, the collectivity of specialists), the organisational location for practice, and the range of governmental and non-governmental bodies that review the specialists' practice. Asking these questions enables us to extend our concern from comparisons between different healthcare regimes to comparisons – commonalities as well as contrasts – between the governing of healthcare and the governing of other fields of human service provision.

## REFERENCES

1 Griffiths R. *NHS Management Inquiry*. London: Department of Health and Social Security; 1983.
2 Exworthy M, Powell M. Big windows and little windows: implementation in the 'congested state'. *Public Administration*. 2004; **82**(2): 265–81.
3 Degeling P, Kennedy J, Hill M, *et al*. *Professional Subcultures and Hospital Reform*. Sydney: Centre for Clinical Governance Research, University of New South Wales; 1998.
4 Strauss A, Schatzman L, Bucher R, *et al*. The hospital and its negotiated order. In: Friedson E, editor. *The Hospital in Modern Society*. New York: Free Press; 1963.
5 Maxwell S, Degeling P, Kennedy J, *et al*. *Improving Clinical Management: the role of ICP-based clinical management systems*. Durham: Centre for Clinical Management Development, University of Durham; 2005.
6 Giddens A. *General Problems in Social Theory*. Basingstoke: Macmillan; 1979. Giddens A. *The Constitution of Society*. Cambridge: Polity Press; 1984.
7 Colebatch HK. Policy, models, and the construction of governing. In: Colebatch HK, editor. *The Work of Policy: an international survey*. Lanham, MD: Lexington Books; 2006.
8 Dye TR. *Understanding Public Policy*. Englewood Cliffs, NJ: Prentice-Hall; 1972, p. 2.
9 Colebatch, op cit., 12.
10 Baggott R. A funny thing happened on the way to the forum? Reforming public and patient involvement in the NHS in England. *Public Administration*. 2005; **83**(3): 533–51.
11 Ibid., 548.
12 Power M. *The Audit Society: rituals of verification*. Oxford: Oxford University Press; 1997.

# CHAPTER 19

# Conclusion: systematisation of clinical care in theory and practice

*Andrew Gray and Pieter Degeling*

In May 2007, the Institute of Public Policy Research (IPPR) published *The Future Hospital*.[1] Its analysis found, *inter alia*, that attempts to redesign services were driven primarily by clinical concerns with quality and outcome rather than resource problems, that clinical engagement with change was undermined by financial and target regimes, that local populations were often distrustful of service redesign that took services away from their local institutions, and that there was a systemic accountability gap at the local level. Thus, although its scope was limited to hospital reconfiguration, the IPPR report reflected developments described and analysed in the chapters of this book. Moreover, the issues raised by the IPPR matched many of those raised by our accounts, most notably the emphasis on local change within impediments of national incentive structures.

This book has been specifically about the systematisation of care: what it is, the experiences of its development and the difference it makes. Although systematisation takes its form in a variety of ways, its essence may be illustrated by two cases (*see* Box 19.1). The differences between the cases lie in the traditional open-ended and emergent character of the patient journey in Case 1 compared with the systematised way in Case 2 the network of required tasks has been pre-planned to optimise their contributions to achieving a specified set of therapeutic goals. These attributes of Case 2 in turn provide people who are involved (either as deliverers or recipients of care) with the basis for monitoring, routinely reviewing and benchmarking care processes within and between clinical settings to the benefit of improved efficiency, effectiveness and quality.

## BOX 19.1 Systematisation: a tale of two cases

### Case 1

A patient visits her general practitioner with persistent pain in her left hip. Six months later, after her third visit, the GP refers her to an orthopaedic surgeon at the local district hospital. Three months later she sees the consultant at the outpatient clinic. The consultant orders tests and arranges a further outpatient consultation in two weeks. At this consultation the patient learns that she requires a hip replacement that will be undertaken six months later. After nine months and two rescheduled operations, the patient is admitted to the orthopaedic ward two days prior to theatre and undergoes tests, many of which are broadly similar to those undertaken at the first outpatient consultation. Following a successful operation the patient is returned to the ward and over the next seven days receives care primarily directed at the healing of the wound and improving her ability to extend her new joint rather than specified mobility on a day-by-day basis. Nurses explain this somewhat loosely linked approach to rehabilitation and discharge in terms of staffing shortfalls in the physiotherapy department and the fact that discharge cannot occur until the consultant surgeon authorises it.

### Case 2

A patient visits her general practitioner with persistent pain in her left hip. At the third visit in the next two months, the GP, following a set of guidelines agreed with orthopaedic surgeons in the local hospital, orders tests and on reading the results refers her to an outpatient clinic at the local district hospital. Within a month the orthopaedic consultant sees her and, on the basis of her test results and his personal observations, he informs her that she requires a hip replacement that they book for two months' time. During this consultation the full care pathway is presented and agreed with her. In accordance with this pathway, on the day prior to admission the patient attends the outpatient clinic for further tests in preparation for surgery. At this time her discharge from hospital as well as her post-hospital rehabilitation is also planned. She is admitted to the hospital on the day of surgery. Her post-operative care in the ward is provided by nominated nurses trained by the physiotherapy department and is structured to promote healing of her wound, proactively build her confidence and enable her day by day to achieve a graduated set of mobility targets. By day four she meets an agreed and specified set of criteria and is discharged by a senior nurse specialist in charge of the orthopaedics ward.

---

Our chapters confirm that the current interest in the systematisation of healthcare is not new but that it has developed new and more positive emphases on the content of clinical care itself. They also show how these new emphases both enhance professionalism and ask it to perform in new ways. They illustrate some of the challenges faced by systematising clinical care and reveal that not all conditions are amenable to its applications. Above all, however, they show that changing clinical care in these systematised ways can improve clinical outcomes and patient experiences.

## SYSTEMATISED CLINICAL CARE: WHERE ARE WE NOW?

The experiences described in this book have provided evidence that a health-care system that is more systematised in focusing on patients and organising its clinical, managerial and financial resources can provide more effective care more efficiently. Yet, while this suggests that improved systematisation is key to implementing government reforms for patient well-being, the reforms have generally failed to address or provide for systematisation directly. Systematisation for clinical improvement places clinicians at the centre of organisational performance and provides them with the means for integrating the clinical, resource and organisational bases of care. This in turn provides the substance and form of *responsible autonomy* as the fundamental principle of *clinical self-governance*. This too has been overlooked in NHS reform.

If previous approaches to healthcare focused on the use of resources by, for example, medicine, nursing, allied health and/or primary versus acute care, systematisation conceives clinical care as batch processing in which the contributions of nurses and doctors (in primary and acute care) are interdependent throughout all stages. Equally, the problems of quality improvement require focusing on the totality of a patient's journey throughout the process rather than solely on what (for example) doctors or nurses do in particular bits of the process. In this regard, a number of chapters hint that it is not the elements of care that define medicine and nursing but the ability and competency of care providers to put together the particular contributions of each professional groupings into a patient-centred process. In other words, systematised care depends for its effects on linked contributions that break down barriers of professional self-interest.

Systematised approaches at various levels of healthcare both depend on authoritative data and information and provide bases for generating, gathering and monitoring new data that can be used to improve care. Hospital episode statistics (HES) provide a good starting point for identifying the clinical conditions for which systematised approaches to their care, such as integrated care pathways, may provide significant gains to patients, healthcare providers and the wider health economy. Moreover, analyses of HES data help identify barriers to systematisation that may arise when, for example, funding systems differentiate between care provision in primary and acute care.

Whatever the potential of HES data and other clinical activity data, the full potential of care systematisation is undermined by a number of data gaps. We do not, for example, have ways of systematically collecting data on the non-clinical experiences of patients and their carers. But, as the chapters on pathways show, ICPs have the functionality to include such experiences. Indeed, the chapters on pathways in surgery argue that patients should be involved throughout the development and monitoring of a pathway. Involving patients who have undergone a hip replacement, for example, not only gives them voice but also helps identify points in existing treatment modalities for specific conditions that produce bottlenecks and duplication, that undermine dignity, that add to risk and/or adversely affect quality. In summary, constructing, implementing and monitoring a patient-centred pathway that is condition specific requires focusing on and communicating with the patient as well as that between primary and secondary care and between members of the multidisciplinary team.

Pathways in surgery succeed, according to our accounts, when they not only fulfil these imperatives but are also disease and team specific, and where there is shared socialisation and development driven by dedicated and enthusiastic champions. However, for some, pathways are more a form of re-engineering the whole of the clinical activity of a healthcare organisation. If our accounts of surgery warn against such a wholesale view, those of long-term conditions (including COPD and CHD) appear more sympathetic to such an approach. The Year of Care model, for example, (1) distinguishes between three levels of the population, (2) integrates both the personal health responsibilities of individuals and their rights to have their voices heard and heeded in the co-production processes, (3) provides a basis for risk assessment and service planning to take place at a population level and an individual level and (4) makes fully explicit both what comprises each of the elements of care (self-management, support and clinical) and how they will be related to each other on a person-by-person basis in ways that enable service provision to be prospectively and proactively designed, explicitly defined, planned and coordinated. The development of such an approach takes time, resources and multidisciplinary cooperation, including on the basis of an understanding of the importance of non-clinical aspects of patient care.

Yet, perhaps pathways for long-term conditions and surgery have more in common than this summary implies. Both are founded on explicit methodologies for stratifying the people that fall within the specified condition and for identifying their clinical and non-clinical needs and wishes. Both require clearly authorised persons to be responsible and accountable for integrating services at the personal level. Both are enacted through a codification that specifies who will do what, why, when and where. And both provide the basis for a system of clinical performance management that is improvement-oriented and occurs as prospectively designed, condition specific care processes are routinely examined and reviewed by the clinicians, patients and carers who are central to their occurrence.

The Integrated Care Pathways Appraisal Tool (ICPAT) can be used to assess such content and quality in ICPs. Its application provides evidence that ICPs are being developed within generally accepted definitions; that is, they have content validity. However, there are shortfalls in their governance and accountability (e.g. audit), service user involvement, staff training, risk assessment and planning across organisations. Such shortfalls imply risks in developing ICPs in isolation from their organisational and patient contexts.

The significant elements of the organisational context in developing clinical work include a clear strategy for the organisation, a model of care pathway development that flexibly accommodates the multiple needs of the directorates, middle managers to interpret data from frontline staff as information for executive management, and an executive team that takes clinical management as seriously as financial status and performance. Strong executive leadership helps to instil a sense of commitment and significance to systematisation as a means to deliver better clinical outcomes, manage its links to other strategies, and forge a common interdisciplinary approach by clerical, medical, allied health profession and nursing staff.

Our chapters have also shown that the integration is not only within a healthcare organisation but also across them, particularly within the care of designated conditions. Clinical networks, for example, have the potential to help develop an improvement culture and build capacity in communities of related practice in which knowledge management and innovation are recognised as managerial priorities in their own right. Clinical network-based systematisation can help develop structures, language and processes to integrate the interests of clinicians and others to enhance social capital for clinical improvement.

Finally, a number of chapters show how care systemisation can challenge (1) the identity of individual professionals (i.e. their perception of themselves, their work and the work of others), (2) who should determine appropriateness, quality, cost and (3) how care process can and should be organised. As we have seen, effective and efficient care delivery necessarily depends on the articulated (i.e. systematised) involvement of not merely doctors and nurses but also of other professions, such as social workers, and patients as co-producers. Hence it is no longer sufficient for the professional to make expert judgements in isolation; team working is increasingly the modal vehicle of health and social care services. By implication, higher education and other providers of learning and development must include opportunities for inter-professional learning and working in both undergraduate and post-qualified programmes. Similarly, systematised care can be a vehicle for making clinical work the basis for capital investment and business planning. The experiences described in this volume imply that capital planning's traditional focus on beds and buildings must give way to an emphasis on the processes by which patients are being treated. In contrast to continental Europe, it is not clear that newly constructed or rebuilt British hospitals, whether commissioned through traditional public or private sector sources of finance, have yet realised the emerging service models inherent in systematised healthcare.

Thus, we have a picture of very considerable development of systematised clinical care that is contributing directly to better clinical outcomes, service experiences and resource use. But it is also changing the way professionals work and placing demands on managers, trainers and planners to engage more actively with service design. Such demands cannot be met without being aware of their implications and conditions. It is to these that we turn in our final section.

## IMPLICATIONS FOR THE THEORY AND PRACTICE OF SYSTEMATISED CLINICAL CARE

We have established that systematisation is not new but intrinsic to health practice and service. It relates to the organisational (both cultural and performance management), financial and clinical dimensions of relationships. However, its current emphases have shifted in a significant direction: from professions and administrative structures to the detailed composition of clinical processes and monitoring and content of clinical care itself. This shift focuses on outputs and outcomes (rather than inputs) and their specified clinical production processes; that is, how we do a hip replacement, a normal delivery, etc. It reinforces the role of frontline clinicians in initiating, framing and maintaining its content. It involves patients, carers and healthcare professionals in multidisciplinary teams, rather than as sub-specialty silos. It develops prospectively and reflects retrospectively. It relies on and mobilises collective performance intelligence, using variation as a stimulant to service development rather than regarding variation as something that is deviant and hence not discussible. It prompts the skills development of practitioners and patients and their carers. It is supported by an authority structure that is focused on clinical production rather than the management of issues.

In these ways systematisation of clinical care stimulates the management of care to effect appropriate balances between individual patient and population-centred care, between clinical and resource issues, between clinical judgement and system capacities, between integration and differentiation, and between clinical autonomy and accountability. Systematisation is *not* top-down standardisation, rationalisation, regulation or knowledge appropriation; that is, it is not a synonym for Fordism, Tailorism or the proletarianisation of medicine. On the contrary, it constitutes a professionally led response to the reform agenda of choice, commissioning, information technology, capital and workforce development, performance management and clinical governance. It is, in short, at once an instrument of clinical and economic change, an arena of collective endeavour by carers and the cared for, a value system and a public policy (part of a wider movement in human personal service encompassing education, social work and criminal justice).

The methodology of systematisation planning first reduces care analytically to its elements and then reworks it to maximise the clinical experience for the patient within the (capital, financial and human) resources available. Its implementation is grounded in what is feasible culturally and institutionally, not just in conservative terms but in what can be developed. Both the planning and implementation are stimulated by forces working with systematisation: (1) the complexities of morbidities, especially comorbidities, and their clinical and social care treatments and support, (2) the scarcity of resources, especially of finance and skill, and (3) the desire to improve patient outcomes and experiences. But they have also to address forces working against systematisation: disciplinary specialisation, payment by results and NHS targets that hinder cross-sector integration, the traditional management suspicions of clinicians, the traditions of professional authority and function, and the almost iconic place of the hospital in our society.

All this calls for some demanding requirements in the healthcare system: (1) technical elements including new intelligence, systems and skills, (2) organisational elements including new structures, processes and resourcing, and (3) political elements including the realignment of power and authority between professionals, mangers and patients. The contributions to this book suggest that, at the local level, the healthcare system is both aware of these requirements and is beginning to provide for them. But this awareness is lacking at the level of policy and service design for the NHS as a whole. Here there remain disincentives, even penalties, for working in this way despite the potential for it to contribute to the explicit higher level goals of a 'patient-led health service'.

## REFERENCE

1 Institute of Public Policy Research (IPPR). *The Future Hospital: the politics of change*. London: IPPR; 2007.

# Index